James Anderson

LSE ASEN
Conference
18 March '94

The Condition of States

The Condition of States

A Study in International Political Theory

Edited by Cornelia Navari

Open University Press
Milton Keynes • Philadelphia

Open University Press
Celtic Court
22 Ballmoor
Buckingham
MK18 1XW

and

1900 Frost Road, Suite 101
Bristol, PA 19007, USA

First Published 1991

British Library Cataloguing in Publication Data

The condition of states.
  1. State
  I. Navari, Cornelia, *1941 -*
  320.1

ISBN 0-335-09668-9
ISBN 0-335-09667-0 (pbk)

Library of Congress Cataloging-in-Publication Data

The Condition of states: a study in international political theory/
  edited by Cornelia Navari.
       p. cm.
    Includes index.
    ISBN 0-335-09668-9. – ISBN 0-335-09667-0 (pbk.)
    1. National state. 2. International relations. I. Navari,
  Cornelia, 1941–
  JX4000.C65 1991
  341.26–dc20   91-2447
                                                              CIP
Typeset by Burns and Smith Ltd, Derby
Printed in Great Britain by Biddles Ltd, Guildford and King's Lynn

Contents

The Contributors

Christopher Brewin Lecturer in International Relations, the University of Keele

John Baker Research Student, the University of Birmingham

John Charvet Reader in Government, the London School of Economics and Political Science

Michael Donelan Senior Lecturer in International Relations, the London School of Economics and Political Science

Mervyn Frost Professor of Political Science, the University of Natal, Durban

Willie Henderson Senior Lecturer in Continuing Education, the University of Birmingham

Christopher Hill Senior Lecturer in International Relations, the London School of Economics and Political Science

Martin Kolinsky Senior Lecturer in Political Science, the University of Birmingham

James Mayall Reader in International Relations, the London School of Economics and Political Science

Cornelia Navari Lecturer in Political Science, the University of Birmingham

Brian Porter Honorary Lecturer and Senior Member of Rutherford College, University of Kent. Fellow of the Royal Historical Society

Philip Windsor Reader in International Relations, the London School of Economics and Political Science

Preface

This is the third production by an inter-university group which first met in 1974 and has continued to meet at regular intervals since to discuss theoretical questions in the study of international relations. The first was *The Reason of States* edited by Michael Donelan (Allen and Unwin, 1978) and the second was *The Community of States* edited by James Mayall (Allen and Unwin, 1982).

Two essays prepared for the present collection have appeared in slightly amended form as journal articles: 'War and the State' by Philip Windsor in the *LSE Quarterly*, **1**, 1 (1988) and 'Liberal States and International Obligations' by Christopher Brewin in *Millennium, Journal of International Studies*, **17**, 2 (1988).

We thank many others for their care in reading essays and their valuable comments.

1

Introduction: The State as a Contested Concept in International Relations

Cornelia Navari

During the last two decades, political theorists who had previously neglected the state have returned to a consideration of it. Marxists, pluralists, political economists and other sorts of social base theorists – theorists who long considered the state to be a derivative of a more relevant social process – have shifted their focus back to the institutional apparatus, an apparatus, moreover, separate from a social nexus.[1] They have declared that the state is something more than a sum of processes, a resultant of class conflict or a product of interest interaction. Some, indeed, have gone so far as to hold that it can think and be for itself. Whether through 'competitive requisites', 'corporatist intermediation' or 'bureaucratic insulation', the state, it appears, can now act independently and on its own behalf.

The 'what' that is the state is scarcely agreed upon by all of these theorists (although, as we shall see, there is more agreement than might be supposed). Generally, however, there is an 'it', generally viewed as a form of agency, generally centred on a bureaucracy or a set of executive officers, which is capable of acting with a degree of 'autonomy', that is, acting independently of a social base, in certain circumstances.

During this rediscovery of the state, scholars concerned with international relations remained somewhat on the sidelines. Indeed, initially, they greeted its rediscovery with some derision.

In part, their scepticism had to do with the fact that the state had never disappeared far below the horizons of their own inquiry. However thoroughgoing neglect of the state in other quarters, those in departments of

---

* Superscript numerals refer to numbered notes at the end of each chapter.

international relations, particularly in British departments of international relations, remained for the most part devoted to it, resolutely opposed to processes, interests where they were not 'national' interests and, especially, classes, and insisted that, for most of the time, the state acted 'autonomously'.[2] Indeed, they held autonomy to be the chief characteristic of a state. (Scholars of international relations have a pervasive tendency to grade the substance of a state by its capability for independent action.) During this period, they were often accused of reification, obscurantism and traditionalism; they became isolated from the mainstream of political science. But they bore these burdens stoically, even with a sense of superiority, and remained firm in their insistence that the thing which fights and which diplomatizes, if considered a form of organization, was unlike other forms of organization, and that this thing had the capability to act and to act in accord with its own reasons.

Of course, this is an exaggeration. Concern with the requisites of capitalism, and even 'economic determinism', challenged the state-centric view, even in Britain, through functionalist and systems approaches: the idea that the state was part of a larger system, part of which was also an 'economic system', clearly subordinated the state to something 'beyond' it, even if not precisely 'within' it. A consideration of social forces and their effects on international relations intensified in the late 1960s, at about the time that some pluralists began to rediscover the state, through transnationalism and the study of international interest groups. But parts of the international relations community also strenuously resisted just these approaches, at least in the degree to which they questioned the state as the main political community or determinate actor, and even conducted resolute campaigns against them.[3] The only new approaches to the state with which, certainly British, mainstream international relations felt entirely happy (and which were incorporated into its own subject matter) were strategic analysis, theories of nationalism, bureaucratic analysis and inquiries into 'political culture', particularly in relation to developing countries – theories which, if they allow one to analyse its processes more sophisticatedly, keep the state intact as a bounded entity, an entity with the capability for free action and, more importantly, as the 'main' actor.[4]

In the circumstances, then, it is not surprising that the new literature on the state was viewed for a long time by many in the discipline as confirming what they had been maintaining all along; and, hence, of little interest.

More recently, however, indifference has been replaced by a certain celebratory union. Social force theorists from sociology departments and state-and-market political economists from international relations departments, formerly little inclined to meet, suddenly have a lot to share with one another.[5] Sociologists seem suddenly to want to know a lot about power, state conflict and even the notion of the national interest, while many international relationists are quite keen on notions of social tension and social particularism.[6]

The cement of these rather unholy unions would seem to spring from the sort of state that a number of social force theorists were busy rediscovering. Very often, the discoveries of the new breed of social theorist were such as to uncover, as was gradually to emerge, some very traditional ideas, ideas in which the study of international relations was itself steeped. Some pluralists, especially economic pluralists, the world economy theorists and a great many marxists, were not just discovering the state. They were discovering the sort of state which lies close to the heart of international relations theorizing on the state: they were discovering the *Machtstaat*.

The theory of *Machtstaat* identifies the essential defining characteristic of the state as power, a power unmediated ultimately by any social force, and a power which welds a potentially troublesome diversity of social forces together and forms the state. It is German theory, and a theory which became inextricably linked with the history of the German Reich, as Michael Mann avers, 'to die with it on the battlefields of the second world war, defeated by Anglo-American liberalism and Soviet marxism'.[7] The 'German idea' did not die everywhere, however. If marginalized in domestic political science after the war, the *Machtstaat* lived on in the study of relations between states. Indeed, there, it was reborn and accomplished something of a victory over pluralism.

The dominant modes of international analysis in the 1920s and 1930s were a 'personalized' nationalism, in which states were assigned psychological and moral characteristics and treated as forms of real persons, and legal and institutional analysis. Pluralism, the idea of self-sustaining and differentiated social forces which invade government, was also, however, present, and had appeared quite early. In 1909, Norman Angell, in the context of an analysis of the world economy, had conjured up the existence of cross-cutting and internationalized social forces which were operating, he maintained, in such a way as to make war dysfunctional, an analysis which restated nineteenth-century liberal theories of *douce commerce* in a modern structural-functional form and which inspired a good deal of éclat. After the First World War, this nascent pluralism was infused with some American 'radical' thought and extended to include the existence of classes. By the 1920s, moreover, political liberals and radicals had been joined in their belief in self-sustaining social forces which could bend states to their will by a new breed of liberal economist, proper economists, concerned to outline movements in the world economy which affected state policy. Indeed, at least in America, liberal economism became the common form of international analysis, while concern with 'divisive' state interests was frowned upon – yet more *douce commerce*. By the mid-1930s, even interest group analysis had put in a tentative appearance.[8] Among all of these approaches, Realpolitik or analysis by strategic calculation of national requisites, was marginal, employed generally only by military historians and military analysts.[9]

But the experience of the war reversed this equation. Hans Morgenthau, whose *Machtstaat* classic, *Politics Among Nations*, appeared in 1948, made the point: natural harmonies, the needs of an internationalized economy, group interests, classes and legal structures did not prevent war coming, did not ameliorate it when it did come, did not fight it and did not win it. It was *governments* which fought it and won it, by intricate calculations as to strategy and tactics, by mobilizing the political, material and psychological resources of *nations*, through appeal to a *national interest*. Victory in war, and the perceived modalities of that victory, established the prime mode of analysing the relations between states in the post-war period: the analysis of the basis of state power, its sources and likely direction, which were generally ascribed, moreover, to national and unifying, not sectoral, divisive or 'international' interests. The new state-centric approach, with its emphasis on rational calculation of the national interest by a wise political leadership, often cajoling or in conflict with a hesitant domestic constituency, in the context of often hostile international pressures, was the *Machtstaat* approach, with its hostility to 'groups', processes and systems. But it is precisely this sort of state which is being rediscovered by the pluralists: a power derived from, and made a resultant of, a potential social division, which welds that division together. After decades apart, machtstaaters and pluralists have joined sides.

Some dimensions of the new realism

Not all recent theories of the state are realist or *Machtstaat* theories. Some pluralist thinkers are toying with revised concepts of 'the public interest' which the state is held to represent and which they use to source its 'relative autonomy'. New-corporatist theory, on the other hand, highlighted the importance of the state as a law-maker: Philip Schmitter, the discoverer of neo-corporatism, saw the corporatist relationship, at least initially, as a form of legal relationship, and state and government as important determinants of it, on that basis.[10] The unearthing of the *Machtstaat* has been due primarily to the new marxists, Skocpol's brand of political sociology and Wallerstein's world systems approach, and it is these with which students of international relations have most concurred.

Claimed to be of interest because they combine some notion of divisive social forces with some notion of autonomous state, each of these approaches conceives the state as a directing bureaucracy, a Weberian rational actor (the rediscovery of the *Machtstaat* has created renewed interest in Weber's account of the state) whose quality is useful because it can be an instrument of decision or 'willing'. This instrument is then put at the service of some concatenation of capital, or of fractions, or at the nexus between the international system and the domestic socio-political order, which position gives it a certain autonomy or will of its own, producing, though not all intended to, the state able to pursue its own purposes. Each arrived at the *Machtstaat* by a somewhat different route, however, and by somewhat different concerns.

It should be said at once that so far as marxism is concerned, there is nothing new in the instrumental view of the state. It lurks constantly on the fringes of Marx's writing, in the idea that the state is an instrument of the ruling class and an instrument of coercion, ideas Marx got perhaps from the Saint Simonians, those early social engineers.[11] In the marxist formulation, state serves capital as an instrument of its collective will, 'knowing' what it requires, and enforcing its will. It is, however, precisely this view which poses the many problems marxists have had with the state, problems derived, moreover, from the postulates of *Machtstaat*, which, contrary to marxist thought, poses the victory of state over society. 'Instrumentalism', confusing the idea that control is essentially social control, confuses, first, because it introduces an alternative mode of social power to the mode of production – the state – and then potentially frees the state from social control, producing a postulate of a power actually severed from society and imposed upon it.

For marxists, workers are not repressed by the state at all but by the requirements of capital. They are repressed by the mode of production, in 'the workplace' or by 'the totality', not by the state. To have them repressed by the state, as if the state could do any repressing, confused the relations of class and state as relations of base and superstructure, because it introduced a structure in between the two, and made its exact setting problematic. Even formulations which posed the legal system as an expression of the mode of production, or as a bit of an add on, did not solve this problem entirely, for to pose even a balance between some repression in the workplace and some repression by public law raised sensitive theoretical questions. Too much repression by the state and the state would start to replace capital as the instrument of social condition maintenance. And this matters not merely because of a theoretical confusion it introduces into the holy writ. The real problem with the instrumental theory of the state, and the locus of the ghostly *Machtstaat* which pervades it, is as follows: since the state is comprehended by marxists as nothing but a system of repression, once it (the repressive state) is freed from its base and maintains the base instead of being produced by it, the secret of social cohesion would in effect lie with a foundationless and 'purposeless' power. It would lie with a state apparatus which could, theoretically, determine its own direction and coerce society into taking that direction.

This is an old concern within marxism, reflected in the debate on the precise nature of oriental despotism.[12] The problem with the concept of oriental despotism, or a state without a class, was that it led to what one recent Soviet theorist, criticizing Kautsky, accurately termed the 'idealist theory of violence', a power which was simply serving itself, a phenomenon which, were it to exist, would serve to falsify the central tenants of marxist theory.[13] It is also the case, however, that it was an exceedingly popular idea in the 'liberal' and post-Hegelian analyses of the Bismarckian state at the time. To German liberals, the Bismarckian state appeared to be just such a state which 'served itself', and it was largely their analysis of that state which led to concretization of the idea of *Machtstaat* from which it entered into international relations as 'power politics'. (It was also the experience of the Bismarckian state that led worried marxists to develop the theory of the 'transitional moment', the theory that the state gained a certain 'illusory' autonomy in moments between the ascendance of one class and another, precisely to repel such idealist notions.)

In the event, the new marxists, in trying to pin down precisely how the modern state serves capitalism, have all too often strayed into realist instrumentalism, and its attendant idealism. Ralph Miliband, generally credited with beginning the marxist rethink of the state, saw capital being served and maintained by the participation of capitalists in the instruments of the state, a participation secured by the 'old boy network' and élite socialization.[14] This theory is not only the purest élite theory and not marxist at all, but it is also deviationally étatist, for by such a theory it is the state which is maintaining capitalism, coloured of course by a capitalist élite. Poulantzas' attack on it was, from a marxist point of view, fully justified.[15] From a realist point of view, however, it deserves to be applauded. Here is the state, which is an instrument of power, defending its power base from 'external' depredation – if not precisely a perfect realist formulation, one none the less with which a realist could live quite happily.

Another route by which realism has invaded marxism is via psephological marxism, or why people vote and who wins elections. Gregor McLennan calls this 'synthetic' marxism, because it synthesizes classic or structuralist marxism with instrumental marxism.[16] According to this school, attractive because it shows how capitalism might be being maintained in a practical manner, longevity has to do with the winning of elections. Here, parties compete in an open manner for the hearts and minds of the people, but the overwhelming advantage goes to the forces which maintain the capitalist system of economic exchange. They have the financial power to choose candidates (of the right sort) and to lobby and campaign more effectively, capabilities which, combined with marginal calculations of individual benefit on the part of voters, ensure the continuation of the 'system'.

In this marxist variant, however, the actors are all highly interconscious. It is, moreover, outright political calculation which induces behaviour which, in turn, produces electoral victories beneficial to the status quo and ensures the continuation of capitalism. Equally, it is the state which is the *efficient* maintainer of the capitalist system. (Such an analysis also, though somewhat incidentally, implies that capitalism is more beneficent than a marxist would generally like to admit because, to be victorious at the polls, it must have produced a range of benefits for at least some strategic voting groups.)

In the political sociology of Theda Skocpol, the political realism is openly acknowledged. She claims the heritage of the 'continental' school and wishes to bring Weber and Otto Hintze back in, as well as the state. In her formulation, state autonomy is defined in the classic *Machtstaat* way as the capability for 'independent goal formation' and, as is made abundantly clear, independence means independence from the domination of social forces. As for the state, it is defined as a 'coercive apparatus that structures relations between civil society and political authority', and the 'who' who does this coercing and structuring is the organized and coherent collectivity of state officials who are, moreover, 'relatively insulated from ties to currently dominating socio-economic elites'.[17] They coerce and structure either to 'maintain control' or to compete more effectively in a world order made up of other similar entities. In other words, the 'what' that they do is defined by competition for advantage in a world of other states, also the classic *Machtstaat* view of the ends of a state. Their participation in a world of states, moreover, leads them to pursue 'transforming strategies', even in the face of 'indifference or resistance'; that is, they push important, recalcitrant or divisive social forces around in order to achieve their ends.

Their 'relative insulation' from social forces is an idea Skocpol has taken from Ellen Trimberger, who developed it in her account of the modernization of Japan and Turkey.[18] In those cases, Trimberger maintained, the state was capable of acting as a modernizer, often against the predominant and powerful social forces in each country, because in each case there existed relatively insulated state élites who owed their loyalties and career progress to the state alone. In the event, 'insulation' is the crucial category in Skocpol's theory, as it is the source of their autonomy. According to Skocpol, their insulation protects them from the taint of sectoral interests, allowing them to see what is required for the good of the state and giving them the independence to accomplish it.[19] Their separation from social forces allows them both to see and to do, and by her reading of history it was precisely states that were lucky enough to have state élites cut off from social forces which were better able to make 'rational' decisions (defined as rational because they are decisions of advantage over similar goal-seeking entities).

Of course, society is important in Skocpol's formulation as the field and matter of the state's activities, and no state can ever get very far from its society. But it is equally clear which is master. In this formulation, state élites (if they are of the right sort) may serve those forces in society which aid modernization or competitive advantage or whatever else the state's position at the 'nexus of international and domestic society' requires, and they may move against those who do not. They are, thus, able to set the agenda in important ways for their large economic groups, who are instructed to do what international competition requires or die.

The actual power which the state operationalizes is not explicitly spelled out in Skocpol's theory, leading some commentators to observe that the theory is not complete. But while it is not spelled out, the importance she gives to rational calculations of advantage, together with the ability to will one's own will and not the will of others, adds up to an entirely coherent theory of power, and a rather famous one. It is Machiavelli's theory: according to the inventor of power, the bases of a prince's power, the bases indeed of all human power, were, first, foresight and, secondly, the ability to will an end separate from the dictates of religion, advisers, nobles or the mob. These two qualities allowed successful princes, or power seekers, to make lucky combinations, to seize moments of advantage and to anticipate dangers; and those who were better at reasoning and willing made better princes (better defined, of course, as who gains the edge or advantage). The state élite's relative degree of insulation gives it precisely these capabilities – it can see and it is free to act in accordance with what it sees – which capabilities it deploys in a machiavellian manner. Skocpol's theory is a perfect machiavellian formulation.

Separation from social forces produces not only the capabilities of rationality and free will, it also produces the coherence of the state apparatus and makes it into a real state apparatus. Were state embedded in society, it would lose its sense of itself as separate from society and no longer be a proper state. (State in *Machtstaat* theory means precisely being free from society.) It would also no longer be free to seek reason, defined as the ability to seek advantage in a coherent way, which is ultimately the definition of the state in Skocpol's theory. According to Skocpol, what makes janissaries is not that they are in the Sultan's service, but that they are conscript Christian children, free from social connections and hence free to do his will. Nor is she alone in seeing advantage in social separation; there are many who would start the decline of the Ottoman Empire with the opening of the janissary corps to locals and 'natives'.

If Skocpol is a realist by intent, Wallerstein appears to become one somewhat accidentally. His complex historical theory intends to set up a system-determinate condition for state behaviour, allowing no room for human agency, much less state agency, or human reasoning and willing. Yet, as the theory proceeds, we begin to understand that both human reason and state agency are integral parts of its determinism, so much so that its 'determinism' becomes somewhat less than thoroughgoing.[20]

The system which is doing the determining in this theory is an autonomously generated system of capitalism. Capitalism, Wallerstein insists, is not a state-based system – there is no such thing as capitalism in one country. It is a world system, which sprang up in the world, in the cosmos Hegel would say, and which produced states in its wake. The crucial thing about capitalism is social differentiation – it produces differences and works because of them. This, Wallerstein insists, is the crucial feature of capitalism, together with exploitation, a classic marxist approach. But for Wallerstein, these are not differences of class or class exploitation. (He began his academic career as an Africanist, and emphasized *ab initio* the striking differences between Africa as a whole and the West as a whole.) The crucial distinction in his theory, and the differentiation produced by capitalism, is that between the centre, or core, and the periphery. According to Wallerstein, the differentiation capitalism produces is not the difference between a national bourgeoisie and a national proletariat; social differentiation *within society* may actually fade away. What capitalism really requires is regional and geographical distinctions. This is because it is a world system and what it is creaming off is a surplus world product. It needs peripheries from which that surplus world product may be extracted. Indeed, it produces peripheries: those areas it exploits to maintain the world system of capitalism as a whole become peripheralized. Finally, there is the state, which is nothing but a product of this process. It is the state's role to keep the periphery peripheralized, a role determined by the functioning of world capitalism.

How, in this scheme, does a *Machtstaat* emerge? How can a free-wheeling knower result from such a deterministic system? It is clear, first of all, that there are states and that these are systems of coercion, in this case the coercion of peripheral areas to keep them in a pheripheral, i.e. exploitable, condition. Secondly, states do have reasons or purposes; it is their job to maintain the capacity of the centre. Thirdly, capacity means the capacity for profit maximization; capitalism works, according to Wallerstein, by a rational calculation as to where profit lies and how to achieve it. The role of the capitalist states is to maintain the conditions of profit maximization, and they develop the capacities to do so – armed forces, the right kind of treaties, etc. This capacity, however, is not determinant: capitalism does not 'know' where it is going or what is required to maintain the right conditions of exploitation. The knowers are, in effect, the state élites and capitalist bosses who, pushed by the system into profit maximization and exploitation though they may be, have to understand the rules of the game and to make choices accordingly.

Because states have to know the rules of the game, there is the chance that they may get it wrong; and, indeed, they do get it wrong. Hence, the changing power ranking of the core states. Other states can, moreover, also change their ranking, rising to the semi-periphery at least.[21] Capacity change is not infinite; each state leadership has a *donné* which is not easily changed, but it can change. Otherwise, why is the coercive, exploitative state required? In fact, while the system determines core, periphery and semi-periphery, who is in each of these categories depends also on luck, skill and timing. What, then, does this make of the international game? It is a game of building capacity in a dangerous environment of competition on the part of rational calculators whose aim is to protect and enlarge their own state capacity, whose major competitors are in fact other major powers, but whose actual capacities depend on forms of imperial reach. Morgenthau could not have put it better.

These new theories of the state do more than revivify the idea of the *Machtstaat*, however. The theorists propounding them have also been expressing a flattering interest in international relations, particularly in the sources of conflict among states. Indeed, the international arena is crucial to some of them. Anthony Giddens and Skocpol, for example, both expressed doubts about simplistic state-society theories of the marxist vein and early in their careers, noting in each instance that the state was itself a source of change.[22] Yet neither wished to drift into 'idealism'. Here, then, was a dilemma: were state actually embedded in society, it could not change, at least not autonomously; were it 'free', they could not be sociologists. However, there was also the international arena: it was precisely the state's participation in an international system of competition which both freed the state élite and yet kept it chained to some social 'reality'. What Giddens and Skocpol have done is to simply substitute external for internal constraints, and external for internal competition, allowing them to square the circle. The historical forms of that competition and/or constraint could then be used to explain social formation and change. In the process, actual historical state competition becomes very important and, though largely as a logical contingent, what students of international relations have to say suddenly becomes of interest.

Their welcome by international relations realists was not due to a mere, albeit incidental, flattery, however. The new machtstaaters, in turn, have posed various solutions to the problem of how to reconcile the self-evident existence of diverse (and represented) social forces with the independent and self-seeking state. They also posed solutions to that allied and most intractable of problems in traditional realist thought, which is how such things as large nation-states, containing a diversity of peoples, can be conceived as having unifying or single interests. The weakest point in realist thought under the pluralist onslaught was the idea of unifying 'national' interests; the new realists have presented to them an interesting menu for selection. (In Wallerstein, the 'national interest' is the maintenance of core capacity; that is, the well-being of a state as an industrial and technological leader. In Skocpol, it is a rational calculation of the relevance for state advantage *vis-à-vis* other states of changing circumstances, particularly as that agenda reflects on the internal constituency of the state: the national interest is determined serially by who has to be pushed around in order to sustain international competitiveness at any particular moment. For the neo-marxists, it is simply the maintenance of some form of capitalist economy.) It is scarcely surprising, all told, that these theorists have embraced international relations or that international relations has embraced them.

None of this mutual dependence should disguise the fact, however, that such theorists are new arrivals to political realism. As political realists, they are, indeed, in their infancy, and are learning more than telling. For example, Wallerstein certainly has a theory of power, which is technological innovation, but he is scarcely the only one with such a theory. It is a classic theory in the *machtpolitik* school. What he needs to tell us is what sort of technological innovation matters, and the conditions for its maintenance. There is, however, already an impressive literature on this subject.[23] Were a scholar of international relations, or politics, or history, interested in this subject, he would not be likely to read Wallerstein. It is equally the case with Skocpol: the notion that a bureaucracy must mediate between the inside and the outside world is scarcely new; it is a truism in diplomacy; and we would not in fact go to Skocpol for illumination of the difficulties of this process. We would go to the new international history or the literature on the new diplomacy.

Moreover, scholars of international relations have been living with realist theories for a long time and it is not clear, at the end of the day, what these theories contribute to their subject, beyond the truism, perhaps, that the state is concerned with its economic base. The problems concerning the national interest remain what they ever were. (Or the old debates about them emerge in new, but ever recognizable forms, e.g. how does a state know what its economic base needs?) Moreover, they are in danger of reintroducing a certain mysticism into the state. What is this power state, where does its power come from? What is the foundation of autonomy? As Michael Mann has observed, autonomy is a quality of behaviour, it is not a theory of power. It is an observation about freedom to act, not a theory of the basis of action. In detaching the state from its social base, the new realists face the same danger all realist theory faces, i.e. turning power into a mysterious quality and of idealizing it.

There is, however, a deeper logical problem with the *macht* or power view of the state. Power, as defined by the machtstaaters, is the capability to cause movement. But that capability is present universally, in all human agencies, including individuals. And because it is so, it can scarcely be the *defining* characteristic of the state. There must, logically, be something else, at least for any theorist who believes a state can choose.

Another view of the state

There is another version of the state used by international relations theorists. It is the view represented in this collection of essays, and it is this other version of the state whose fate is being considered here. In the present climate of social forces and coercive states, it is scarcely a fashionable view, but it underlies many of the assumptions with which international theorists work, it dominated the subject during the first phase of its existence as a discipline, during the inter-war period, and is closely associated with its origins as a subject, which were in international law.

In this view, the state is not 'power' *vs* 'people'. It is not a condition where the people are either a disaggregated mass or a collection of self-referring groups pushed around or served by a coercive apparatus. In this view, the people are an association for, among other things, discussion of public affairs and for making determinate decisions about their regulation. In this view, the people are a political community. In this view, moreover, power is not a force. It is an articulated set of institutions with certain 'powers' or rights – power is government – and government is not an imposition upon the political community but is contained within it. Moreover, the power that the state expresses is not a disembodied form of 'state' power, but precisely a social power.

What contains government and gives it form, what indeed forms the association of the state and gives it power, is not interests or classes or pluralities, nor is it a coercive, knowing force. It is a legal order. In this view, states as governments and states as associations or political communities are creations of laws, customs and practices. Laws, customs and practices create the political community by, among other things, securing rights, a decision-making 'process', parliaments, representation (and even interest groups), while they create government by assigning and diversifying the decision-making process. In this view, power is to be comprehended as legal power. According to this view, the legal order of the state serves as a collection agency of social power. It absorbs the diverse powers in society and directs them, generally to a purpose, generally also to changeable and multiple purposes. In this view, the state is not *Machtstaat* but *Rechtstaat*. In it, a legal order simultaneously calls up government, citizenry and power, and creates a relationship between them. In this view, the autonomy of the state is a simple legal creation, an attribute of sovereignty.[24]

This view of the state is sometimes called an 'associational' view. In it, the state is a form of corporation, in a very generalized legal sense of corporate personality, a body created by law with officers which act in its name. This corporation then establishes relationships with other corporations. It can also take on duties and obligations towards other corporations, which are generally seen as duties of the whole, in the degree to which the officers carrying out these duties have been so authorized. But equally, the state is nowhere the same thing. It is in fact a series of quite distinct corporate entities which are distinguishable by different allocations of authority, by different allocations of the social right, and by the different purposes they have elected to serve.

Why particular states have the legal forms they do, the customs, regulative practices and guiding conceptions, is one of the perennial questions this school asks itself. And it has given many different answers, including social forces, international competition, historical development and political culture (formerly in disfavour, but now coming back into fashion). One of its abiding concerns, however, and its major analytical purchase, is with the law-making right itself. It identifies the state and locates its distribution of power by spotting the extent and depth of the law-making power, how it is impinged upon, how it is expressed, and how it changes. (If Machiavelli is the father of all machtstaaters, the *Rechtstaat* is the legacy of Montesquieu.)

What is to be made in this view, then, of the state-society distinction? Because, according to this view, one cannot determine a society without determining the rules or practices of a society, the state–society distinction cannot be a real distinction. It must therefore be an analytic distinction. We may further suggest that it is a distinction created to do specific kinds of work. One property this distinction allows is the assignment of a limited domain to the state; it also allows for meaningful discussions on what ought to be government's proper concerns. (Without hypothesizing the state-society distinction, such a discussion would be impossible in the modern secular order.) Yet another is to get analytical purchase on the question of how states come to serve different and changing ends: by freezing a picture in time, by abstracting something called 'society' from another historic agency called 'government', by observing changes in both, while focusing on rules and practices (which become 'the state'), it establishes a field for causal explanation. (For the political scientist, the state–society distinction is a *sine qua non* of causal explanation, as it establishes a number of distinct agencies which can affect one another, which can 'cause' causes.) The category 'society' is also a 'residual' category: society is what public authority fails to touch or fails to alter, and which hence 'falls outside' the domain of the state; hence, in some arguments, sexuality, parts of the family, most forms of criminality and political dissent. (Indeed, these have become the particular concerns of some sociologists, precisely because they appear to be pure social forms, untouched by the state or resisting it.)

The conception of the public authority as a corporation produces a unitary conception of rule making, despite the diversity and complexity of actual decision making. From the international and legal point of view, the state speaks with one voice; this is integral to its definition as a legal person. Authority may reside with many agencies within the political community, but which is to be identified as final authority is an entailment of this mode of political organization, certainly for the purposes of international law making. In international law, government and the effective agency of the state, indeed the sovereign power, is located by locating the treaty right. (And some have argued that locating the treaty right locates the effective sovereignty of the state.) Thus, for the student of international relations, the relevant groups and forces, those elements of political culture and of the abstracted society which matter, are those which impinge on the treaty right.

But the unitary conception of the state is no mere legal or analytical convenience. More importantly, it derives from the modern concept of sovereignty as expressing a 'public power'. In contemporary civic orders with secular bases, in civil orders dominated by the idea of a power which ascends from some community, be it a national community, or the proletariat or citizenship within a civic community, the community is expressed and realized through the notion of a public sovereignty, or there being a (single) public power in which all citizens share. The unitary conception of the modern state was enormously strengthened by the notion of a communally based public power.

The second important characteristic of a state from the legal point of view is the nature of state jurisdiction. The latter is, indeed, very important for understanding the modern form of political association which is the state. By the legal concept of the state, indeed the modern meaning of the state, authority is exercised over territory, and only incidentally over people. There is a territorial domain in which certain laws operate which apply only over those in that territory. Thus, legal conditions and the operative rules of existence alter with territorial shifts. (Equally, however, it is possible for legal conceptions to shift, to divide, to encompass partial or open web legal orders, through which a legal community can be enlarged to include others for defence or economic purposes, and for the concept of a territory to include multiple territories, accordingly.)

The association between the concept of 'political community' and the state is a necessary association, in the sense that law-making is the way a political community expresses itself, and the government is a law-making agency. It is, however, neither a timeless association nor an uncontested association. There have been other sorts of political communities, and other ways of producing law and protecting culture or civilization or the word of god or the good life or interests, rather than the unitary authority-territorial way of so doing. Indeed, some people would go so far as to maintain that states are rather bad carapaces for political communities: anarchists, for example, and some religious groups, believe that political communities are more properly contained within universalizing – not territorial – associations. Certainly, the degree to which political authority ought to be centralized is contested, and whether even a plurality of legal orders might not serve the modern political community as well or better than the unified legal order. None the less, the territorial state with a unified government which produces a single law for a (single) citizenry remains closely associated with our modern ideas of a proper political community, and has been so for some time, particularly since the nationalist movements of the nineteenth century. It is widely accepted that to constitute a genuine political community is to have a territorial domain, in the first instance at least, with a recognized and more or less recognizable, more or less unified, government which serves the citizens within that domain; and the possession of territory and a discrete set of institutions which can be identified as 'government' is widely held to be essential in the constitution of such a community.

It is this state with which the present venture is concerned, the state as a political community, and as a particular kind of political community, one which is territorially located, with a more or less delimited set of persons distinguished from the citizenry by the name of government, and which is conceived as a law maker. What it is concerned to ask is, how is this state doing, viewed from the perspective of international relations?

Understanding the state

Understanding the state by viewing it as one among many is not a new perspective. When Hobbes defined the laws of nature and the state of nature, when Rousseau determined the meaning of the particular will, these definitions were made comprehensible and complete by viewing the state as one among many. The definition of an imperial state or the test of an ideological state are also achieved from outside, by observing how states act towards one another. (We test the quality of their democracy only occasionally by this method, but their marxism rather obsessively.) We also test their ability to change and adapt.

Viewing the legal, associational state from outside involves attention to the changing patterns of government induced by international participation, attention to the different routes of access opened to groups by such participation, and attention to the scope of government 'at home' as revealed by its dealings with other governments: the density and complexion of the bonds which tie citizen to government are revealed when a government is in dispute with other governments. How the idea of territorial authority is doing in the face of widespread participation in norm- and rule-setting international organizations is also clearly pertinent, as are its powers *vis-à-vis* large private corporations that operate internationally. But certain perspectives are particularly state-revealing.

An obvious case is the state and war. When states go to war, they are required to mobilize, or to guard from mobilization, large parts of the social, political and economic resource. What they choose to mobilize and what to guard reveals their ideas of themselves as political communities and their notions of the fulcrums of their social orders and their powers. More particularly, the course of war tests the capacity of states, the nature of loyalty and the quality of their institutions. (This was why nationalist theorists so often considered war the real test of national qualities.)

Another is the area of state acquisition. An important feature of the post-war world has been the creation of 'new states', new jurisdictions and new powers, as a result of decolonization and the handing of those powers to newly authorized agents, identified as a political élite in former colonial countries which then had the task of winning loyalty and creating new political communities. They brought to that task certain conceptions and institutions: How have they fared? How many of these conceptions and institutions have stayed intact? More particularly, how have these new experiments affected our understanding of what is required in order for there to be a state?

What we have done is to choose a few such critical viewing places where some aspects of different sorts of state-legal communities may be thrown into relief and where some generalities attempted without straining credulity. Such a method, which involves a series of 'cuts' on the state, aims for no general theory. On the contrary, it is intended, as the *Rechtstaat* idea always intends, to differentiate.

What ought to be done about the condition of states?

Integral to the legal, associational view of the state is the question of values, or the great 'oughts' which the state serves. Why this is so is not easy to explain, at least not in any brief compass. Logically, we might point out that the positive law concepts on which the modern state is built pose the law as an empty box, to be filled by human agency. Accordingly, if the state were to serve no moral purposes, it would serve by reduction only prevalent social forces. Historically, we might say that the legal view of the state was the creation of a deliberate historical development in self-determination, intimately involving the separation of the state from society. This separation was not a natural fact but a human creation, out of a desire for what can only be termed the good life, placed now on a secular foundation. That foundation demands, as a practical inference, a continuous evaluation of the state, and turns the state into a sort of continuous transformational device which mediates between events, forces and goods. Philosophically, we might say, in consequence, that no amount of state pathology can answer all the questions we have about the state.

For the associational state viewed in its relations with other states, there is one overriding moral question: what Hoffman has called duties beyond borders. This is not an incidental question to what a state is. It is a constitutive question. How a state chooses to define itself to outsiders, how indeed it defines outsiders, will largely determine what a state is, since its definitions establish the boundaries of the association. And how to think about insiders and outsiders is one of the most pertinent questions involved in any political theory. Indeed, it is political theory, and every theory of political association has an answer to that question.

The associational view of the state is often considered the same as the contractarian view. But contractarians are not the only rechtstaaters. Hegelians, rationalists and natural law theorists all hold views of the state which identify it with a legal order, view government as the creation of a legal order and the constitution of the laws as central elements in defining and shaping the political community. The collection closes with three essays, one in the hegelian tradition, the second by a libertarian and a third in the natural law tradition, which consider the question of duties beyond borders and the thorny issue of 'insiders' and 'outsiders'.

Notes

1 The onset of the marxist rethink of the state is generally credited to Ralph Miliband's *The State in Capitalist Society* in 1969; but in the American pluralist tradition, problems with the group approach were signalled even earlier, by Joseph La Palombra to the American Political Science Association meeting in 1959, who called attention to 'a vast network of quasi-corporatist relationships' in Italy, France and Great Britain: 'The Utility and Limitations of Interest Group Theory' *Journal of Politics* 22, 1 (1960), pp. 29–49.

2 The American case is ambiguous. American scholars were the first to apply interest group analysis to foreign policy studies and pioneered the application of bureaucratic and process models, rarely making use of any explicit notion of the state. But assumptions concerning a 'national interest' remained, despite the dominance of pluralist assumptions in policy studies, and accounts of the international system displayed the unitary actor perspective, so pervasively indeed that John Vasquez, for one, has consistently denied that American scholarship in international relations showed any significant deviation from the state-centric approach, and that American employment of systems analysis was but a continuation of the state-centric approach in a different guise: *The Power of Power Politics* (Pinter, 1983). The realist approach in America is also maintained by the concern to properly counsel leadership: see S.M. Hicks 'Influencing the Prince: A Role for Academicians' *Polity* 15, 2 (1982), pp. 279–93.

3 In English letters, note Hedley Bull 'International Theory: The Case for a Classical Approach' *World Politics* 18, 3(1966) pp. 361–77; F.S. Northedge 'Transnationalism: The American Illusion' *Millennium, Journal of International Studies* 5, 1(1976), pp. 21–8; and H. Bull 'The State's Positive Role in Human Affairs' *Daedalus* 108 (1979). In Britain, during the 1960s, to be labelled a functionalist, transnationalist or system theorist involved extreme professional risk.

4 See, esp. W. Olson and N. Onuf 'The Growth of a Discipline: Reviewed' in Steve Smith ed. *International Relations, British and American Perspectives* (Oxford, Blackwell, 1985) pp. 1–28.

5 Note, for example, the realist Susan Strange 'Supranationals and the State' in John Hall ed. *States in History* (Oxford, Blackwell, 1986) pp. 289–305.

6 See Martin Shaw ed. *War, State and Society* (Macmillan, 1984) for the new school of historical sociologists in their new concern with international relations; while B. Buzan and Barry Jones eds *Change and the Study of International Relations* (Pinter, 1981), for their part, include an essay by John Maclean on 'marxist epistemology'. Maclean reviews some of the new reunion literature in

'Marxism and International Relations: A Strange Case of Mutual Neglect' *Millennium, Journal of International Studies* 17, 2(1988), pp. 295–319.

7 'The Autonomous Powers of the State' in John Hall ed. *States in History* (Oxford, Blackwell, 1986).

8 The classic interest group analysis of American foreign policy is an inter-war work: E. Schattsneider *Politics, Pressure and the Tariff* (New York, Prentice-Hall, 1935).

9 The author reviewed *Foreign Affairs* during the inter-war period, looking, in vain, for examples of the famous dispute between 'realism' and 'idealism'; it was simply not there, due mainly to the paucity of realist theory, which was specifically nominated, when it did appear, as 'German' theory.

10 'Still the Century of Corporatism' *Review of Politics* 36 (1974) pp. 85–131.

11 I find F.A Hayek's argument compelling: *The Counter-Revolution of Science* (Indianapolis, Liberty, 1979).

12 The most recent discussion is Brendan O'Leary's *The Asiatic Mode of Production* (Oxford, Blackwell, 1989).

13 V.N. Nikiforov *The Orient and World History* (Moscow, Nanka, 1975), introduced into the current debate by Ernest Gellner 'Soviets Against Wittfolgel' in John Hall ed. *States in History* (Oxford, Blackwell, 1986) pp. 78–108.

14 *The State in Capitalist Society* (Weidenfeld, 1969).

15 *Political Power and Social Classes* (New Left Books, 1973).

16 For a good discussion of this and indeed many of the new state theories, see Gregor McLennan, David Held and Stuart Hall, *The Idea of the Modern State* (Milton Keynes, Open University Press, 1984).

17 'Bringing the State Back In' in Peter Evans, Dietrich Reuschmeyer and Theda Skocpol, *Bringing the State Back In* (Cambridge University, 1985) pp. 8–9.

18 *Revolution from Above* (New Brunswick, N.J., Transaction Books, 1978).

19 Op. cit., note 17, pp. 10–12.

20 The theory was originally laid out in *The Modern World System* 3 Vols (San Diego, Academic Press, 1974–89), but has been summarized in *The Capitalist World Economy* (Cambridge University, 1979).

21 'Dependency in an Interdependent World: The Limited Possibilities of Transformation in the Capitalist World Economy' *African Studies* 17 (1975), reprinted in *The Capitalist World Economy* (Cambridge University, 1979).

22 See A. Giddens *A Contemporary Critique of Historical Materialism*, esp. Vol. 2 *The Nation-State and Violence* (Polity, 1985); and T. Skocpol 'A Critical Review of Barrington Moore's Social Origins of Dictatorship and Democracy' *Politics and Society* 4, 1(1984) pp. 1–34.

23 See Gautam Sen *The Military Origins of Industrialisation and International Trade Rivalry* (New York, St Martins, 1988), 'Introduction' and 'Bibliography'.

24 One should note that Michael Mann's by now well-known thesis on the source of the state's autonomy, as an attribute of the 'legal arena of the state', expresses much the same view: op. cit., note 2.

2

Reality and Illusion in the Acquisition of Statehood

Willie Henderson

State creation, as a result of the break-up of imperial systems, has been an important feature of the post-war era and continues to be so. The focus of this chapter is not the detailed history of decolonization, nor is it the various ways in which statehood was achieved.[1] Rather the concern is with what it was that was obtained, or thought to have been obtained, by and through the achievement of statehood.

Different ways of achieving statehood undoubtedly left their mark on what it was that was thought to have been obtained. Those who fight a protracted war of liberation can be expected to feel differently about the achievement of political control over their territory from those to whom negotiation was an effective choice. Expectations of the likely rewards to individuals and groups might be more difficult to satisfy in the former case than in the latter. (Recent political differences in Zimbabwe are partly explained by differences in the commitment of activist forces during the war against the Smith regime.) Also, the key assets of statehood, an intact administrative system and useful physical infrastructure functioning in a way capable of sustaining contemporary needs, were more likely to be available to those states where negotiation was possible.

The timing of independence is also an important factor. Imperial withdrawal, as exhibited by the self-conscious and maritime imperial systems, extended over a 30-year period and nationalist agitation over an even longer period. Given recent problems experienced by the French and British over the political future of fragments of their former dominions, the process of withdrawal is not, even now, finally concluded. (The continued case for further development of the Australian constitution is less dramatic than the Falklands War but is, none the less, also part of the story of institutional adaptation.[2]) Over this time span, there were important changes in the conditions within which state creation took place, which affected the scope and timing of decolonization among Imperial systems. French experience of military defeat in South-East Asia coloured their domestic political attitudes towards decolonization in North and West Africa. Such attitudes influenced the possibility of negotiation and hence the kinds of outcomes open to the various parties involved. So unwilling were the Portuguese, even in the face of costly wars, to yield up the autocracy, that a coup in Portugal was required to produce a withdrawal from Africa. The British had accepted, in domestic politics, by the late 1950s that decolonization was in their own interests. Such domestic acceptance was more difficult in France until promoted by de Gaulle after his return to political leadership.[3] It was only faced in Portugal after a military coup. Myths of assimilation, or incorporation, and of minority domination proved too strong to be easily adjusted. At the international level, the political balance shifted towards the USA and the USSR, and both held anti-colonialist views. From time to time, the United Nations also effectively promoted the decolonization issue.

At a regional level, decolonization in southern Africa, complicated by the existence of a legally constituted and formally independent South Africa, with its own longstanding political and territorial ambitions in the region, was not an identical process to what had taken place earlier in English-speaking West Africa. Settler regimes, such as Algeria for the French and Rhodesia for the British, were difficult to handle, given both their political influence through highly organized pressure groups in metropolitan political circles and their strategic command over domestic resources within the territories concerned. And Hong Kong, though it has the economic capacity for statehood along lines similar to that of Singapore, has had to accept the prior claims of China (a political empire older than that of the British) over its territory.

Southern Africa was more problematic not simply because of a settler presence in Rhodesia, Mozambique and Angola and an ambitious South Africa, but also because of the weak nature, by comparison, of the other regional candidates for statehood. The presence of India within the international community of states involved changes in the international system quite different from the achievement of statehood by entities no bigger than, and in many cases much smaller and considerably poorer than, (say) the Birmingham conurbation.

Nevertheless, it is still possible to attempt some generalizations about the acquisition of statehood because of the very nature of the state. Some common properties were assumed to be confirmed and conferred by the state-making process. In the case of state-making within the Common-wealth, the kinds of moves made during the process of getting out reinforces this notion of something common having been achieved. Several decades on, it is possible to ask whether assumptions made by participants in the process of state making and the structures achieved, served their intended purposes.

What did a new state gain when it achieved statehood?

The starting point for the discussion must be former status within the imperial systems. Colonial entities within the British Empire were not of equal political or legal status (nor economic status for that matter, but the question of economic status can be postponed). Some were crown colonies with longstanding legislative councils and partly indigenous administrations; some were protectorates in which the exercise of power by an expatriate administration was sustained, and in the case of Bechuanaland and Swaziland for example, constrained by domestic political systems firmly under the control of a colonially supported aristocracy. Where white settlers existed in significant numbers, it was possible to find at the beginning of the decolonization process, advisory councils selected on the basis of racial segregation. Sierra Leone, Zambia and Nigeria are examples of countries which encompassed shortly before the process of internal institutional change, both crown colony and protectorate, though the experience of being treated as one entity had been lengthy. In Bechuanaland, modern Botswana, the division between the northern and southern protectorates, first made at the end of the nineteenth century, still had lingering administrative significance, and considerable political significance, 4 years before self-government in 1965.

Within each of these various kinds of entities, change was taking place according to a different pace, depending largely on the economic status of the country and the degree of education and, hence, on the aspirations of the élite. Ghana was already an independent state before government by decree had been abolished in the High Commission Territories in southern Africa. Portugal's writ in Mozambique, notwithstanding claims of centuries in Africa, hardly ever applied in northern Mozambique.

A new state then acquired control over the territory administered by the colonial administration with little regard for the historical, economic, political and social basis for viewing a territory as one entity. Generally, protectorates were tagged to the crown colony with which they had usually been associated and constitutional development applied to the new entity as a whole. And certainly, Acts of Parliament in the 1890s had removed, for the administration of justice and hence for most aspects of government and administration at the time, any barriers to the exercise of sovereign powers on the part of the Imperial Parliament and locally delegated administrations. In practice, however, particularly in those societies where rural economic life was the key to well-being, politics were a local concern (being about access to arable land, water, grazing) with local interest groups and loyalties that predated the colonial state. This sense of autonomy was not easily removed. It was, not unnaturally, greater or less depending upon the financial, and hence administrative, resources available to the colonial authorities.

Protectorates, then, tended to be absorbed directly into the new unitary state often leaving, as in Western Province in Zambia, local people with a sense of political frustration and hence creating problems for the concept of a loyal opposition, a premise upon which constitutional evolution in British territories was built. Nigeria was an exception, because specific federal arrangements were made to accommodate the northern protectorate, though this was not simply because of the power of the emirs. Federalism was also a recognition of the economic, religious and ethnic differences that existed within the vast territory that was to become Nigeria.

Botswana, in contrast, is an example of a protectorate that survived to statehood, with the title Protectorate dropped, at the request of the new government, only on the advent of self-government. In the case of Bechuanaland, however, a southern part of the original territory deemed to belong to the Tswana and given the name British Bechuanaland was transferred to Cape Colony in the 1890s. It was assumed, upon the formation of the Union of South Africa, and specifically written into a codicil to the Union's constitution, that the High Commission Territories would be handed over to South Africa at some stage subject to the agreement of the chiefs, and thus the union would be completed. This uncomfortable solution did not appeal to the ruling aristocracy within the three small countries. The idea finally died, for the British at least, when it was clear that there was no long-term future for a constitutional settlement based on any idea of transfer. (The nature of the relationship between a small dependent state and a powerful neighbour had to be faced elsewhere; for example, Nepal in relation to India. The problem in southern Africa was not simply because of size but because of the growing unacceptability of apartheid.) South Africa did not cease to be interested in controlling events in the region simply because of a proposed or actual change in the legal status of the High Commission Territories, though initially such changes had to be accommodated in the strategies adopted in its search for regional security.[4]

Despite occasional unrest and disaffection, colonial regimes in Africa, though founded on force and autocracy, were subject to periods of stability. The point about force was well understood from the very outset of Edwardian imperialism, by Sir C. P. Lucas. Writing on keeping the Empire, he said:

> The dependencies of Great Britain, as opposed to the self-governing Dominions, like the Roman Provinces, have, speaking generally, been held by force, open or in reserve, but by force perpetually receding into the background as good government has produced goodwill.[5]

Where goodwill was lost, force again came into its own, a trade-off not unknown in modern Africa.[6] The empire had to be garrisoned and sometimes a police force was not enough. Local security forces were created to serve local needs, albeit within the imperial system. What happened to such forces as the institutional framework for controlling them changed was not an unimportant issue. Where the forces and resources were large, as in the case of the ill-fated Central African Federation, the fact that Southern Rhodesia inherited much of the infrastructure and equipment of the airforce was not without significance in terms of the confirmation of regional power. But it was the size and ethnic composition of the defence forces that posed, for some leaders at least, a problem. As independence approached in east Africa, Julius Nyerere was one who questioned the need to take the forces as part of the inheritance.

Where there was an army, it was inherited or absorbed (the most striking problem being assimilation of nationalist freedom fighters in Zimbabwe into the conservative ranks of the existing armed forces). Troops old and new needed to be socialized into new loyalties.

Former holders of civil power within the domestic arena of the colonial state had also to be contended with. Constitutionally, this problem was tackled directly by the colonial authorities themselves before they departed the scene. Political and constitutional evolution implied that chiefs, local kings and the aristocracy be removed legally from centre-stage, to be replaced by the new nationalist groups. This issue was first tackled in Ghana, but had to be repeated in many countries. Until shortly before self-government, the *dikgosi* (chiefs) in Bechuanaland had been the main source of domestic political representation, and although they were effectively challenged by newly formed political parties, after 1961 it was left to the British administration to 'jolly them along' a road that was to lead to their loss of power. Although they lost much formal power through constitutional change particularly at the local government level through measures introduced during self-government, they continued to have local authority and patronage. However, it was not until a considerable time after independence that their final constitutional status was resolved. Compromise rather than direct confrontation was the basis of tackling the problem of chieftaincy in that country. In Uganda, where the kingship of the Kabaka was a powerful factor in domestic political life, the British-enforced compromise made in order to hurry the country into independence intensified rather than resolved domestic conflict. It was the independent state that moved, with violence, to end the significance of the kingship as a force in domestic politics. Tensions between the King and the politicians continues to be a significant factor in politics in Lesotho.

In terms of trying to manipulate the process of political development, traditional authorities were probably less of a stumbling block, in the short run, to the achievement of some sort of temporary consensus than settler communities whose economic position and access to right-wing groups in the UK could potentially lead to blockages in the change process. Rhodesia and Kenya are the two outstanding examples of settler power, but settlers were not without influence in Swaziland and Northern Rhodesia. In Kenya, where concerns were primarily economic, the solution to settler interests in the long term was to buy them out through international aid. The white community in Rhodesia, unlike the community in Kenya, had been given effective control of the territory in the 1920s and the move from minority to majority rule required an extensive war, sanctions and two transitional sets of constitutional arrangements (internal power sharing and the internationally recognized settlement with a period of special protection for the minority community). Other foreign minority groups were unable to secure such favourable treatment from the former imperial authorities. Former legitimacies and loyalties, on the part of the indigenous population, could not be so easily disposed of. Local rulers and nationalists could make common cause against the British but short-term agreement did not necessarily lead to long-term stability as old patterns of behaviour re-asserted themselves on independence.

As the prospect of statehood approached, the colonial entity went through a series of political stages, referred to as a process of constitutional development. Just as Edwardian commentators on empire drew on the Roman Empire as a source of comparison, and perhaps even inspiration, so too did nationalist politicians look for historical precedent against which to measure the success of the movement towards independence. At the beginning of the state creation process, particularly in Africa, the model that many politicians both locally and in the imperial country had in mind was that of the change from crown colony to dominion status that had taken place in countries such as Canada, Australia and South Africa. The Congress Party in India saw itself as a product of English education and its concern with the historical unfolding of the theme of freedom. India had already contributed to this process by accepting the idea of a Commonwealth with the British monarch as its head, while achieving independence with a republican constitution. The Commonwealth was seen by 1957 as a mechanism for helping to regulate the economic relations between the sterling area and territories moving towards independence. Later, the wheels of the constitutional development model were well oiled through practice elsewhere.

As a result of sometimes acrimonious negotiations, usually after a lengthy period of nationalist agitation, both within the particular country and in London, the new state acquired a liberal, democratic constitution, a judiciary in principle free from political interference, a governor-general and prime minister (only later a president and rarely an executive president), a parliament, cabinet, a leader of the opposition, a central bank and appropriate currency, a system of local government introduced late in the colonial period, a national anthem and a flag. In the process of constitutional development, party politics played a prominent and exciting role in the struggle to identify a legitimate group to whom the constitution and state machinery could be entrusted. Government by political participation through multi-party elections replaced government by administrative fiat or self-government under constraints imposed by the extra-territorial authority.

If many new states in Africa later became one-party states, it must be remembered that the colonial administration for most of its existence found the no-party state and autocratic rule to be politically convenient. Westminster-style confrontational politics had little chance, in most places, of replacing the carefully manipulated, non-democratic, consultation politics of the colonial regime. Few serious observers of constitutional evolution thought that it would guarantee political stability. Its primary role was to facilitate a tidy exit for the British administration along lines acceptable to public opinion and to meet international criteria for entry of the new state into the international community. But this should not be taken to imply scorn for tidyness. Tidyness was important to all parties concerned including the competing contenders for domestic power. Whereas there was eventually a tidy political settlement in Mozambique (and in Zimbabwe), Angola was more or less abandoned by the Portugeuse and the ensuing lack of territory-wide legitimacy on the part of the government allowed scope for external manipulation and warfare.

From the imperial viewpoint, constitutional development was a requirement for independence, though in the late 1940s the Colonial Office was only feeling its way towards a set of political reforms suggested as capable of satisfying the demands of educated political activists. Democratic elections served the need of testing claims to legitimacy coming from the new parties and interest groups, traditional leaders and specific ethnic or racial groups. Where colonial constitutional practice enjoyed long periods of stability, as in, for example, the Bechuanaland Protectorate, constitutional development had to be hurried along both by internal pressure from those groups anxious to assume power and by external encouragement. Between 1961 and 1966, the people of Bechuanaland experienced three major constitutional changes, the relocation of the administrative capital (at last within their own borders),[7] and the accompanying move from secretariate to ministerial government implied by constitutional change. In Bechuanaland, as elsewhere, the key change came with the arrangements made for the establishment of the self-governing constitution.[8]

In the years following independence, self-government was not given much political analysis, because full sovereignty is what normally counts with respect to statehood, but, in terms of the development of domestic political life, change from government by officials to government by elected representatives on the basis of universal suffrage was of major significance.

As with the establishment of a new basis for political life in Eastern Europe, the first brush with democratic politics has great significance for future developments. During self-government, the UK typically retained control of certain reserved powers, the most important of which was the power to control questions of security, both domestic and cross-border security, and all aspects of foreign relations. Naturally, nationalist politicians at this stage, especially with independence now within range, saw the right to exercise an independent foreign policy as an important expression of statehood, rather than as a potentially costly activity yielding little in the way of tangible benefit.

Even when recognizing the power of the political forces that nationalist movements managed to harness, there was a lingering unwillingness to conceed the autocracy. Internal self-government was often a two-stage process, with the governor retaining the right to preside at ministerial meetings, and the title 'cabinet' and even of 'prime minister' being withheld, for as long as possible during the transition period. Presidents-to-be were, in the early days of self-government, 'Leaders of Government Business' or 'Chief Ministers'.[9]

Territorial integrity and constitutional development were not the only formal criteria of readiness for what was called independence. A third, and one which was initially of considerable concern, was that any newly independent state should be seen to be economically viable. In granting independence to Newfoundland without paying adequate attention to the question of economic viability, the UK acted unwisely and had to resume responsibility with considerable embarrassment until such times as arrangements for the territory to join with the rest of Canada were worked out. The international discussion of colonial matters during the Second World War had stressed the costs of colonial administration. In the period of economic austerity that followed, the British found it necessary to reconcile the need to reinvest at home and the need to accommodate the investment needs of the colonies in an international context within which capital resources were scarce. Some thought had therefore to be given to economic and financial conditions.[10]

Economic viability might seem a straightforward enough concept, not capable of much evolution. Given that most colonies were poor, economic viability could not, and did not, imply a specific level of economic well-being, not at least in any direct sense. Viability was taken to exist whenever local taxation could support the administrative machinery required to sustain an independent government on the constitutional development model.

This criterion was subject to modification as the pace of decolonization quickened, as it was inevitably bound to do so. Aspirations changed within countries as those still to finish the process became anxious to catch up, while the controlling power felt more and more that it was in its own interests to divest itself of responsibility.[11] New solutions to non-viable countries had to be found. The change came through changed aid relationships. If the criterion of economic viability applied to both the recurrent budget and the development budget, few countries in Africa, even today, could be classified as economically viable. International aid, other than from the UK, meant that only some of the development budget need be financed from domestic sources. There were, however, countries such as the Gambia and Botswana, which achieved independence without being able to balance the recurrent budget (in other words without being able to pay for all the manpower and materials consumed by the administration on a day-to-day basis) from domestic resources. The UK guaranteed to provide grant in aid to such countries until they could finance administration from domestic sources alone. Sir Seretse Khama did not achieve domestic financing until 7 years after the granting of independence. He is known to have felt much more confident in the pursuit of Botswana's developing foreign policy once this domestic source had been secured.[12]

The relationship between nationalist agitation, constitutional development and the development of mass political parties is a complex one, as each activity fed off the other. Constitutional development helped identify new groups with whom the expatriate government could legitimately cooperate, and who would eventually acquire on behalf of the new state whatever it was that was on offer. Constitutional development implied not only a staged move from unrepresentative or less representative government, but also time within which to settle administrators and politicians into new roles.[13] Although those who participated in the process recognized that it left many questions unresolved, constitutional development was deemed capable of producing constitutional government (i.e. the rule of law), a loyal opposition and a loyal civil service capable, under ministerial direction, of impartial administration carried out in the national interest. At the same time, it was rarely felt that the constitutional rules would be fixed for all time.

The goal of this process was legal independence. In other words, an internationally acceptable settlement that freed the former colony of external control and confirmed on a new government authority for all internal and external affairs, even in those instances where the capacity to execute effectively such responsibility was questionable. Colonial people may have been seeking freedom and independence, but what the new state gave them was sovereignty; that is, the right to make their own laws and enter into their own treaties, together with domestic mechanisms, and access to international mechanisms, to help articulate such sovereignty.[14] In the beginning, in order to protect this legal independence, new states in Africa had little choice, initially, but to build upon the connections with, or made by, the former colonial power.

Thus the new sovereign entitles were expected to honour treaties and agreements made by the previous regime and to agree to the conventions and protections afforded by the body of international law that they had no direct part in making. However, once in the international arena, and bolstered by increased numbers, the new states sought to assert influence through such institutions as were available to them. During the Rhodesian crises, the black Commonwealth states (not just in Africa but also in the West Indies) made considerable use of the Commonwealth to enforce British Government commitment to 'No Independence Before Majority Rule'. Indeed, the New Commonwealth changed the Old Commonwealth and the strains led, as at Singapore in 1971, to the expectation that either Britain, or some of the African states, would split the organization.

Accommodation to new states was also made within the United Nations with institutions like the United Nations Conference on Trade and Development (UNCTAD), the United Nations Educational, Scientific and Cultural Organization (UNESCO) and the United Nations Industrial Development Organization (UNIDO) either changing or being brought into being as a result of their involvement. The Organization of African Unity (OAU) and the Non-Aligned Movement were similarly products of the new states, though perhaps the proliferation of new international meeting points was a measure of frustration rather than of purposeful action. It took some time for the new states to work out, among themselves, strategies for successful joint diplomatic action.

As part of the mechanics of independence, formal agreement had to be reached with neighbouring states on the precise definitions and mapping of boundaries. Territorial integrity did not imply precise and enforceable boundaries. In some instances, it was difficult to reach acceptable agreements; for example, the existence of a border between Bostwana and Zambia somewhere in the middle of the Zambesi was accepted by Botswana and Zambia in the face of South African and Rhodesian opposition. On the whole, lack of agreement at the edges was not allowed to hold up the acquisition of sovereignty.[15] Problems and disputes at the edges were postponed until later. In any case, real border controls and significant meaning was often lacking as people crossed borders at will.

There can be little doubt that the main acquisition of those who gained power was the control of a reformed government machine, recently established along ministerial lines, and control over a recently re-organized system of local government through a body of colonial and self-government legislation that was largely intact and that vastly extended the role of government in the new state.

Nationalist politicians and writers had long argued for more and better paid indigenous involvement in the colonial administration at all levels.[16] This meant that there were enormous expectations of new labour market opportunities to be satisfied. While there was an enormous pressure for 'Africanization', there was in almost every case in British Africa, a carry-over of personnel from the outgoing regime. Indeed, as the role of the state in relation to economic life had been changed during the process of political development, so the demands for state manpower also changed. This led to an increase in overseas recruitment for the services of technical experts. The foreign autocracy had gone, but the numbers of foreigners present increased. At the same time, the expansion of the domestically recruited civil service meant that the new rulers had to come to terms with the interests of a young and strategically placed group of educated people whose aims and objectives were not necessarily the same as those of national economic development. The likely reaction of civil servants to issues of state policy were important political issues in their own right.

However, the post-colonial state was expected to maintain the commitments of its predecessor not only with respect to international agreements but with respect to contractual agreements such as the payment of pensions to retired, or soon-to-be-retired, civil servants recruited on permanent and pensionable terms. Although some objected, it was in the interests of the new politicians to agree, as the civil administration and external agreements helped fix the state.

As decolonization proceeded, another criterion came to the fore, though it was not an additional criterion, rather a re-emphasis of territorial integrity. This was the concept of self-determination, promoted by both nationalist politicians opposed to multiracialism and by the United Nations. This certainly was not intended to imply the breaking up of the colonial entity into its pre-colonial constituent parts, but simply to insist on the transfer of power to the indigenous populations rather than to settler or other alien communities and on a common roll suffrage rather than on the basis of constitutional guarantees to minorities. This was of particular importance in east and southern Africa. It also has had application to South Africa where the government in the 1960s and 1970s pursued a policy of granting independence or self-government to Bantustans. It was important, especially in the context of southern Africa, that states met the criterion.

Entry into the international community was largely by legitimate sponsor – the former colonial power usually supporting the application to join the United Nations and with additional diplomatic support from other Commonwealth countries. Entry into the Commonwealth was not a problem, although entry into the United Nations for some of the weaker states could have been difficult. Botswana, Lesotho and Swaziland were much criticized at the OAU on the eve of self-government and critical voices were expected at the United Nations upon independence, though in the normal run of events, sponsorship was not a problem. Botswana did at least look like a state, had a legitimate sponsor, had experienced constitutional development on the basis of self-determination and, in addition, was in possession of contiguous territory. Across the border where the idea of an independent Tswana homeland (later created and named Bophutatswana) was being promoted, contiguous territory, self-determination and legitimate sponsorship were all lacking. To the north, where the settler regime in Rhodesia was in a state of rebellion, the regime could command, for a while, considerable internal resources but access to external support, both diplomatic and material, was limited by a lack of legitimate status. Neither rebellion by a white minority nor sponsorship by South Africa were internationally acceptable routes to securing full sovereignty. Latterly, the process of constitutional development came to be applied to Namibia, but only after a guerilla war and direct United Nations involvement.

Access to the world system of states was available on the basis of assumed international equality. At the same time, new states obtained access to the recently created international aid system (designed initially to cope with potential power vacuums in Europe after the Second World War but capable of adaptation and extension to deal with potential power vacuums elsewhere on the withdrawal of imperial power) but on the basis of being clients and recipients rather than as equal partners. Aid, of course, had been provided by British sources under Colonial Welfare acts, but the new states now found access to wider sources of aid, both bilateral and multilateral, as well as from sources where ideological competition was also taking place. This choice of funds co-existed with a very favourable international financial regime, especially during the major period of state creation (1957–66) and for some time after, especially when the period is compared with the international financial concerns after 1973 and again after 1979 (both periods of oil price increases and of recession or of rising real interest rates leading to payments problems). In the earlier period, the international community could afford to treat generously even the less likely candidates for statehood. The embarrassing riches of short-term and long-term credit was not necessarily in the long-term interests of the new states as some, like Ghana, discovered fairly rapidly.

Policy assumptions and policy guidelines

In addition to an initially favourable international environment, constitutional structures and rising expectations, the new politicians came to political independence with certain assumptions and objectives. These established policy guidelines, which, despite differences of conditions, time and even place, were remarkably similar across states.

Perhaps one of the most important assumptions was that new territories were poor because they had been colonies. If they ceased to be colonies through the acquisition of statehood, then they could also escape from poverty. The proposition that countries were poor because they were colonies was one that the generation of new nationalist leaders felt to be the case. If the new bureaucracy could mobilize domestic as well as international savings, through the formulation of a development plan based on a development strategy, then increased real income could soon be achieved.

With these aspirations towards increased living standards (felt also by the wider population) went the idea that the state was concerned not only with the simple administration of justice and incremental improvements in communication, education and health, but with the promotion and management of economic development or with what came to be called modernization. The idea of state responsibility for development was not simply a post-colonial idea. Some responsibility for what came to be called development had been accepted by the UK and France in the 1940s; and some colonial administrations had been aware, much earlier, under particular governors, of notions of co-ordinated development before the terms were fashionable. However, when the term 'development' had been used it tended to mean opening up areas to white settlement. In contrast, during the 1920s Guggisberg of the Gold Coast developed a remarkable policy of government for and by Africans and a planned approach to government expenditures.

Ideas of state responsibility for welfare had clearly influenced the first generation of independence politicians from their student-day contact with UK domestic political change and moves in the UK towards a welfare state. Colonial paternalists in government and church were often suspicious of capitalistic involvement in the colonial economy. This suspicion of capitalism, seen as the force behind colonialism, was shared by many of the new leaders who, while contributing little of a fundamental nature to the analysis of colonialism (except perhaps Nkrumah's analysis of the neo-colonial state), were anxious to use the state and state activity to create wealth. State activity, big pushes (i.e. large quantitative increases in domestic investment) and market manipulation, were thought to be the only ways to secure rapid increases in living standards. This investment, when it took place, tended to be urban-biased and industrial, whereas the bulk of the growing population lived on the land. For the period 1961–6, Ghana provides the best example of such thinking being applied in practice. As an illustration of the claim that policy assumptions and guidelines have a common element, large urban-based conspicuous consumption projects (such as the Sheraton Hotel and the international sports stadium) have been undertaken recently in Zimbabwe.

Few states opted for an overtly capitalistic ideology, Kenya and Botswana being the obvious exceptions. In West Africa, where there was a trading tradition, the formal mercantile structures were expatriate in origin and the existence of domestic traders and an extensive, non-formal trading sector did not give rise to outwardly biased economic policies as it did, say, in the case of Singapore. Colonial economic structure was itself so obviously externally biased that outwardly oriented policies were perceived as maintaining poverty. Tanzania managed to combine socialist ideology with an emphasis on rural production. Leaders in most states found it necessary to articulate some kind of collectively approved ideology, such as African socialism, that helped illustrate and simplify ideas concerning the future society.

There was an implicit assumption that states could effectively and efficiently control economic transactions both within their borders and with the rest of the world through price fixing, import licensing and the creation of public monopolies, despite the fact that such activities are costly in scarce administrative resources. (Paradoxically, colonial administrators, particularly in Tanganyika but elsewhere also, did not much relish market forces nor rich farmers either.) In practice, attempts to manipulate and control economic life were costly in economic and administrative terms. States could and did control the exchange rate but found it difficult to control cross-border smuggling of both goods and foreign currency. Domestic black markets were also difficult to control as illicit sources of goods and lack of effective rationing devices led to market erosion of fixed prices. Where economic good-fortune had given rise to financial reserves, in Ghana and Zambia – and later in Nigeria through oil exports – such reserves were rapidly liquidated. Nigerian politicians found it difficult to resist spending both sustainable income and windfall economic rent earned from the export of oil, whereas politicians in the economically open and vulnerable state of Botswana managed, throughout periods of windfall earnings, to resist the temptation to over-extend the budget.[17]

With these views went the notion that building-up the state and state institutions was both a means to an end (economic development) and an end in itself through employment generation. In Africa, the state became the largest, single employer of labour. Some new states attempted to resist spending large sums of money on the newly inherited defence services; only a few, like Botswana, managed to postpone the establishment of a defence force (rather than a small paramilitary police force) until long after independence. Where resources were constrained and defence expenditures threatened as a result of International Monetary Fund (IMF) structural adjustment policies, the army tended to be a source of discontent and adept at securing its own interests. The proposition that there was always a military reason for unrest, rebellion or takeover in the case of coups in West Africa is one that is generally accepted.

The need, in the face of rising expectations, and growing numbers of educated school leavers, to be seen to be tackling the problem of unemployment without sanctioning wholesale wage cuts in the statutory sector of the economy, was a profoundly difficult problem to solve. In looking for solutions, attention was drawn away from output towards employment. In most countries, the fact that the private sector was largely foreign-owned meant that the state could, with little organized domestic challenge, gather developmental policy and implementation under its wing.

In addition to economic and statist assumptions, there were also important political and cultural ones. Most nationalist leaders felt that nationhood was a necessary basis for statehood, in the short-run as well as in the long-run. The nation-state concept assumes some kind of unity of sentiment, supported and sustained by commonly accepted symbols. Empire had been strong on common symbols in terms of the Crown and of the responsibilities of groups rather than states towards it. The new state needed potentially powerful symbols. Nkrumah's black star state and the selection of Ghana as the name to replace the Gold Coast, despite the fact that the Ghanaian Empire has been an interior state far from the Gold Coast, shows how important the symbolization was. Political energies, as a matter of necessity, had to be directed into creating some means of establishing a sense of common destiny. In acquiring the state, it was thought useful to mould a nation. It was also thought that nation-building would be popular. In the context of unequal development, where some had the wealth and others the symbols, such popularity was always likely to be dubious, once the initial objective of independence had been obtained.

The cultural aspect of nation-building, illustrated very strongly by the choice of the names Ghana and Zimbabwe, was the reassertion of the African personality and culture, often languishing under the unsympathetic assumptions of westernization through colonialism. But there were problems of conflict among the objectives of modernization, which tended to challenge traditional practices, and promotion of African cultural values which potentially reasserted them in the face of the challenge from modernization. Similar conflicts exist between nation-building and the reassertion of the historical experience. The historical experience within each new state in Africa had often been one of conflict prior to, or exacerbated by, contact with whites. Some states in South-East Asia could reasonably call upon even older empires for their sense of nationhood, though this in itself has not guaranteed political legitimacy. For these reasons, modernization, nation-building and the reassertion of the validity of the African historical experience did not always sit comfortably side by side. Clearly, there was need for a sense of balance among these objectives.

Reality and illusion

These, then, were the structural transformations and policy assumptions. Any attempt at understanding what happened to territorial authority in the transition from colonial status to making sovereignty work (rather than simply attaining freedom or independence) must take into account the tensions between legal authority and actual real-world conditions of competing legitimacies and power (domestic and international); between the aspirations and illusions that state-makers shared and the reality of state capacity.

All states were, in theory, equal members of the international community.

At the same time, there was clearly an international pecking order. Although states were not divided into 'civilized' and 'barbaric' as they had been in the nineteenth century, international classifications had been drawn-up in order to determine which qualified for what kind of international subsidy. The language of classification changed as the new actors expressed preferences for neutral terms both in terms of higher and lower ordering but also in terms of East–West divisions. Thus a terminology moving from underdeveloped to developing countries, from recently emerging nations to countries in the Third World. Such states as were guided by good judgement (together perhaps with some good luck) and sound diplomacy used the right of access to the community of states on an equal basis as a way of changing their position in the pecking order.

In Africa, among the new states themselves, differences in state capacities were not immediately understood and accepted. Nkrumah successfully exploited, though at some cost, Ghana's position as the first black African state to gain independence within the Commonwealth. Such a leading position did not survive economic decline and his removal from the scene. At the same time, the OAU, designed to increase African influence and to provide a focus for new loyalties, acted, during the 1960s and 1970s, in respect of policy towards Rhodesia, as if all member states stood in the same physical and practical relationship with minority-ruled countries. It was in the early 1970s that black-ruled states in southern Africa initiated and defended their right to develop regional lines of action based on what it was possible for each state to achieve in the context of South Africa's dominant regional position. The Lusaka Manifesto of 1969 was the starting point of a process that led later to the formation of the frontline brotherhood when Seretse Khama joined Kaunda and Nyerere in a search for purposeful diplomatic action.

The making of African foreign policy within international fora in Africa was further complicated by communication and political constraints on foreign ministers. Few could make policy commitments or adjustments without referring back to their ministries and head of state. Delays at crisis meetings became the norm. This sort of behaviour has continued to hinder the development of Nigeria's potential to become a significant foreign policy actor in Africa. Up to 1970, there was little recognition in the OAU that states in Africa had different capacities to cope with the problems created by the existence of minority regimes in southern Africa. States in southern Africa needed to clarify their interests and did so in terms of the Lusaka Manifesto. Later, in attempting to formulate and co-ordinate international policy towards the various parties in the Rhodesian war, after the collapse of the Portuguese in Africa, the diplomatic task in southern Africa passed from the foreign ministers to the state presidents of Botswana, Zambia, Tanzania, Angola and Mozambique. It was only through such personal diplomacy that urgency could be accommodated and difficult issues resolved.

Although states were small, this did not exempt them from trying to secure favourable external environments. In southern Africa, it had always been clear that diplomatic alliances were essential for the small countries. Botswana first sought negotiation alliances with Lesotho and Swaziland concerning the re-negotiation of the Customs Union with South Africa but, once this was accomplished, had to turn northwards, looking first to Malawi (finding Banda's idea of alliance with South Africa unacceptable) and then to Zambia. Faced with challenges to sovereignty both from South Africa (which wanted to treat them as Bantustans) and freedom fighters (who wanted to use them as jumping-off points for cross-border penetration) the small countries had to think very hard about capacity and useful alliances. That they had a degree of freedom is evident from the differing choices that they made.

This process of adjustment took place elsewhere. It had been assumed that patterns of regional cooperation worked out in east Africa in colonial times would continue; in the short term they did not, in the longer term they changed. The different ideologies and differing allocation of benefits from regional cooperation meant that the sovereign governments looked for new associations. Changed political status implied a progressive reassessment of needs and a wider range of diplomatic possibilities. Not only was the potential recognized, changed patterns of association were achieved. Few could have foreseen in 1965, either Botswana and Tanzania as equal partners in the search for solutions to conflict in southern Africa, or the development of the Southern African Development Co-ordination Conference as a way of focusing questions of regional economic development without the disadvantages to sovereign entities that a customs union implies.

Interference across international borders was not restricted to southern Africa. Border disputes, refugees and open conflict appeared in other regions, e.g. as between Chad and Libya. In the beginning, the OAU found it more difficult to secure agreement among its members than had the colonial monopolists among themselves.

As it happened, the international legitimacy of new states was quickly accepted. Biafra, unlike Bangladesh, did not make it to statehood but even those small states, such as Lesotho and Chad, that had seemed unlikely as candidates for independence in the early 1960s, found support from being part of the international community. All small states had, however, to find ways of coming to terms with the economic and military might of powerful neighbours anxious for some control over political developments.[18]

To fail as a government did not imply failure as a state. Ghana has survived as a state entity despite economic failure in the context of an unsympathetic international financial climate. Uganda has survived internal political barbarism, invasion and the collapse of the formal economy. Tanzania incurred considerable costs during the invasion of Uganda. Dennis Austin has pointed out that the existence of such costs, and the prospect of further costs, was a factor that made annexation an unlikely option. In southern Africa in the nineteenth century, colonial administrators were warned against incurring further responsibilities because of the likelihood that new territory would mean additional costs.

On the domestic front, the new state assumed public power but frequently neither the constitution, nor the nationalist movement, was enough to establish the reality of that power. Despite the formal downgrading of chiefs and other institutionalized remnants of colonially sanctioned authority, political control was not easily achieved along liberal-democratic lines or, in some cases, on any other lines. Underlying regional or ethnic interests, with or without chiefly government, had to be accommodated or confronted. Command over new institutions and over new sources of office, of patronage and even over domestic resources (in some countries the state obtained control of mineral rights for the first time on independence), all led to potential increases in competitiveness among groups that predated the state. Consequently, instability and threats to the constitution from both opposition and government parties or through military intervention gave rise to constitutional modifications, either through one-party systems (usually popularly sanctioned) or through the temporary eclipse of parties and constitutional arrangements as a result of military coup. The state in Africa was not a monolithic, purposive institution, but often an unstable coalition of particular interests. In a sense, constitutional development continued, even in those states – Gambia and Botswana – where the multi-party ground rules have been adhered to, as a pragmatic search for effective rules to govern new interests was followed. Care must be taken to distinguish unstable coalitions of particular interests, the search for new rules to govern interests and instability as such.

On the economic front, where statist assumptions and aspirations had been strongest, considerable adjustments had to be made. Some states were surprisingly successful at bringing to life a level of economic development that would have been thought highly unlikely on the eve of independence: Botswana is the best example. Others, well placed on independence with educational, financial and productive resources, destroyed their growth potential through economic and political mismanagement. The Ivory Coast made an economic success on a resource base very similar to that of Ghana, whereas the economy of Ghana has been in difficulties for the last 20 years or so. A relatively large bureaucracy and the exercise of political power on the basis of legal independence was not sufficient as a basis for increasing economic development. Those who looked outwards and blamed multinational corporations were less successful than those who looked outwards and sought new export markets and new sources of investment.

The gulf between rich states and poor states was not, and could not be, plugged by official aid in countries that chose inappropriate investment strategies. To promote development, policy needed to be both more refined and more selective, and policy makers needed to be much more aware of what a given state or a given economy could do efficiently. Countries are poor for reasons that have to do with resource endowment (climate, rainfall, natural resources, supply of trained and educated labour), domestic economic policy and with how that economy is directed in relation to world markets in general and the exchange value of the currency in particular.

Reappraisals have had to take place. Tanzania has recognized that some mistakes have taken place on the road to socialism. Ghana is currently experiencing a reconsideration of the role of the market and market forces as ways of allocating resources and of enhancing growth. Outside actors, such as the IMF, have had a part to play in this reassessment.

Political independence did not lead to what has been called, by some, genuine economic independence. States have had to learn to live with the power of multinational corporations, some using them as a vehicle for increased prosperity (though controlling and taxing what they can), others continuing to challenge their monopolistic powers through the alternative of state monopoly. Some states have come to realize that dependency/independence is less important than the generation of domestic incomes through whatever means is available, while others still struggle with the notion of a national economy.

Despite numerous internal problems, in most cases territorial integrity has been maintained. True, some states, such as the Sudan and Uganda, riven with religious and ethnic conflict, have at times come close to disintegration, but in others some kind of sense of belonging to a wider polity has slowly emerged. Engagement in the state-making process has been painful, and in some cases tragic, but there have been considerable achievements. Survival has not simply been about being buttressed by international aid or international legal institutional arrangements. In cultural terms, for example, sovereignty has meant a reconsideration of the black African contribution to culture, with a refocusing on African studies and on the African contribution to other cultures (particularly through the black presence in the USA). Problems with the adaptation of culture patterns to new behaviour and new expectations have also given rise to new forms of the novel, critically appraising issues in African society. At the same time, exchanges at the political, party, diplomatic and university levels, have given rise to a growing understanding within Africa of the realities behind other states. The dispersal of economic refugees from Ghana throughout southern Africa has also raised an awareness of comparative political cultures and the possibility of political regimes operating without the widespread use of the dash. It is difficult to imagine any of these changes taking place without the support of statehood.

Given the artificiality of the colonial entity, it is hardly surprising that the process of constitutional development did not give rise to a sense of belonging to one polity. It has taken time to learn to live domestically. The nation-state formula suggests that some national interest in political life can be discovered and used as the foundation for political consensus. If that interest does not exist but a dominant culture does, what can be expected is a kind of stability accompanied by cultural hegemony. If there is no dominant culture, then all that can be hoped is that good sense creates some kind of national interest, if only because no-one can think of a suitably constituted alternative state. While it is true that some countries, at some stages, have come close to splitting, there can be little doubt that working compromises over the years have led to some sense of commonality and hence to some kind of nascent political culture even if only at the level of recognition of this is how we do things in this country.

The tension felt between state sovereignty and state capacity still exists. While Botswana is theoretically equal to Nigeria, it cannot afford the same degree of diplomatic representation nor the same level of defence expenditure, though its strategic vulnerability in southern Africa requires policy towards securing a safer external environment within which to operate. Small countries have little choice but to react to regional events. The quality and timing of their reactions can make a difference to their position. It is in exercising such careful choices that smaller states can discover some reality in their sovereignty.

Was the game worth the candle?

Is it enough, when thinking about the reality and illusions of statehood, to concentrate largely on the capacity of state machinery to produce economic or military well-being? If we focus solely on tensions between state sovereignty and state capacity, then the product is likely to be a very gloomy view of the state in Africa. In the 1930s, when countries were driven in on themselves through protectionist measures designed, in vain, to cope with falling incomes and rising unemployment, empires were thought to be more liberal than nation-states because they had to reconcile somehow the commercial, industrial and political interests of so many different elements in the system. In a decolonized world, and one in which change is rapid and often unexpected, in which powerful states exist with little obligation to accommodate the smaller ones, small states and weak states must compete as best they can for space in the international pecking order and seek what alliances they can.

However, the emergence of other new states, of alternative sources of aid and of new institutions, has in turn led to an increasing choice of partnership in various kinds of alliances. If a world of large powerful states has reduced the chances of small states effectively expressing their sovereignty in international decision making, then this has been offset, to some extent, by the increased choices of diplomatic, trade and aid contacts, which has in turn allowed other opportunities for expressing sovereignty. And if Zimbabwe has more choice of alliances than UDI Rhodesia, so too, in a curious way, have countries like Sweden, Denmark and Canada. Decolonization has meant more space for the smaller state, at the cost of greater unpredictability perhaps, to operate in than the imperial monopolies ever did.

It is not only externally that the gloomy view has less gloomy aspects. Within states there is a growing understanding of the nature of the political culture that has been achieved and a growing number of critical voices assessing that culture. Notions of what it is to be an unsuccessful polity, and hence ideas as to what success might be, constitute an important subject in the writings of African novelists. Even where the state has failed to promote economic efficiency, the concern is now on how to improve economic performance rather than on how to put the clock back. What has been stripped away are the illusions about state building or easy assumptions about political and economic life.

At the individual level, the concept of being Ghanaian or Zimbabwean (even if there is conflict) is probably more satisfying than the idea of being a native of the Gold Coast or a black Rhodesian. The difference has little to do with state capacity but with the notion of participation. Given a Zimbabwean state, the potential for the individual citizen is enhanced as new kinds of discussions are entered into, new choices faced. This potential exists even where economic success is problematic or where the system is a one-party system. It is hard to imagine, for example, the Rhodesian authorities raising the consciousness of black, rural women. Fully participating citizenship adds a new dimension.

For those interested in the moral validity of states and state action, however, the notion of capacity remains important. In the twentieth-century meaning of the term 'state', it is not possible to separate the idea of capacity from the idea of sovereignty which it both informs and constrains. Sovereignty implies the capacity to secure some degree of human welfare, and while no list may be readily agreed, security from starvation must be an absolute minimum. Capacity and sovereignty do not imply autarchy; no poor state, and few rich ones, can hope to achieve even minimum welfare ends without alliances, access to international finance and financial cooperation, and a network of international agreements. What they both imply is the ability to enter into such arrangements in the pursuit of welfare ends. Even within this notion, it must be recognized that states have unequal capacities and the concept of capacity is a useful one, even if measurement is difficult, for both commentators and practitioners to keep in mind.

The plight of famine victims in Africa also raises questions about government responsibility, government-to-government responsibility and the responses of private people, besides reminding us what expressions like capacity and sovereignty mean in terms of human welfare. Even if states had similar capacities to look after the welfare of their citizens, they are likely to display different degrees of willingness to do so. The framework for famine relief and control in India was established in the earlier years of the twentieth century. The principles of famine control cannot therefore be remote and difficult ones. The economic capacity to realize them is likely to be available internationally if the domestic will is also available.

Are we dealing in some states with questions of capacity or questions of willingness? States come in a range of conditions and from a variety of historical starting points. It might be useful to be able to distinguish questions of willingness from questions of capacity. Capacity implies the ability to make some rational decisions about resource allocation together with the ability to preserve groups in the population from at least accidental harm. Uganda under Amin or Ethiopia under its marxist regime would seem to have neither the will nor the capacity for fulfilling even such a minimalist list.

The concept of capacity has then this other important function. It allows us to distinguish between ability and will. States with similiar capacities might well have different wills to action. This distinction is important surely for any concept of responsibility. The state that does not assume the responsibility to build a capacity to protect its citizens from accidental harm is unlikely to be a successful state, and where the minimal list is not achieved, arbitrariness and force will be to the fore, and good government will, itself, inevitably recede.

Where the willingness to improve economic welfare has existed, as it clearly has in Ghana, Zambia and Tanzania, the state, for whatever reason, over-reached itself and over-estimated its capacity to provide sustained increases in living standards on the basis of the economic and political programmes that each pursued. In making an evaluation of the notion of responsibility, then, any failure in such countries is an empirical one, rather than a failure of will.

The revision of ideas on the relationship between the state and society that is currently taking place in many countries in Africa is not unique to that continent. It is part of a much wider revision that is taking place in Eastern Europe and elsewhere, where there exists a popular demand for economic progress. In the late eighteenth century, Adam Smith set out the state's role in making and maintaining the market and of prohibiting rent-seeking economic behaviour. That role is being rediscovered in many polities. No doubt the process is painful, carrying with it in some African countries a feeling that adjustments to problems of indebtedness and over-valued exchange rates recommended by outside agencies such as the IMF, implies financial recolonization, as domestic policies become subjected to determination, once again, by outside forces. A better test of such policies from the point of view of what it means to be a state is their implications for enhanced economic growth and increased domestic capacity in an interdependent, international system.

Notes

Sources: Muriel Evelyn Chamberlain *Decolonisation: The Fall of the European Empires* (Oxford, Blackwell, 1985); John Darwin *Britain and Decolonisation: The Retreat from Empire in the Post-war World* (Macmillan, 1988); Prosser Gifford and W. Roger Louis eds *The Transfer of Power in Africa* (New Haven, Conn., Yale University, 1982); Henri Grimal *Decolonisation: The British, French, Dutch and Belgian Empires 1919–1963* (Routledge and Kegan Paul, 1978); J.D. Hargreaves *Decolonisation in Africa* (Longman, 1988); Charles Harvey and Stephen R. Lewis Jr *Policy Choice and Development in Botswana* (Macmillan, 1990); A.H.M. Kirk-Greene *Africa in the Colonial Period, 3: The Transfer of Power*, Proceedings of a Symposium held at St Antony's College Oxford, 1978; A.N. Porter and A.J. Stockwell *British Imperial Policy and Decolonisation*, Vols 1 and 2 (Macmillan, Cambridge Commonwealth Series, 1989); Dorothy S. White *Black Africa and De Gaulle: From the French Empire to Independence* (Philadelphia, Pennsylvania State University, 1979).

1 For example, by political and nationalist agitation; by negotiation, sometimes with considerable unwillingness on the part of numerous political actors involved and sometimes with a surprising sense of common purpose; by revolution; or even through abnegation of imperial responsibility.

2 Fortress Falklands seems out of step with the main thrust of Britain's record of imperial withdrawal. The existence of settlers and/or interested third parties complicates the issue both in the Falklands and in Hong Kong.

3 For details of decolonization in French West Africa, see Yves Person 'French West Africa and Decolonisation' in Prosser Gifford and W. Roger Louis eds *The Transfer of Power in Africa* (New Haven, Conn., Yale University, 1982) pp. 141–72. See also Dorothy S. White *Black Africa and De Gaulle: From the French Empire to Independence* (Philadelphia, Pennsylvania State University, 1979). The Suez crisis helped the British to think through the resource implications of not decolonizing.

4 In 1963, Verwoerd even went so far as to offer to lead the High Commission Territories to independence under South African leadership along Bantustan and traditional native democracy lines.

5 C.P. Lucas *Greater Rome and Greater Britain* (Oxford University, 1912) p. 161.

6 For an analysis of the factors that encouraged stability, see J.D. Hargreaves *Decolonisation in Africa* (Longman, 1988) Ch. 1 'Conditions of Tranquility in Africa'.

7 From the Imperial Reserve in Mafeking, South Africa, to a newly planned administrative headquarters in Gaborone (then Gaberones) in the southern part of Botswana. This new town was tiny. It is now the fastest growing city in sub-Saharan Africa.

8 For a summary of the type of administrative reforms that were implied by political reform, as recommended by the Colonial Office to colonial governors in 1947, see Cranford Pratt 'Colonial Governments in East Africa' in Prosser Gifford and W. Roger Louis eds *The Transfer of Power in Africa* (New Haven, Conn., Yale University, 1982) p. 254.

9 Kwame Nkrumah became Leader of Government Business in the Gold Coast in 1951. This unwillingness to concede the title Prime Minister applied even late in

the decolonization process. During talks in 1963, leading to the development of the self-governing constitution for Bechuanaland, the colonial authorities approached the negotiations with reservations about the title of Prime Minister and a desire to maintain the influence of the Queen's Commissioner for as long as possible within the internal transition allowed for in the transfer process. The Batswana negotiators managed to secure the title from the outset of the self-government package.

10 For general considerations of policy issues involved from the UK's point of view with respect to wider issues in investment policy, see Document 72 'The United Kingdom's Role in Commonwealth Development' in A.N. Porter and A.J. Stockwell *British Imperial Policy and Decolonisation* (Macmillan, Cambridge Commonwealth Series, 1989) Vol. 2

11 If nationalists thought they were poor because they were colonized, then the British came to the conclusion that they were poor because they were colonizers! The idea of the internationalization of the 'colonial burden' had been opposed by the British and Free French when first suggested towards the end of the Second World War. Dropping the alleged burden became a factor in the conversion of the Conservative Party to decolonization. For details of the internationalization issue, see Henri Grimal *Decolonisation: The British, French, Dutch and Belgian Empires 1919–1963* (Routledge and Kegan Paul, 1978) Part 2.

12 Willie Henderson 'Seretse Khama: A Personal Appreciation' *African Affairs* 15, 1 (1990) pp. 27–56.

13 The time period for the transitional arrangements very much depended upon the starting point and the initial assumptions. Nkrumah became Leader of Government Business in the Gold Coast in 1951 and Prime Minister of the independent Ghana in 1957. Seretse Khama became the first Prime Minister of Bechuanaland in March 1965 and Executive President of independent Botswana on 30 September 1966. In the former case, the process in Africa was uncharted; in the latter case, the process was already well-understood.

14 Those responsible for the development of policy in the UK were very much aware of the differences between freedom as 'the civil liberties of individuals' and 'the independence of states'. Lennox-Boyd, Secretary of State for the Colonies, made the distinction in October 1958 and added 'The truth is that the citizens of British dependent territories enjoy civil liberties far exceeding those of any Communist country, and indeed exceeding what is possible that some may enjoy under independence'. In close proximity was the following: 'We have got to face it, that although the facts of the modern world clamour for the notion of inter-dependence, the psychology of political evolution may tend to follow the sequence: dependence, independence, interdependence.' Document 74 'Imperium et Libertas', Extracts from a speech by the Rt Hon. Alan Lennox-Boyd, Secretary of State for the Colonies, 9 October 1958 in A.N. Porter and A.J. Stockwell *British Imperial Policy and Decolonization* (Macmillan, Cambridge Commonwealth Series, 1989) Vol. 2, p. 492.

15 This problem was not unique to Africa. India achieved independence without clear-cut agreement as to the precise location of its borders with China. In Central America, Belize's validity and border has never been fully accepted by the Guatemalan authorities.

16 In the 1920s, Lugard held that educated Africans had a right to 'a sphere of civic usefulness': F.D. Lugard *The Dual Mandate* (Edinburgh, Blackwood, 1923). In the late 1930s, the view was that educated Africans should concern themselves with the business of the relevant native authorities: see Cranford Pratt 'Colonial Governments in East Africa' in Gifford Prosser and W. Roger Louis eds *The Transfer of Power in Africa* (New Haven, Conn., Yale University, 1982) pp. 249–81.

17 For an analysis of the policy development process in Botswana and of its remarkable economic success, see Charles Harvey and Stephen R. Lewis Jr *Policy Choice and Development in Botswana* (Macmillan, 1990).

18 Swaziland and Botswana showed themselves to be very skilful, though by using different policies, in avoiding unwelcome South African intervention. Lesotho has been less fortunate. The relationship between independent Namibia and a reformed South Africa still has to be worked out.

3

The Variety of States

James Mayall

Variety may be the spice of life, but for political scientists it poses problems. What is it they are looking at? When they open the atlas they are confronted with a political map which divides the populated area of the globe into 150 or so separate units, popularly referred to as sovereign states, or even more inaccurately as nation-states. These units vary enormously in land area, population, exploitable and exploited reserves, and cultural and political institutions. Some are democratic, others totalitarian, and here and there are survivors of an earlier age, states that appear to belong to a particular ruling family, caste or clan. Societies also divide in many ways – agricultural and industrial, developed and underdeveloped, landlocked and maritime, old and new. It is by no means obvious that either states or societies have a common identity which will allow a comparison or enable us to answer how, in general, states (and state systems) relate to society.

The standard definitions of the state – the executive committee of the ruling class, or the monopolizer of legitimate violence, or the guarantor of civil society or of the self-determining national community, or the agency for effecting the social and economic transformation of society – are not particularly helpful. Given certain assumptions, any one of them may hold for some states, but none for all. They also contradict one another. Indeed, if everywhere, in the capitalist and communist as well as in the transitional world of the non-aligned, there is a prevailing sense of despondency in state theory, it is because, whether the state is viewed as oppressor or liberator, it is failing to deliver what the rival definitions promise. It very often fails to monopolize violence and it almost never presides unambiguously over the progressive transformation of society. How, then, can we say anything sensible about the variety of states?

One possible approach is to put aside the contested question of definition and to concentrate instead on some comparative questions about actual states. For example, we might reasonably ask what kind of state is necessary for the creation of market society and its liberties; or what are the consequences of dependence on a single export crop for the capacity of the state to engage in successful economic planning; or whether war and the preparation for war are necessary prerequisites for the emergence of a strong national identification of a people with their government; or why post-colonial states have found it so difficult to maintain democratic institutions; or why socialist states apparently cannot devise legal mechanisms for a peaceful and orderly transfer of power. And so on. If we proceed in this way, it may be argued, it is the problem which has a fixed identity rather than the state itself and their variety need no longer bewilder us.

From the standpoint of international theory, however, this approach has a double disadvantage. First, it necessarily ignores the fact that all empirical enquiry rests on some *a priori* or metaphysical assertion about the nature of the world and/or its purpose. Modern economic enquiry, for example, was built around a belief in the natural harmony of interests. This belief could yield an investigation into comparative costs within a competitive market, but it was only when the deliberate pursuit of full employment, an equally elusive concept, was substituted for the idea of natural harmony, that it made sense to ask questions about the composition and distribution of national income.[1] Similarly, problems of the kind which suggest themselves when we confront the modern state all rest on an unstated assumption about its nature and legitimate purpose. In the twentieth century, the Western conception of the state has established an intellectual hegemony. It is viewed as a rational system of centralized authority whose sole justification is to provide the population with a range of public goods. One can argue, as marxists and Liberals do, about the circumstances under which these functions can be performed; but not that the state exists for some entirely different purpose altogether. The disadvantage of this conception, from the standpoint of theory, lies in what it obscures. It correctly identifies the dominant framework within which modern political debate is conducted, but fails to account for the possibility that there may be states which rest on quite different *a priori* assumptions. In these states, the political idiom is likely to be borrowed, magpie-fashion, rather than internalized within the political culture.

The second disadvantage of the problem-solving approach for international theory follows from the first. Paradoxically, it cannot be used to solve what is arguably the central question of international relations: is it possible to envisage an international society in which the threat of war has been abolished or significantly reduced and in which serious efforts are made to improve the material well-being of the masses of the world's population? If we take the public commitments of those who speak in the name of the state, as set out, for example, in the United Nations Charter, the answer will presumably be in the affirmative. But, notoriously, the UN Charter was drafted in the language of political liberalism and on the mistaken assumption that democratic government would establish itself as the norm rather than the exception. The Charter establishes the 'constitution' for what would have been, had it ever existed, an international civil society of great force. That it does not exist may be explained very largely by the fact that very few states conform to the conception on which the Charter is based. It is for this reason that, from the standpoint of international theory, variety is part of the problem, not the solution.

In this chapter, I propose to examine the nature of this problem. The central questions which it addresses are these: is it possible to have an international political society in which the major participants are radically rather than superficially various, and is the contemporary world characterized by such radical variance? (I shall use the concepts of international society and state system interchangeably.) For such questions to be intelligible, it is clearly necessary to specify both what is meant by international society and what is to count as radical variance.

By international society, I do not mean merely an empirically observable set of interactions which are systematic in that they are patterned and regular over time and systemic in that they together constitute the environment within which the individual states live and to which their governments must react. I mean also, and more importantly, a set of ordered relationships and institutions which constitute a common commitment and rest on shared, if minimal, values.[2]

Specifying what is to count as radical variance, which would threaten an international system constituted in this way, is more difficult. The difficulty stems from the method of abstraction and reduction on which all Western theorizing depends.

The vulnerable point in the picture of the Western state (and its state system) is the alleged separation of the polity from society, just as the vulnerable point in the liberal economic system is the separation of the economy from the polity. In both cases, coherence and explanatory power is purchased at a price. In neither case is any attention given to the social and historical preconditions which justified and supported the separation in the first place. It is not the variation in the outward forms which the state can assume, e.g. between federations or centralized authority, that challenges the possibility of a shared value commitment. It is the absence, in some societies, of the conditions for supporting the divorce between state and society/economy and polity, at all.

The traditional picture of state and state system

It follows that an attempt to locate the problem posed for international relations by the existence of the variety of states must start with a brief sketch of the state/society relationship in the traditional picture. Within this tradition the relationship can be expounded purely theoretically, although there is also a lively historical debate about how it came about. At the outset it is worth repeating that the theory claims to be universal. Despite the familiar criticism that its main ideas are Eurocentric, it is presumably on its universal appeal that its current status rests.[3]

In theory, the relationship has an essentialist and an historicist aspect. In its essentialist aspect, the purpose of the state is to provide the security and welfare of the people; but the state is not a synonym for society, it is the agency of government. It must, therefore, have a monopoly of coercive authority and the right (and capability) to raise the necessary revenue to discharge its functions within its territorial jurisdiction. As there can be only one final authority in any country, the only kind of association between states that is possible is one based on formal equality, mutual recognition and reciprocity. But outside the sphere of government, there is the private domain of civil society in which the individual retains his natural rights and sovereignty. Such, in synthesis, is the mainstream account of the state and state system within Western political theory. The theory is essentialist in that, in principle, it applies anywhere, anytime, being derived not from special circumstances but from a view of human nature.

The historicist aspect has been grafted on to the theory more recently. Originally, the ultimate justification of state and international society was derived from their place in a wider God-given design. Seventeenth-century social contract theory does not directly challenge this legacy of natural law. Indeed, it builds on it. One consequence of the Enlightenment and the French and American revolutions, however, was to sever the connection between political legitimacy and any form of argument from design. From the end of the eighteenth century, the state increasingly justified itself as the engine of a social teleology – in the first instance to create the conditions of human liberty, and then progressively to put an end to privation and create the conditions of plenty.

Two consequences flow from this historicist evolution. First, the legitimacy of the state comes to be grounded on a fundamental egalitarianism, i.e. states which exist to preserve a particular social hierarchy are regarded by political pluralists as much as by marxists, as anachronistic. Secondly, and in consequence, new questions arise about the legitimacy of any state within international society. In the original essentialist version, these questions did not have to be asked. All sovereigns recognized one another by virtue of their sovereignty. The relationship of state to society was not an issue. If they went to war (and they did) it was about other things

– territory, dynastic rivalry, the balance of power, etc. With historicism, the question of whether or not a state is pursuing progressive social goals enters the international equation.

Because Western political theory reflects its essentialist origins as well as its historicist trappings, there is no agreement on this question. The majority probably continue to hold that membership of international society is decided by external criteria, i.e. it embraces all self-determining entities, and therefore intervention against such entities is ruled out – regardless of the quality of their social and political arrangements. There are those who contend, however, that only like-minded states – those which protect the fundamental human rights of their citizens – can form a genuine state system, because they are only genuine states. In relations between these states and others, there may be, under certain circumstances, a positive duty to intervene, and certainly if interest dictates intervention, there is no fundamental objection.[4]

If we ask why the tradition evolved as it did, we must necessarily look for an answer beyond the theory itself; in other words, to whether social and economic conditions shape and limit the possibilities for political organization (and therefore also theory)? If they do, as materialist thinkers maintain, then the co-existence of a variety of states would clearly challenge the possiblity of a single international society or system. It may be no accident that Soviet ideologues clung for so long to a classification of states – capitalist, social democratic, socialist, etc – in terms of their alleged 'objective' progress towards the ultimate goal of communism. The fact that communist ideology, at least in its Soviet version, is currently in such deep trouble, does not dispose of the problem. We know that the development of political liberalism accompanied the breakdown of traditional argicultural society and the emergence of industrial capitalism. We do not know the causal relationship. It may be that, as idealist thought would suggest, authoritarian industrial societies can transform themselves politically as a result of an intellectual conversion to pluralism. But we do not yet know whether it will happen.

Whatever view we take on the materialist/idealist divide, two points can be made about the circumstances in which the Western tradition evolved. The first is that it was under conditions that varied enormously except in one important respect: the Western world was composed of agricultural or commercial societies.[5] Indeed, the early modern state has been described both as an armed warehouse for guarding the agricultural surplus, and as a protection racket. Once centralized institutions were developed, such a surplus was necessary to support the activities of specialized classes – the aristocracy, armed forces, priesthood and bureaucracy – and the exercise of power to protect their interests had to be legitimized. Political theory, on this view, developed as an ideological justification for centralized authority against the claims of other regional, clan or kin-based systems. In order to extract the surplus, moreover, the military potential of such groups had to be broken. In all modern states, society has to be disarmed; where families or clans can organize for battle there may be a political system but there is no state and there is consequently no need to draw a distinction between civil society and the state. For the development of Western state theory, therefore, agricultural society was a necessary precondition; industrial society was not.

The second point about the Western tradition is that the breakdown of traditional agricultural society, the growth of industrial society and the rise of historicist thinking, all appear to be closely related, even if we do not fully understand how. Modern nationalism, the idea that the society and the state should be culturally indistinguishable, and that the state should guide the progress of the nation out of the undifferentiated past and into the historical future, has arisen in societies undergoing rapid economic and social change. The belief in, and demand for, an historically achievable social progress has, of course, destroyed the distinction between state and civil society in some social orders. Even in Western industrial societies, historicist ideas of social progress have led to new accommodations in the relationship between the state and citizen. No doubt this version rests ultimately on an *a priori* assumption – the idea of economic development and growth is no less metaphysical than that of full employment – but in the meantime its cash value for practical men arises from its activism: states are called upon to do something to make life better in a material sense.

It is the modern industrial state which has developed and extended the egalitarianism of modern society. Again, it is difficult to sort out the metaphysical and material components of this apparently universal drive for equality. But, from a sociological perspective, legal and functional egalitarianism provide a necessary basis for a society predicated on the need for (and possibility of) continual change and innovation. The increased differentiation of modern industrial societies paradoxically requires universal literacy and basic education.[6] At the level of governmental organization and decision making, efficiency demands that the ruling profession shall be as open as possible to talent and that decisions should follow, so far as is possible, from a 'rational' calculation of the national interest. Within this world, decisions are not meant to be influenced by considerations of personal advantage or privilege.

So far as the state system is concerned, the logic of industrial society is contradictory. On the one hand, the need for markets, raw materials and the advantages to be derived from large-scale and rationalized production supports the drive towards the integration of the world into a single market order governed by universal rules. Within this order any exceptions arise from technical rather than political or cultural considerations. The classification of states under this imperative is according to their ranking in the economic league table. On the other hand, the survival of pre-industrial rivalries, and the need to define the national interest in increasingly egalitarian (and competitive) terms, reinforce the tendency in industrial societies to domesticate foreign policy.[7] If, as Susan Strange argues, the name of the game is increasingly competition for world market shares, international politics, unlike many pure games, has a prosaically functional purpose – to maintain or improve the well-being of the population.[8]

The impact of social and cultural heterogeneity

There are two negative points to note about the relevance of this background picture to the non-Western world. First, it is not self-evident that the most obvious line of demarcation, the fact that in the West the majority live under conditions of wage employment and are engaged in manufacturing industry or the provision of services, while elsewhere the majority live within an agricultural economy, is itself a barrier to the universalization of the state and state system. A centralized state rests in the final analysis on agriculture, not on industry, although the co-existence of the two types of society clearly has a decisive bearing on the foreign policies and priorities of the two types of state.

Secondly, even where the Western model of the state does not fit, the external dominance of the form is generally sufficient to impose its values, or at least to ensure that values derived from other ways of life and organization will be recast and synthesized with it. For example, pastoral nomads generally make bad nationalists and citizens, not least because they are extremely difficult to disarm.[9] However, when they come into conflict with the ambitions of the state, as in Baluchistan or parts of the Sahel, they quickly absorb and adopt the aspirations and language of national self-determination.[10]

Despite such evidence of adaptability by both state and society, it seems clear that the co-existence of a wide variety of state/society relationships makes for incoherence in international society and sets limits to the possibility of evolving a securely anchored value consensus for the international community. The relevance of the Western background picture to the non-Western world is, therefore, open to doubt. However, the substitution of historicist for essentialist values in the Western political tradition also suggests a scheme which may be useful in measuring the impact of these disturbing influences.

Three kinds of radical variance can be observed. The first derives from survivals from earlier systems in the contemporary world, the second from the problems of government in transitional societies where the traditional pattern of civil relations and political authority is breaking down but has not given way to a Western distinction between civil society and the state, and the third from the presence of states whose vision of the future positively enjoins the obliteration of this distinction.

'Anachronistic' states

The past lives on in the present everywhere and despite revolution. But certain kinds of civil/political organization are plainly incompatible with the concept of a modern centralized nation-state. Two spectacular examples of such incompatibility are Chad and Lebanon. The statehood of both these countries is very largely fictitious, although the reasons in each case are different and so consequently are the implications for their international relations.

In Chad there is not now, and so far as I know never was, a centralized state at all; nor was it a single self-determined entity in any sense. Like most other African countries, Chad owes its existence to an accident of colonial history, in this case to the fact that the south of the country, which was economically useful to the French, was pacified, while the north, which was largely desert and the home of the Tuareg and other nomadic herdsmen, was merely contained. The colonial state was never self-financing and no serious effort was made either to tax the population in the north or to disarm them. The consequences for the post-colonial 'state' are well known. The central administration of the territory has only been maintained by outside subvention – the civil service was paid first by the French and then by the Libyans and now (presumably?) by the French again. Since its independence in 1960, the country has also been almost continually wracked by civil war.

Civil war may be proof of the breakdown of a state but not of its non-existence. In Chad, however, the war has several anachronistic features. In the beginning, it was a struggle between north and south, ostensibly over the monopoly of power held by the Christian south at the expense of the Islamic north; conceivably at this stage it might have been regarded as the struggle to establish a modern state in the conventional mould. But for the past decade it has been a struggle between northern factions for power over the south. No policy objective or social programme distinguishes these factions, with the result that they enjoy considerable freedom in securing and dumping external patrons as their fortunes in the internal struggle wax and wane. Moreover, there seems to be no basis on which a permanent victory or even a lasting accommodation can be achieved. The international result has been to make Chad a dangerous political vacuum at the meeting point of what by comparison seems the relatively stable state-centric worlds of north-west and central Africa. Where territorial boundaries have little social meaning, trouble tends to spill over and cannot easily be bottled up. Inevitably, other African and non-African countries are drawn in but because the advantages of ruling Chad are so negligible, all (including Libya) try to limit their liability, with the result that they keep the pot brewing without ever putting the lid on.

Although the conflict between Muslim and Christian is also a feature of the Lebanese crisis, Lebanon represents a different kind of anachronistic legacy. In Chad, because there was no state, there was no political problem of state and society to resolve. The Ottoman Empire, on the other hand, had an elaborate system of civil political relations, which operated on very different principles to those prescribed by the Western model. (The nearest contemporary example is arguably South Africa, which may be one reason why it was widely regarded as anachronistic within the modern system).[11] Broadly ethnic and/or religious communities enjoyed civil and religious rights but no political rights. This system proved viable until the Ottoman Empire came under the influence of a modernizing nationalism. In most parts of the empire, most dramatically and bloodily, with the liquidation of the Armenians in Turkey, the dominant community simply took over the state without making any notable concessions to the political rights of non-national citizens. In the Lebanon, however, the balance of communal power and external interests was sufficient to produce an accommodation under which the spoils were divided. With the breakdown of this accommodation once Lebanon became the centre for the Palestinian struggle with Israel, the functions of the state (minimal policing, taxing, the administration of law and defence) reverted to the communities. Lebanon, like Chad, became a battleground where social life continues despite the State (or what is left of it), not because of it.

A third form of challenge to the idea of the separate state, and state system, is represented by the non-conformist tradition in Islam. The fact that under Islamic law there is no justification for the separate territorial state suggests that there is a built-in tension within modern Islamic society between the political injunctions of the faith and the secular principles of modern state theory. In principle, it also means that there is no place in the Islamic political culture for the notion of a secular civil society.[12] Nor is there an equivalent in Islamic political theory to the principle of *cuius regio eius religio*, the direct forerunner of the principle of 'non-interference' in domestic affairs within the modern state system.

For the most part, Muslim states have had little difficulty in accommodating themselves to the practice, as opposed to the theory, of the Western tradition.[13] The tension surfaced only when the ambitions of the Muslim brotherhoods became uncontainable or when, as in Morocco, nationalism and Islam could form an alliance on the question of irredentism, or when Muslim leaders, e.g. Numeiri in the Sudan and Qadhafi in Libya, were pursuaded to support openly the political aspirations of minority co-religionists in neighbouring states, overriding the conventional injunction to non-interference. By contrast, the Iranian Revolution questioned the legitimacy of the state system in both theory and practice.

So far, the implications of Iranian fundamentalism for the Islamic world have probably been more serious than for international society in general. In relations with the non-Islamic world, it is possible to retreat towards the original position which allows co-existence with infidels. Indeed, this retreat has already partially taken place. The Iran/Iraq war dragged on for 8 years and achieved nothing, partly because in a conflict between believers such worldly concessions were not available. Exhaustion finally forced the Iranian Government to accept the ceasefire negotiated through the UN Security Council, but the strength of the fundamentalist faction in Iranian politics frustrated attempts to translate it into a peace agreement.[14] Ironically, Iran emerged as the 'winner' only because Saddam Hussain, the ruler of Iraq, himself flouted the most basic rule of international society – respect for state sovereignty – by seeking to liquidate Kuwait in the summer of 1990. Faced by nearly universal condemnation at the United Nations, and a formidable international force quickly assembled in Saudi Arabia, he conceded to Iran everything for which Iraq had fought.

Transitional societies and 'Prebendel' states

Many non-Western states share in some degree one or other of the characteristics described under the previous heading but are accommodated within the dominant framework without presenting it with an anachronistic challenge. Yet in their ways of operation and decision making, they often present a different 'rationality' to that which is taken for granted in industrial societies. This alternative 'rationality' in turn constitutes a different kind of challenge which can be viewed along two overlapping dimensions.

The first dimension is formed by the concept of transition. As in the Ottoman Empire, many traditional societies were relatively self-contained socially and culturally, regardless of whether or not they constituted a self-determining entity in the political sense. This self-containment gradually broke down as they were drawn into the web of international economic relations, either as a result of coercion, as when hut taxes were imposed to ensure that able-bodied men offered themselves on the labour market, or indirectly. After 1945, the process was carried further as governments everywhere aspired to industrialize and modernize their societies, engaging in universal literacy campaigns as a first step.

Traditional society was also pulverized by the population explosion and the associated drift from the land to the cities. Social attitudes and state capabilities often did not evolve in step with changing conditions: tribal associations grew up in the new cities as people tried to deal with the insecurity of urban life. In parts of Africa, sectarian churches proliferated for the same reason: the state itself which often controls access to the modern sector of the economy was regarded as a prize to be won, and neither the individual citizen nor the social and economic class counted for much in the competition. This may seem paradoxical, as both soldiers and politicians, the two groups usually involved, generally spoke the language of nationalism and the national interest; but it is not because those whom they claimed to represent did not.

Lenin called the state the executive committee of the ruling class – it existed simply to protect their interests and to promote their accumulation of capital. In some Asian and Latin American countries, this is a fair description of what the state actually is. In others, as the new educated élite perpetuates itself, it may be what it is about to become. But in many, the state is still a prize to be won; both society and society/state relations are in flux. This is the context in which the 'prebendel' state flourishes and it is its luxuriant growth which constitutes the second dimension along which the challenge to the Western tradition must be viewed.[15]

In the agricultural polity, which provided the setting for the development of Western political thought, a settled population had to be capable of producing a tappable and taxable surplus. It is a depressing feature of many Third World states that society cannot feed itself and that in pursuit of the prize of state power agriculture is neglected. On the other hand, the farming of offices, the defining activity of the prebendel state, is often extremely advanced.

As in all societies, greed is no doubt part of the explanation. But there is no reason to believe that vice and virtue are distributed any differently in the southern and northern hemispheres. A more plausible explanation may perhaps be sought in the social context of transitional society. A common feature of many traditional societies is that family obligations of a mandatory, or quasi-mandatory, nature extend much further than they do in industrial societies where the standard unit is the nuclear family. (In Sweden, it is rapidly becoming the one-parent family!) Under pre-industrial conditions, the discharging of these obligations by the powerful presumably did not impose unbearable strains on the society, because social and educational opportunities and horizons were circumscribed. Under modern conditions, the discharge of family obligations can become very expensive: the big man in town is no longer required merely to provide shelter for a country cousin; he has to purchase food for him in the market, or put him in the way of employment so that he can support himself, or even, if he shows promise which may reflect well on the family, educate him at a foreign university. The greater his ambitions, the more clients he is likely to attract and the more important it can become for him to secure an office which will provide him with access to additional income. If, for example, he is in a position to grant contracts, he may be able to extract a rent for himself, i.e. a bribe. But since the number of such lucrative positions is limited, the competition for them is intense: the big man will himself need a patron, or if the stakes are really high, an alliance with other families or tribal or regional groups to divide the spoils.

Corruption is endemic over much of the Third World and its denunciation is the common coinage of political battle. Yet a change of regime, loudly trumpeted in the name of purification, generally results in a change of beneficiaries, not the restoration of the rule of law. Political hypocrisy, of course, is not a monopoly of developing countries. The difference between political venality elsewhere and the practice of politics in the prebendel state lies in the absence of an external standard against which corrupt behaviour can be judged. Within all the great religious communities which preceded the rise of the national state (and facilitated its establishment), the wielders of political power could be criticized from the standpoint of holy writ, and/or by its learned guardians. Learned guardians are not required within secular nationalism, and consequently where constitutional behaviour is not already well established, there is no politically authoritative tradition from which the abuse of state power can be criticized.

What are the implications of prebendelism for the state system? The most obvious is perhaps to undermine the commitment to a genuine international community based on the acceptance of common rules. Where the state itself is the prize, the external world will be regarded as a taxable resource by the victors, and as a court of appeal by the losers. For some of them, it may also hold out the promise of physical sanctuary. Because the point of office-holding is to extract personal advantage from the patronage it bestows, one might expect the foreign policy of such states to be arbitrary, contradictory, volatile and incoherent. Alternatively, as many dependency theorists maintain, foreign policy may be under the control of a comprador bourgeoisie, i.e. up for sale to the highest bidder. Very often, indeed, this seems to be the case. And it is not easy to see how the mould can be broken. This is because the prebendel state does not conform to either of the operational models that can be derived from the traditional theory of the state and state system discussed in the first section of this chapter.

The first 'realist' model is of independent self-determined and ultimately self-sufficient units that can feed and defend themselves, pursuing their interests and rivalries across international boundaries. The second 'liberal' model qualifies this conception of self-containment with the idea of specialization and an international division of labour which develops as a result of technological innovation and market laws, rather than as a result of victories and defeats in the power battle. But most prebendel states are not self-contained in the realist sense – they can frequently neither defend nor feed themselves. In the domestic political battle, moreover, the rewards from administering their dependence on the outside world are such that, despite the rhetoric, there is little incentive to change the situation. To do so would, after all, require a clear conception of the entity to be defended. Nor, again despite the rhetoric, are office-holders receptive to allowing the international division of labour to be decided by market laws – to do so would be to deny themselves the rent on which they rely to fulfil their ambitions and discharge their inherited obligations.

There is a serious difficulty in assessing the nature of the challenge that prebendalism poses for the state system. No doubt it is true that the logic of decision making in such societies is often less transparent and less obviously connected with the issue at hand than in states where there is a long standing constitutional tradition. In such states, the discretionary powers of the political class and the bureaucracy are more or less successfully limited by law. But beyond this, the distinction between the two kinds of states is one of degree. If, then, the state system is viewed in terms of the realist model, in the last analysis, bipolarity survives; dependence and subservience is not confined to the developing countries.[16] If it is viewed from a liberal perspective, the motives for interventionary behaviour by Western states may be different, but the outcome is remarkably similar.[17]

Totalitarian utopianism

It is also this idealized theory, in which a world of separate but constitutional states agree to govern their relations under common rules, that was until very recently (and is arguably even now) challenged by the communist bloc. Such states posed practical problems for their ideological opponents: closed societies are by definition non-transparent and it is notoriously difficult to understand where in such political systems power and authority is located and how decisions are taken. In practice, the challenge was limited because externally the behaviour of communist states was generally cautious and predictable. In communist societies, civil society was quite deliberately subordinated to the party and the state. It is not surprising, therefore, that they respected power when it was ranged against them and exploited such opportunities for expanding their own interests and long-term aims, as were offered them. Industrialism did not, in and of itself, force constitutional convergence with capitalism, as some theorists hoped it would. Indeed, so long as the state system is not required to evolve an international civil society, in which for example individuals could take action against their own governments over the denial of human rights, communist states need have no difficulty in supporting the principles of the traditional state system.

The leaders of the communist world buttressed their suspicion of the outside world with a conviction that they represented the historical destiny of mankind. This combination of fear and self-righteousness posed two actual, as opposed to purely theoretical, challenges to the contemporary state system. The first was the technical problem of promoting economic relations between societies which were organized along quite different principles.

The debate about the granting of most-favoured nation status (MFN) to centrally planned economies is perhaps the best illustration of this inherent difficulty. The Soviet Union often called for an international economic order based on the principles of reciprocity and non-discrimination. It also insisted that these liberal concepts could be translated into the principle of mutual advantage, on which Soviet foreign economic policy was allegedly based. But while this might be true of reciprocity, non-discrimination cannot be reduced to mutual advantage. The latter concept is designed for use in state-to-state relations, the former depends on the existence of a civil society as well as a state. The separation between the two may be very imperfectly maintained even in the West, but to make legal sense of the MFN principle, private interests must still have access to foreign markets on equal terms. The bilateralism which characterized the external economic relations of the centrally planned economies thus created a formidable obstacle to their integration in the multilateral market order. When the Soviet Government expressed an interest in joining the General Agreement on Tariffs and Trade (GATT) in August 1986, US officials ruled it out on the grounds that the Soviet trade system was 'in fundamental, practical and philosophical contradiction to GATT rules'.[18] The USA has now lifted its veto on Soviet membership for political reasons, although the question will only be considered if and when the Uruguay Round of multinational trade negotiations is completed some time in 1991. Even now, it is uncertain how quickly the Soviet economy can be made to conform to GATT.[19]

The second communist challenge to the state system was more fundamental and more familiar. The ideological contest between socialism and capitalism had a deeply paradoxical impact on the participation of socialist states in international society. Their participation was dependent on a static interpretation of international law and the conventions of diplomatic life. The imperatives of co-existence, and their own minority position within the system, militated against foreign policies which were too blatantly designed to serve their historical vision of the future. At the same time, the official ideology of these states was dynamic. From this point of view, they were waiting for the others to catch up, and reserved the right to give the evolution of 'objective' conditions in these societies a helpful nudge whenever the opportunity offered. Because the existing system lacked any final legitimacy, it could only be endorsed provisionally. The inevitable consequence was to cast a permanent doubt in the minds of Western governments over Soviet, Chinese and Eastern European intentions and commitments.

How much has changed? The pace and scope of political transformation in the Soviet Union and Eastern Europe is such that it is difficult to be confident about its long-term consequences for international relations. On realist assumptions, the 'opening up' of the socialist world may lead to a measure of trust between East and West (particularly if progress is made on arms control) and some limited cooperation between them. Indeed, this has already occurred. Since 1985, there has been more cooperation between the five permanent members of the Security Council over peace-keeping in the Third World than in the previous 40 years. On this view, international politics may become less 'ideological' but is unlikely to remain harmonious for long because the underlying strategic confrontation is rooted in geopolitical and state rivalries. Even if what Pierre Hassner calls 'the growing allergy to nuclear weapons' leads to the de-nuclearization of central Europe, there is no guarantee that this will not merely make the world once more safe for conventional war.[20]

On liberal assumptions, on the other hand, the rapid decay of the socialist system, above all of its domestic legitimacy, has put the issue of genuine international community on the political agenda for the first time since Immanuel Kant published *Perpetual Peace* in 1795. It is much too early to say which of these visions most accurately forecasts the future trajectory of world affairs. It seems intuitively unlikely that Fukuyama has correctly identified the end of history. He is probably right to claim that, for the time being, 'the triumph of the West, of the Western *idea*, is evident first of all in the total exhaustion of viable systematic alternatives to Western liberalism'.[21] But this triumph on the level of ideas provides no guarantee that the Western model will be successfully emulated elsewhere on the level of institutions and political culture, or that it can be proofed against internal decay. What it does seem safe to say is that if Mikhail Gorbachev's 'common European home' is to be translated into a reality, that is if Europe from the Atlantic to the Urals is at last to become a genuinely sociable place, two developments will have to be secured. The first is that civil society, separate from the state, will have to be reconstituted in the East and maintained in the West. The second is that government, in East as well as West, will have to be limited in its ambitions and accountable for its actions. It also seems safe to assume that, without success in Europe, the main battlefield of two world wars, there is little prospect of constructing a wider international civil society.

Notes

1 Joan Robinson *Economic Philosophy* (Watts, 1962) Chs I and IV.
2 Hedley Bull *The Anarchical Society* (Macmillan, 1977) Ch. 2; James Mayall '1789 and the Liberal Theory of International Society' *Review of International Studies* 15 (1989) pp. 297–307.
3 I have discussed this claim more fully in 'International Theory and International Society' in Michael Donelan ed. *The Reason of States* (Allen & Unwin, 1978) pp. 122–41, and in *Nationalism and International Society* (Cambridge University, 1990) Ch. 2
4 See, for example, James Lorrimer *The Institutes of the Law of Nations* (Edinburgh, 1883) Vol. 1; for a contemporary and less extreme treatment of the same theme, see Roy E. Jones *Principles of Foreign Policy: The Civil State in its World Setting* (Oxford, Martin Robinson, 1979).
5 Ernest Gellner views platonism, which is often taken as the starting point for the development of Western political thought, as 'the supreme expression of agro-literate man, of a society endowed with a large and steady food supply, capable of sustaining a minority elite endowed with a high culture, and also endowed

with writing and hence the capacity to codify, formalise and preserve its ethos and cognitive capital' *Plough, Sword and Book: The Structure of Human History* (Collins Harvill, 1988) p. 118.

6 Ernest Gellner *Nations and Nationalism* (Oxford, Blackwell, 1983) pp. 35–8.

7 An illustration of the contradictory logic of industrial society in international relations is provided by US policy (and to a lesser extent that of the other Western democracies) in the Uruguay Round of multinational trade negotiations under the auspices of the GATT. On the one hand, a major US objective is that the newly industrialized countries should 'graduate' to division one in the league, i.e. accept the obligations of GATT membership, rather than continuing to claim trade concessions negotiated for developing countries as a whole. On the other hand, the industrial countries themselves – not least the USA – have frequently taken the lead in ignoring GATT rules, whenever they perceive a threat to their interests, and despite their continued insistence of their importance.

8 This is the central argument of work on which Professor Strange is currently engaged and which she expounded in preliminary form at a London School of Economics seminar in March 1990. International theorists have long been attracted to metaphors drawn from the kitchen and sports field. Few, however, refer to the most sensitive account of the 'play' metaphor, perhaps because it suggests ways in which modern politics have departed from one of the central characteristics of all games – namely, that they should take place in a space and under rules which can be differentiated from life in general. See Johan Huizinga *Homo Ludens: A Study of the Play Element in Culture*, translated by R.F.C. Hull (Routledge and Kegan Paul, 1949).

9 Cf. Rene Lemarchand's description of the area in northern Chad occupied by Libya: 'population movements back and forth across the Chad/Libyan frontier – some traceable to the caravan trade, others to the rhythm of seasonal migrations and the exigencies of nomadic life, others still to the spread of Islam – have been going on for centuries. The history of the region is pre-eminently the story of societies in movement. The concept of a frontier as a precise, identifiable line of demarcation between territorial units is thoroughly alien to Sahelian societies; not only does it do violence to the mode of life as nomads or semi-nomads, but to their mode of production and mode of transportation (camels are notoriously unmindful of geographical boundaries)' *The Green and the Black: Qadhafi's Policies in Africa* (Bloomington, Indiana University, 1988) p. 107.

10 They are encouraged to do so, moreover, by the current principles of international behaviour. These strongly support the territorial *status quo*. See Robert Jackson 'Quasi-States, Dual Regimes and Neo-Classical Theory: International Jurisprudence and the Third World' *International Organization* **41** 4 (1987) pp. 519–50.

11 Hugh Seton-Watson *Nations and States: An Enquiry into the Origins of Nations and the Politics of Nationalism* (Methuen, 1977) p. 370.

12 James Piscatori *Islam in a World of Nation-States* (Cambridge University, 1986) pp. 40–45. Piscatori's general thesis is that although non-conformism is powerful in the Muslim world, it is a minority position. The majority of Muslims, he believes, have accommodated themselves, in theory as well as practice, to the system of international relations based on territorial pluralism and international law.

60 The Condition of States

13 Ibid., pp. 144–5.
14 See Gary Sick 'Trial by Error: Reflections on the Iran/Iraq War' *Middle East Journal* **43**, 2 (1989) pp. 230–44.
15 The concept of a prebendal state was adapted by Richard Joseph from Max Weber. See his 'Class, State and Prebendal Politics in Nigeria' *Journal of Commonwealth and Comparative Studies* **21** (1983) pp. 21–38. His use of the term is somewhat inaccurate as Weber used it to describe the way in which officials were granted a source of revenue for life, in the same way as canons in medieval Europe drew prebends from ecclesiastical lands. Political systems in Africa are not sufficiently stable to guarantee anyone an income for life. On the other hand, the appropriation of state revenues for personal gain, and for the discharge of personal rather than public obligations, *is* a crucial aspect of African politics. The concept of prebendalism accurately captures a situation in which office-holding is very often the principal way of accumulating wealth. See also Rene Lemarchand 'The State, The Parallel Economy and the Changing Structure of Patronage Systems' in Donald Rothchild and Naomi Chazan (eds) *The Precarious Balance: State and Society in Africa* (Boulder, Col., Westview, 1988).
16 Most realists would accept Raymond Arons's definition of the international system as being bounded conceptually by the possibility of a general war, and the great powers as those whose rivalries are most likely to lead to such a war. In this sense, despite the partial disintegration of the Soviet Empire and the decline of US economic hegemony, their effective nuclear duopoly still defines the contemporary system. Other states can pursue independent policies only to the extent that they do not directly threaten the vital interests of the two superpowers. See Raymond Aron *Peace and War* (Weidenfeld and Nicolson, 1966).
17 For example, many office-holders in the Third World who publicaly oppose the Multi-Fibre Agreement (MFA), which limits Third World textile exports to the West, are known to be privately in favour of the Agreement. This is partly because it provides them with a competitive advantage over new entrants to the market but also partly because owners of MFA quotas can obtain a rent by auctioning them off in a secondary market. Western governments are opposed to the system in theory, except as a short-term defence against market disruption, but in practice have worked tirelessly to establish the Agreement as a permanent shield for their declining textile industries which they have rescued with public money.
18 *Neue Zurcher Zeitung,* 24–26 August 1986.
19 The experience of GATT with surrogate formuli for non-discriminatory MFN treatment does not suggest that it will be easy. In the 1970s, Poland, Hungary and Romania were admitted to GATT under a variety of special arrangements. It is now widely admitted that none of these provided other GATT members with a satisfactory *quid pro quo*, for their own extension of MFN treatment in Eastern Europe. See James Mayall 'The Soviet Union and GATT' in David Baldwin and Helen Milner eds *East–West Trade and the Atlantic Alliance* (New York, St Martin's Press 1990).
20 Pierre Hassner 'Responses to Fukuyama' *The National Interest* No. 16 (Summer 1989) pp. 22–4.
21 Francis Fukuyama 'The End of History' *The National Interest* No. 16 (Summer 1989) p. 3.

4

Foreign Policy and the Domestic Factor

Brian Porter

It is widely, and doubtless in certain circles wistfully, supposed that there was once a 'golden age' of foreign policy in which the policy maker, usually a European aristocrat, conducted his country's relations chiefly with an eye to preserving the balance of power and without reference to anyone other than his sovereign and perhaps a senior colleague or two in government. A despatch would be sent here, a warship ordered there, with the assured Olympian professionalism of an airline pilot calmly adjusting his controls to the needs of navigation or changes in the weather, regardless of any opinions on these matters that might be entertained by those whose fate rested ultimately in his practised hands. Of course, the picture was never quite like that, but there is in it a sufficient approximation to the world of Metternich, Palmerston, Bismarck and Salisbury to allow us to take the measure of the changes which have taken place between then and now, and in particular to see what developments in the domestic sphere may have contributed to these changes.

The old European system

There is a sense, of course, in which all foreign policy is of a domestic character, for the men who make it will, for the most part, reflect the ideas and values of the society in which they move and of which they are the product. If we wish to understand the diplomatic history of nineteenth-century Europe, we must first look at the political and social world from which it arose. What was the background of these men? What were their aims, interests, fears and priorities?

They were drawn, almost without exception, from the highest social class of their respective countries. The states whose destinies they controlled were, with few exceptions, monarchies with powerful dynastic and military traditions. The making of foreign policy was part of the royal prerogative, and for monarchs and their chief ministers a jealously held preserve. Early foreign policy was essentially dynastic policy, designed to ensure the security of the dynastic state and enhance the glory of its ruler. In Europe, most dynastic states had evolved, or were evolving, into nation-states, but the tradition persisted. Foreign policy was designed to further the interests and prestige not so much now of the dynasty as of the state itself; it was still 'high politics', pursued and performed on traditional lines and by the narrowest and most exclusive of élites. Within the continental arena, the supreme aim was to preserve the balance of power, in which task there was constant need for manoeuvre, for alignments and realignments, made through appraising changes in the distribution of power, and by realists uninhibited by sentiment, horror of war or ideological affiliations. Above all there was no attempt, as there had been in Napoleonic times, and as there was to be again, at European domination; the restrained and subtle hegemony exercised by Bismarck over the Continental Powers from 1871 to 1890 was the nearest approach to it. It was, in truth, a profoundly conservative order, maintained and operated by men who had no desire to embark on courses which might destroy it, and with it their own social class, its privileges and power.

During the last quarter of the century, however, great social forces began to transform the political character of the states constituting the system, and hence the system itself. With the development of transport, the growth of industry, the drift from the countryside to the towns, and the spread of literacy, the local loyalties and deferences and religious submission characteristic of feudalism were nearly everywhere giving way to the emotional identification of the individual with the nation or nation-state. The phenomenon of nationalism, which hitherto had primarily been associated with the bourgeoisie, increasingly permeated all classes of society. Even the 'establishments' – monarchs and their governments – found themselves for the most part imperceptibly and unconsciously adopting its values and yielding to its imperatives. And if individual men were resistant to the change, the procession of the generations was not, which accounts for the very different political outlook of the young Kaiser William II and many of his contemporaries, from that of Bismarck, and hence for the old chancellor's fall from power. From the 1890s on, much of the conservative restraint went out of the system. There was a hardening of attitudes. Ambitions, jealousies and phobias began to sour, then embitter, the feelings one nation had towards another. Great armaments programmes were cheered, and sometimes demanded, by the publics. The traditional class of statesmen who made foreign policy, and the ambassadors and their staffs who carried it out, attempted to cope with the new climate in the old style, but the forces which beat upon them, and sometimes within them, were too strong. Visitors from overseas were appalled at the feverish warlike atmosphere; it was, said Colonel House, writing to Wilson from Berlin in the spring of 1914, 'militarism run stark mad'.[1]

The peoples of Europe, in the grip of forces they could scarcely understand, and which perhaps, as yet, no-one has fully understood, were, in a sense, responsible for the First World War. But they did not see themselves as being to blame. Were they not rather, as many saw it, simply the victims, the source of an almost inexhaustible supply of cannon-fodder for the cynical and ambitious élites who had regarded the management of relations between nations as their exclusive birthright, and who, in bungling the whole process, had brought untold suffering upon the common people? The First World War thus gave immense impetus to demands that foreign policy should be subject to democratic control, and in all states enjoying freedom of expression, the whole field of foreign affairs, including war and its preparation, was scrutinized, debated and made the object of popular movements and pressures, to a degree never previously known.

The First World War, together with the Russian Revolution, also had the effect of blowing the old system apart. Pre-war Europe, despite differences in the traditions, constitutional structures and ethnic make-up of its member powers, was much more homogeneous than post-war Europe. Before 1914, despite conflicts and rivalries, all were playing the same game, talking both figuratively and, in diplomacy, literally the same language, abiding, broadly, by the same rules. After the war no such consensus obtained. New dictatorships arose, based on mutually hostile philosophies, and even those liberal states whose democratic traditions were deep-rooted enough to ensure constitutional continuity, were now having to cope with the rise to power of sections of society that had never previously held power, with all that that meant in terms of political inexperience and naïvety.

In assessing the impact that these great changes had upon foreign policy, and the problems they gave rise to, it would be convenient to classify states into three main types. The first we shall consider is the autocratic state – autocratic, that is, in its institutional structure and authoritarian in its political culture. The second type is the 'citizen state', and the third is the 'authoritarian democracy'.

The autocratic state

States of this kind are characterized by a ruler or executive unrestrained by constitutional checks or by anything in the way of public opinion which, so far as it exists at all, is either rigorously suppressed or mobilized and manipulated to serve official purposes. It might, however, be useful at this point to draw a distinction between the natures of Hitler's and

Stalin's dictatorships, between, that is, 'revolutionary' and 'conservative' autocracies.

Hitler's rule was always more populist than Stalin's; indeed, he came to power by voicing and exploiting some of the deepest grievances, born of a thwarted and humiliated *hubris*, in the German national psyche. When the Fuehrer harangued his massed gatherings, he established a palpable psychological bond with his audience. The whole Nazi phenomenon was the product not simply of an economic crisis, but of a national emotional crisis engendered by defeat. And Nazi foreign policy, both in its aims and in its conduct, was as much a part of that phenomenon as the rest. When a senior official in the German Foreign Ministry remarked to Ribbentrop that Bismarck would have taken years to consolidate his position before making another move, 'Then', Ribbentrop retorted, 'you have no conception of the dynamics of National Socialism'.[2] Conservatives in general operate on a longer time-scale than revolutionaries, for they see themselves as serving interests and undertaking responsibilities which preceded them and which will outlast them. Revolutionaries like Hitler, having no social lineage, and conscious of their role as unique and opportunistic agents of urgent historical change, will be prone to take inordinate risks, and feel impelled to act quickly if they are to act at all.

Seen in this light, Stalin appears not as a revolutionary but as a conservative of almost Bismarckian proportions. He effectively crushed the original revolutionary tradition, and those who represented it, out of the Soviet system. He made no attempt, as did the Fascist dictators, to articulate the unspoken desires and fears of the populace. He made the international communist movement strictly subordinate to Soviet state interests and treated it, if need be, as expendable. Above all, he recreated, in his own person, and in communist guise, the czardom in its most absolute and draconian form. Such ultra-conservatism inevitably had important consequences for Soviet foreign policy. Like any monarch, Stalin seems to have been primarily concerned to pass on his inheritance, entire, to his successors. Despite his awesome personal and institutional power, and the brutal realism with which he advanced that power into the heart of Europe, he yet took no great political risks, nor – and in this he resembles Bismarck – did he have any inclination to go adventuring into the world lying beyond his immediate sway.

The test of how far an autocratic government can ignore public or powerful sectional opinion is provided by the foreign policy *volte face*. When, for reasons of high politics, the hated enemy overnight becomes the loyal ally and friend, with none to gainsay the change, then we may discount any extraneous influence on official decisions. A prime example is the Ribbentrop–Molotov pact of August 1939. The move was as astonishing in its apparent suddenness as it was in the way in which it reversed all former attitudes and policies towards the other power. Only governments having the whip-hand of their peoples can perform such feats, and it is noteworthy that in justification Stalin was given to cite the precedent of Tilsit, an example from a pre-demotic age. Yet even so, unless such measures are taken primarily to placate the other party, the totalitarian government would seem not to take its population for granted; it requires its acceptance and approbation, and so all the political, propaganda and cultural resources of the state are geared to backing the new tack – with, in the case just quoted, the film *Alexander Nevsky*, designed to awaken Russia to a new Teutonic menace, at once withdrawn from Soviet cinemas, and a performance of Wagner's *Ring* made the highlight of the ensuing Moscow operatic season.

The reason why revolutionary regimes remain nervous of their populations, even when they have them under firm control, arises from their having no natural and undisputed legitimacy. A new legitimacy has to be provided that is founded upon the revolutionary ideology, with this itself enforced and made universal by police surveillance and terror. But terror is an inefficient tool. It destroys the fabric of society, dampens initiative and blights talent. Most revolutionary governments prefer in the end to base their authority increasingly upon traditional notions of legitimacy entertained by the bulk of those whom they rule. Thus Cromwell was tempted to take, and Napoleon actually did take, the crown. Notions of legitimacy are, however, liable to change, and a traditional regime relying upon an antiquated form of legitimacy will be at as great a risk as a revolutionary one whose legitimacy has still to prove itself. The legitimacy of monarchy in the Middle Ages was unquestioned. It was sanctioned both by prescription and by religion; but the Enlightenment intellectually, and the American and French Revolutions practically, knocked these two props away. During the Metternich era, there was an attempt to return to the legitimacy principles of the former age, but the upheavals of 1830 and still more 1848 revealed how inadequate these had become. Ultimately, the Metternichian order was no more successful at maintaining itself through a network of government spies and police repression than was its communist successor over a century later. During the ensuing decades, the military monarchies of Europe (with the exception of the Hapsburg Empire which, by reason of its ethnic diversity, was unable to make this final leap) discovered a new basis for their legitimacy by identifying with the increasingly chauvinistic nationalism, including, as with pan-Slavism, religious nationalism, of their peoples.

A regime of uncertain or weak legitimacy that allies itself with chauvinistic nationalism may well be tempted in its foreign policy to embark upon popular but perilous courses. For Napoleon III it was, perhaps, as much an imperative as it was a temptation. The Second Empire was founded upon a *coup d'état*, the dynasty was *arriviste*, the first Napoleonic epoch a fading memory. Disadvantages such as these mattered little so long as the regime brought glory and prestige to France, but during the 1860s one humiliation followed another. Finally, allowing themselves to be out-manoeuvred by

Bismarck, and bowing to the popular mood, Napoleon and his ministers declared war on Prussia, and the downfall of the Empire followed swiftly upon the capitulation at Sedan. The pattern has often been repeated, for a questionable legitimacy, whether or not buttressed by terror, is the weakest feature of any autocratic or authoritarian regime, and a setback which a Philip II or a Louis XIV could survive with impunity will often be sufficient to bring such a regime down. Thus: 1917–18 saw the fall of virtually all the monarchs and monarchies associated with defeat in the war; the rule of the Greek Colonels was unable to survive the Turkish invasion of Cyprus in 1974 (repeating the fate of another Greek regime and from similar causes half a century earlier); and the fall of the Argentine junta quickly followed the surrender to the British of Port Stanley. Even Nasser felt obliged to resign as a result of the crushing Israeli victory of 1967, but that he was persuaded, and was able, to resume power proves the point: he was the embodiment of the new and potent legitimacy of that Arab nationalism which he had done so much to foster and foment; anything or anyone less would have been swept away. As for the Japanese, their ancient monarchy survived the Nemesis of 1945 for profound nationalistic, cultural and psychological reasons; it possessed a legitimacy of truly medieval invulnerability.

The contrast between this last example and the great bulk of Third World states, particularly those which have come into being during the latter half of the twentieth century, is instructive. In such states there is little or no national, social or ethnic cohesion, so that cliques and groups, some civilian, perhaps even more military, with now and then the charismatic 'strong man', rise to, and fall from, power with bewildering frequency. The inherent weakness of these regimes is such that they cling to whatever will give some basis of legitimacy to their rule. Sometimes it will be dogmatic Marxism, as with Cuba, Guyana, South Yemen and Ethiopia; sometimes a rigidly enforced and all-pervasive Islam as with, although in very different ways, Saudi Arabia and Iran; yet again it may be traditional African paternalism as witness Kenyatta's Kenya and Banda's Malawi, or even Voodoo as in 'Papa Doc's' Haiti; almost always it will take the form of 'anti-colonialism' or 'anti-imperialism' with the West as the convenient whipping-boy and South Africa as the inevitable pariah. On occasion, the plight of the Third World government is so desperate that it hazards all on a single throw and attacks a neighbour. Thus Sukarno 'confronted' the British in Borneo, Idi Amin invaded Tanzania, and – a classic example of a discredited regime's attempt to survive – the Argentine junta launched the nationally popular (until things began to go wrong) assault upon the Falkland Islands. One of the major misjudgements in the case of the last was that the cause of 'anti-colonialism' would bring general international support, but most Third World regimes were more concerned with the threat the Argentine action posed to the fragile world political and legal order, and hence to their own security. It is for the same reason that they have been most reluctant to give any sort of support to minorities and causes with which they might be expected to have a natural affinity and sympathy. The southern Sudanese and the Biafrans, in their struggles for self-determination, received no effective help from other African states.

All of these examples illustrate the truth that, even in autocratic states, the peoples themselves are players in the game, and only when rulers, governments or regimes are genuine expressions of the underlying will, self-image and sense-of-being of peoples (and in large areas of the Third World a popular self-consciousness has barely got beyond the tribal or local stage), only then are they likely to survive defeat in war, or ultimately prove effective in their policies and governance. With the swift collapse of so much autocratic government in 1989, there was much talk of 'people power', but there has always been 'people power', just as there has always been 'people pride' and 'people hate'. The much stiffer fight that the French put up against Bismarck's armies after the fall of the gimcrack Second Empire was a reflection of all three. And, on occasion, the absence of them can turn state policy into a fiasco, as when the Italians fought Mussolini's war against Great Britain (an historic friend of Italy) with a marked lack of enthusiasm or resolve, and were sent reeling back into Albania following the Duce's ill-judged attempt to conquer Greece. Great revolutions, too, are products of 'people power', as are (as Tolstoy recognized) the eruptions of energy which invariably follow, whether they take the form of Napoleonic conquests or the rapid industrialization of a Bolshevik Russia. Foreign policy, like the wars which result from it, is much of the time comparable to the wash of ships crossing and re-crossing the ground-swell, but sometimes – and when it is, it is unmistakably so – it is of the ground-swell itself.

The 'citizen state'

The states in the second major category we shall consider are democracies both in structure and in spirit. They are 'citizen states' and are natural republics, although representative and egalitarian monarchies of the Scandinavian type may be not dissimilar. The USA and Switzerland are good examples, their character being derived from a Lockian view of society as a community of property-holders in whom is vested sovereignty. Government in such states has traditionally been viewed as an unfortunate necessity, whose chief function is to maintain liberty and uphold the law, but of which, in most respects, the less the better. Naturally in this type of society the interests of the individual, particularly in the realm of economic opportunity, are put at a premium, although in practice economic opportunity has not infrequently meant economic exploitation. They are, indeed, not only 'citizen states' but supremely 'business states'.

Not surprisingly, the USA, the creation of men imbued with the ideas and ideals of the Enlightenment, and Switzerland, which had given birth to Rousseau and shelter to Voltaire, felt no inclination to sympathize with, or to partake in, the hitherto accepted way of conducting international affairs. Was not war primarily 'the sport of kings', and of aristocrats, a glorified extension of hunting, jousting and duelling, with the maintenance of the balance of power, in the name of which most wars seemed to be fought, but a gigantic confidence trick practised upon gullible populations who had to bear the cost in taxes and lives? Do away with monarchs and the monarchical system and the world would revert to a state of primordial harmony in which men would be free to pursue the acquisition of wealth and other agreeable habits of civilized life. So felt the Founding Fathers of the USA. So, in England, felt radicals such as Price, Paine and Cobbett, and later the 'Manchester School' of free-traders led by Cobden and Bright. But it was no more easy for England to withdraw from the European system than it was for her radicals to exercise power. The USA and Switzerland, however, could: the one by following the advice of her first president in his farewell address not to become embroiled in European affairs, and the other by maintaining for nearly two centuries the tradition of an alert and defended neutrality.

During the nineteenth century, and into part of the twentieth, Americans were able to continue to take a detached and high moral view of Europe and its bad old ways, themselves giving primacy to domestic politics with its emphasis upon the rights of the individual and the cultivation of 'the good life'. For them foreign policy was for little more than preserving detachment from the international system or opening up commercial opportunities abroad – this again reflecting a concern with promoting 'the good life'. Indeed, the low political status which foreign policy was for long accorded in the USA is indicated by the frequent practice of appointing as ambassadors elderly businessmen whose chief claim to preferment in the diplomatic calling seems to have been the extent of the largess they had contributed to the president's electoral campaign coffers.

A tension between the Lockian ideal of minimal executive government (as in Switzerland) and the need for a strong presidency able to exercise influence in an international system which had become global, with even the most powerful of states strategically vulnerable, has increasingly affected the US political scene. Woodrow Wilson, like Roosevelt after him, became a world triumvir in the wake of world war, but under Harding and Coolidge the presidency lapsed into virtual nothingness. No modern president could play so negative a role again, but the 'imperial presidency' of Roosevelt to Nixon has been much impugned not only for being alien to the spirit of the American republic, but specifically for its waging war without first obtaining the approval of Congress. Such initiatives, particularly following the eight-year trauma of Vietnam, brought their reaction, and Congress has since taken steps to reassert itself and, particularly through the War Powers

Resolution of 1973, passed over Nixon's veto, recover its Constitutional function as the war-sanctioning branch of government. This return to a more thoroughgoing separation of powers reflects the essential ambiguity at the heart of American democracy: on the one hand, the state, the 'USA', and on the other the nation, 'America'; the former associated with government, law, politics, 'Washington' and fully involved in the wider world; the latter an ideal, a set of values including an instinctual suspicion of government, politics, 'Washington', and, most of all, the non-American world. Presidents can never ignore this powerful tradition, and may occasionally be the product of it. It is the basis of that favourite American myth, going back to Lincoln or even Jackson (and forward, one might add, to James Stewart and Gary Cooper), of the honest, plain, all-American frontiersman or provincial entering politics to 'clean-up' a capital sunk in corruption and sophistication. It is in Congress, however, that this outlook of 'middle America' or 'the silent majority' finds its true focus. And although most Congressmen soon shed whatever provincial 'innocence' they may once have had, there is still a lot of it about on which their electoral fate must ultimately depend.

The implications for foreign policy, and the course of history, may be momentous. By seven votes the Senate failed to ratify the Treaty of Versailles and thus deprived the League of Nations of the membership of a state whose strength and influence were vital to it. Again, it was his assessment of the same mood in the country and thus in Congress which discouraged Roosevelt from declaring war on the Axis Powers before Pearl Harbour. Roosevelt's cautiousness, although born of one of the shrewdest political instincts in the nation's history, has led some Americans to rate him, as a president, below Truman. The reasons are interesting. As a patrician he could defer to, but not identify with, the American people whose unsophisticated opinions he saw as having to be brought round to the presidential view of things before the time was ripe for action. Truman, however, who was of the people, might plausibly have said, 'Well if I think so, then everybody thinks so', and have taken firm action – as he did over the atomic bomb, the Berlin blockade, NATO and Korea – confident that he and the country would be of the same mind.[3] Nevertheless, Truman was fortunate in being the beneficiary of a change in the public mood: the reaction, after the Second World War, against isolationism which, it was now widely believed, had helped to produce the conditions which led to war. Perhaps Wilson in his championship of the League had been right after all, and an expensive film idealizing him was released by Hollywood on the eve of the birth of the United Nations. This new body was greeted with enthusiasm in the USA and maintained its popularity for the first 15 years of its existence – until the newly emancipated Third World states with their largely anti-American and anti-capitalist attitudes began to transform the character of the UN and particularly the General Assembly. The growth of this post-colonial hostility, and such specific humiliations as the seizure of the 'spy ship' *Pueblo* by North Korea, the collapse of the whole Indo-China strategy in 1973–5, and the taking hostage by Iran of the American diplomats and their detention until the end of the Carter presidency – all this without the world's most powerful state being able to do anything material about it – helped lead to a resurgence of such characteristically 'middle American' attitudes as a desire to withdraw behind the impregnable defences of a land beyond which all was at best unreliable and at worst alien and evil. This neo-isolationism, although never as strong as the isolationism of the inter-war period, might be detected in some of the policies of Ronald Reagan, a president whose unprecedented electoral popularity signified how well he embodied and represented the instincts of 'middle America'. The SDI programme of interceptor satellites was a return to the idea of 'fortress America' and the measures to counter communism in the Caribbean and Central America but a refurbishment of the Monroe Doctrine.

This desire for withdrawal, rooted in the belief that America was a land apart, a new experiment in social organization, had another aspect which is now chiefly of historical interest. As befitted a citizen state, the USA for long had a tiny army grossly incommensurate with its size, wealth and industrial power. When need arose, as in 1861–5, 1917–18 and 1941–5, the nation raised from its citizens mighty armies which on completion of the task in hand were at once disbanded. The Clausewitzian idea that war was the conduct of policy by other means was anathema to the liberal spirit in which Americans had been reared. Rather, war was a sort of social conflagration which had to be put out, and thoroughly so, with all possible speed. To approach war in any other way, and in particular to manipulate it for political ends, was to practise imperialism; it was what the Europeans were always doing and it was what George Washington had warned his countrymen not to get involved in. Thus in the closing stages of the Second World War the American leaders, including Eisenhower in the field, paid scant heed to Churchill's urgings that the Allies should forestall the Russians in the race for the capitals of central Europe.[4] In American eyes there was no race, only the winning of the war. And the war won, massive demobilization could not be curtailed. Said Truman of the years 1945–6: 'That was the time when Congressmen in Washington joined in the call to "get the boys back home", and our influence throughout the world . . . waned as the millions of American soldiers were processed through the discharge centers.'[5] This failure of the Americans to think politically allowed Stalin – who never thought in any other way – to dominate central Europe. The lesson was not lost upon them; it also did much to consolidate, by emphasizing the need for a strong executive in a world of *realpolitik*, the Rooseveltian heritage of the 'imperial presidency'.

Nevertheless, despite this late adoption of sophisticated realism, essential to a superpower playing a pivotal role in the international system, the American habit of judging issues in moral terms, and responding accordingly, is a continuing fact of political life. The administration may or may not be morally motivated, but even when it is not, and self-interest prevails, it will usually try to present an issue in a moral rather than a pragmatic light and thus appeal to an instinct which has entered deeply into the national psyche. There are, however, two springs to this instinct which exist in uneasy alliance and may, on occasion, find themselves in conflict.

First, there is the Protestant ethos which permeates American capitalism, even, in an extreme form, associating individual enterprise and success in business with divine grace, together with the belief, likewise derived from the Puritans and from biblical fundamentalism, that Americans, like the children of Israel, are a 'chosen people', morally superior to others and with a unique destiny. This tradition, which provided an ethical basis for isolationism, although probably less self-confident and widespread than once it was, still forms a significant ingredient in the outlook of 'middle America'.[6] Its influence upon the American world-view, and hence on US foreign policy, has been considerable. It lay behind the notion of communism, not as a response to great social and economic inequalities, but as an evil conspiracy which had to be 'contained'; and it led to the characteristic idea of American wars as 'crusades', the object of which was not political adjustment but liberation. The unconditional surrender of the enemy – the idea was Roosevelt's – appealed naturally to the inheritors of this tradition, whereas the concept of limited wars did not. To limit war smacks not simply of using it for political rather than moral ends but, particularly if the 'wicked' remain inviolate and unpunished after the war, of compromising with evil. The same principle underlay that rule of the American cinema that the law-breaker should never escape his just deserts. Thus many Americans found the inconclusiveness of the Korean War hard to take, one of the consequences being the long delay in the recognition of communist China. Neutralism, too, was regarded by Dulles and many of his countrymen as being morally suspect, an attitude which led to a coolness in American relations with India.

The other great strand in American moralism was born out of the humanist values of the Enlightenment, expressed in a yearning for brotherly relations between peoples, and of the Christian Gospel, with its injunctions to succour the needy, feed the hungry and live in charity with one's neighbours. Great acts of economic generosity have in part sprung from this tradition, which was also aroused to a heightened sensibility, leading to a growing movement for peace, by the latest means of waging war, and the human, social and ecological costs of those means, in Vietnam and Cambodia. Here, more than anywhere, the tension between these two great moral traditions reached breaking point, and in doing so nearly broke the nation itself in two.

The authoritarian democracy

The third type of state we shall consider may be called the 'authoritarian democracy', that is, a state which is democratic in structure but which yet enshrines traditions and attitudes born of the ancient monarchy or oligarchy from which it has evolved. Such states usually have a strong class basis to their society, and the character of their education, institutions and, at least in its higher ranks, civil service, is often markedly élitist. Great Britain is one example of the species, France another. The former has been described by the scholar-journalist, Neal Ascherson, as 'an unreconstructed *ancien régime*'; the latter might well be termed 'a reconstructed *ancien régime*', for in the guise of de Gaulle's Republic the old monarchy of France, although in elective form, seems in many ways to have re-emerged. Foreign policy formulation in such countries is a traditional skill practised by men who, even when drawn from radical parties, tend to be the more conservatively minded members of those parties, and whose permanent officials are, in any case, not likely to encourage radical innovations.

In these circumstances, a gap is likely to open up between the professionals and the public – or at any rate movements of opinion within the public. Such a gap has, however, been more evident in Great Britain than in France. Following their defeat in 1870–71, the French realized that the crude enthusiasms which had characterized public opinion under the Second Empire had been one of the ingredients in the disaster. Hence there was some attempt to educate at least the professional classes in international realities. The École Libre des Sciences Politiques was founded in 1872 for this purpose and the Quai d'Orsay, conscious of the importance of public support for its policies, established a press bureau – as did the Wilhelmstrasse. The British Foreign Office, however, seems increasingly to have resorted to secrecy, particularly in the decade prior to the First World War. This was in part due to the peculiar temperament of the Foreign Secretary, Sir Edward Grey, a nature-lover and, for a politician, almost a recluse, but partly also due to the fact that the bulk of his own Liberal Party did not understand his foreign policy, and to the extent that they did understand it, did not like it. The problem was that *realpolitik* and liberal democracy make uncomfortable bedfellows. Sir Robert Ensor, historian of the period, after stating the imperatives of British foreign policy in the run-up to the First World War, commented:

> . . . while successive prime ministers, foreign secretaries, and foreign office officials knew these things, the majority of members of the houses of commons elected in 1906 and 1910 were almost totally unalive to them. Before 1906 the relatively aristocratic parliaments were largely recruited from families with a traditional interest in foreign affairs. Palmerston or Disraeli debated such topics before a knowledgeable assembly. After 1906 it was not so and Grey worked under handicaps in this respect shared by none of his predecessors.[7]

Dissent, of course, at bottom religious, but invariably having a political expression, has a long and honourable history in the Anglo-Saxon world and, indeed, it helped form the character of the USA and lies at the heart of American isolationism. In England, it manifested itself in a radical critique of foreign policy from the days of the American Revolution, with which to a large degree it sympathized. It was against wars fought in the interest of the balance of power, and it was against alliances with powers which persecuted their populations. Gladstone took advantage of it in his 'Midlothian campaigns' with their impassioned denunciations of Turkish barbarities. But not until the twentieth century when the extension of the suffrage brought new classes, and particularly the middle and lower-middle 'dissenting' classes, to legislative power (the 1906 Parliament had in it more Non-conformists than any other before or since), did it become a factor with which the formulators of foreign policy seriously had to concern themselves.

The nub of the problem is that dissent, traditionally unhabituated to power, tends to see the international world as but an extension of the domestic world; indeed, it projects on to the wider spheres of national, and even international, politics the standards and decencies of private, middle-class, originally pietistic Protestant, life. Behind a Donald Soper, a Michael Foot or a Tony Benn there is usually, either currently or ancestrally, a Non-conformist background. Defence is not their *métier*; disarmament, particularly nuclear disarmament, appeals to them both on ethical grounds and for reasons of social priorities. Some have adopted pacifism, and by taking their stand upon the Sermon on the Mount have argued that even international society may be transformed by non-resistance to evil and the ethic of example. This is not a point of view for which there has ever been much sympathy in ruling circles and the type of man entertaining it would be singularly unfitted, in the last resort, to have charge of his country's destiny.

Faced with dissent, and with the uncertainty and confusion it will cause in the public mind even when it is a minority view, those in the authoritarian democracy charged with making or justifying foreign or defence policy will resort to certain stratagems. The simplest will be to reveal nothing, as Attlee did when his government, mindful of the outcry with which it would be greeted by many Labour supporters, developed in secret the atomic bomb. Another tactic, used by Sir John Simon in his speech to the League Assembly over the Manchurian Crisis, will be to bury the issue in words, to voice support for some principle like collective security, but in effect do nothing. Yet a third response, when action is unavoidable but when the real motive will be controversial or widely judged as reprehensible, will be to concoct a different motive, or fall back on a subsidiary one, more likely to win general support. Thus, an example of a false motive was Eden's claim that the Suez invasion had been undertaken 'to separate the combatants' rather than, as was clear to everybody, to seize the Canal and hopefully achieve the downfall of Nasser. And, as a classic case of justification by secondary motive, there was the reason given for Britain's going to war in 1914: not the military commitment to the French in the interest of preserving the European balance of power, but the German invasion of Belgium, news of which the Cabinet received with profound relief – here at last was a motive and a cause for which even 'dissent' might support the war.

As with sex, so with politics: when their conduct falls short of the moral norms expected of them, the British tend to retreat into either reticence or humbug. It is a characteristic which the French, who soon made no bones about colluding with Israel over Suez, and who went through the whole charade only at British insistence, find baffling, exasperating or funny. In their own case, there has been less occasion, with the exception of the traumatic years from the Popular Front to the Liberation, for disagreements and dissensions. Whatever their ideological stance, the French are inclined to unite around the idea of the national interest with little controversy over the direction in which that should be pursued. Certainly, the French Left seem to have none of the inhibitions and ambiguous feelings about their country, its power and status, so characteristic of the British Left.

Great Britain and France are old monarchies in which the conduct of relations with other sovereigns was part of the royal prerogative. Both have inherited therefore a secretive, élitist approach to foreign policy, recalling, for example, in France the '*secret du roi*' or personal policy of a Louis XV, or in England the management of the state by Queen Elizabeth and Lord Burghley, for whom government was a 'mystery' into which common eyes should not pry. The contrast in both cases with the USA is a striking one. There the people, it is felt, have a right to know; there the servants of the state do not form a mandarinate of self-perpetuating influence, but, with successive administrations, fluidly interchange with the universities, with business and the law; there the legislature is not, through the discipline of party, and except at rare intervals, virtually powerless to check the executive, but exercises a potent influence in focusing and expressing, in all its many interests and manifestations, the popular will. How constitutional structures and practices bear upon the making and conduct of foreign policy is something we shall now consider.

Constitutions and institutions

Foreign policy is normally determined by the executive, but might be modified or even invalidated by the legislature. Thus although President Wilson signed the Treaty of Versailles, the USA did not, owing to the Senate vote, become a party to the Treaty. Where the executive alone is involved, everything will depend upon those who constitute it, the nature of their tenure, and the machinery of advice. There will always be the possibility of discontinuity. This is most likely in the case of a change of regime, particularly when, as with the coming to power of the Bolsheviks in Russia, or of Hitler in Germany, a new and revolutionary ideology is involved. But a change of ruler alone may be sufficient. One of the most remarkable examples of this is from the age of autocratic monarchy. At the most critical juncture of the Seven Years' War, when Prussia lay at the mercy of four powerful enemies, predominantly the Russians, and Frederick the Great was in such despair that he contemplated suicide, the death of the Czarina Elizabeth and her succession by the immature and volatile Peter III who ardently admired the Prussian king, wholly transformed the situation. With Russia now a benevolent neutral, Frederick could wring an advantageous peace out of near disaster. Hitler in his Berlin bunker even took brief comfort from this story when learning of the death of Roosevelt. Although any such hope would naturally prove chimerical in the twentieth century, changes in the executive not only of autocratic regimes but of the most stable and well-ordered democracies may, in less dramatic ways, determine the goals, and affect the style and direction, of foreign policy. And in democracies there is an added complication, for the constitution itself, in accordance with which these changes occur, may well affect the policy-making process.

An American president performs his role in the chronological straitjacket of the four-year term, renewable once only. It is often remarked that in his first term a president's eye is on re-election, and in his second, on history. This may affect his foreign no less than his domestic policy. Moreover, a president will choose his own advisers and, if he is unused to the Washington scene, will be inclined to do so from among friends and supporters from his home state. These men, like their master, know that they may have only four years in which to make their mark. The result will be a tendency towards thematic and episodic policies, often tailored to short-term electoral advantage, such as it is difficult to find a parallel to in, say, the British parliamentary system. Thus Nixon will always be associated with *détente* with China, Carter with human rights and the Camp David accords, Reagan with enhanced defence expenditure and a certain predilection for such 'Rambo'-type ventures as the Grenada operation and the Libyan bombings. Research has shown that this last kind of action, provided that it is quickly over and incurs but few casualties, will raise a president's stock in the opinion polls, whereas a sanguinary, drawn-out affair will depress it. This incessant polling has introduced a new element in the making of policy in democracies.

Apart from the accession to power of de Gaulle in 1958, which put French foreign policy on an altogether more grandiose and independent footing in keeping with his own vision of the uniqueness of France, a vision which to a large degree his successors have retained, the succession of prime ministers in Great Britain and of presidents in France seems to affect the continuity of foreign policy less than is the case with presidential change in the USA. This is partly due to the smaller size and greater centralization of the two European countries – in the USA, a president from the Pacific seaboard is unlikely to see the world in quite the same way as one from the Atlantic seaboard – but partly also due to the influence of permanent and specialist civil servants of high rank. The USA has no real equivalent, and great was American astonishment at the Potsdam Conference when, following the change of government in Britain, Attlee was seen to be flanked by the same two advisers as had accompanied Churchill.

The degree to which foreign policy is affected by the views and attitudes of foreign offices, the services, the intelligence agencies and other governmental bodies, is an immense subject which can be but touched upon here. The institution will not only have evolved its own professional traditions, but also reflect the values of that class from which mainly it is drawn. The personnel of the foreign offices of the Western liberal democracies are invariably a middle-class élite with, usually, experience of diplomacy. Their natural approach to problems is to solve them, and to crises to manage them. It is behaviour characteristic of the satisfied, with resort, often enough, to the 'fall-back' position. The line taken by the British Foreign Office towards Argentina over the Falkland Islands dispute in the years before the 1982 war was entirely of this order. Indeed, diplomacy as an emollient has become so ingrained an idea among its Western liberal practitioners that Harold Nicolson took it as a norm for all diplomacy. It is the politicians, bred in a somewhat rougher school, who occasionally prefer – not always wisely – a stiffer line of policy and who may well ignore or bypass their professional advisers. This Roosevelt often did with the State Department, preferring to recruit his own men, such as Harry Hopkins, and omitting to invite to the main conferences his Secretary of State, Cordell Hull. This, too, Bevin sometimes did with his officials,[8] and it is notorious how much Eden was at odds with prevailing opinion in both the Foreign Office and the Diplomatic Service over Suez.

If foreign offices and diplomats incline to peaceful solutions (a tendency which also reflects their close involvement today in economic relations and export promotion), the military, particularly the chiefs of powerful and self-confident armies, navies and now air forces, will often, in approaching an international crisis, opt for the arbitrament of force. Thus during the Cuban Missiles Crisis, Kennedy was advised by American service chiefs to 'take out' the Soviet missiles by a 'surgical strike', and in answer to the anti-communist revolutions which swept central and eastern Europe during the last months of 1989 leading Red Army generals proposed 'sending in the tanks' as had been done successfully in Czechoslovakia in 1968. In both cases, the civilian heads of government rejected advice that would have had damaging and probably catastrophic political consequences. But even when political control is firmly maintained, the military may exercise, particularly in countries where they enjoy high status, a considerable measure of, and perhaps crucial, influence. The great Bismarck, a scion of their own caste and having, however much they might have disagreed over some things, the ultimate confidence of the king, had found it increasingly difficult during the wars of 1864, 1866 and 1870–71 to impose his will upon the Prussian generals. In the war with Austria, they had wanted a triumphal advance upon Vienna, and the Chancellor, who had no wish unduly to humiliate the other leading Germanic power which, with his characteristic foresight, he saw as a potential ally, had to exercise all the forcefulness of his formidable personality to dissuade them. Again, in 1887 he reacted sharply when he discovered that the military in Berlin and Vienna were intriguing to bring about a war with Russia, and wrote to his ambassador in Vienna: 'We must both take care that the privilege of giving political advice to our monarchs does not in fact slip out of our hands and pass over to the General Staffs'.[9] After Bismarck's fall in 1890, there was no-one of sufficient authority to impose political rationality upon a regime whose foreign policy was increasingly subject to the dictates of strategy and whose character became more than ever one of militaristic *hubris*. In the Schlieffen Plan by which, in a two-front war, France was to be knocked out first in an encircling advance through Belgium, the General Staff dictated the political decisions which determined the shape of the First World War – decisions which, in effect, were to bring down the German Empire. Indeed, by the end of that Empire the military, through the supreme unchallenged authority of Hindenburg and Ludendorf, had become the real government of the state. The German story – like the Japanese a generation later, and the Argentinian later still – is an object lesson in what may happen if the military are allowed to become virtually an independent force within the state or even take over the state itself. If the Western democracies have hitherto avoided such perils, this is not because they have lacked their own share of political warriors, but because these have never been allowed to have their head. One thinks of Admiral 'Jacky' Fisher proposing in Edwardian drawing rooms the 'Copenhagening' of the German fleet, of General 'Old Blood and Guts' Patton avid to continue his final advance into Stalin's territory ('and if the Russians didn't like it let them go to hell'[10]) or, more serious than either of these, of the desire and design of MacArthur in 1951 to enlarge the Korean War into a full-scale conflict with China and possibly the Soviet Union as well. All three eventually went too far and were promptly relieved of their commands.[11] In the case of Truman's courageous dismissal of MacArthur, the president had the advantage of being the constitutional commander-in-chief, but there will always be a wave of animus against 'interfering civilians' in such circumstances, as there was against the politicians, or 'frocks', in the Britain of 1914–18. This is a characteristic right-wing reaction, and a storm of obloquy broke over Truman. Republics as firmly based as the American, or constitutional monarchies in which nationalistic impulses and military loyalties are channelled into a politically innocuous direction, are usually able to withstand such pressures and discontents, but it is a different story where the Army has been the only alternative to corrupt or ineffectual civilian government – a common Third World experience – or even sees itself, as in Argentina, as the embodiment of the national idea and the custodian of the national honour. The temptation then may be to embark upon risky irredentist adventures, as did the Argentine junta over the Falklands or the Greek Colonels over Cyprus, or to impose political 'order' and cultural uniformity – objectives to which the military mind is notoriously attracted – upon a heterogeneous populace or a recalcitrant minority. Either way, war, whether international or civil, may well ensue, and civil war, by eliciting the sympathy of kindred ethnic groups for the oppressed people, by encouraging the state's enemies to help the rebel side, or simply by creating the need for foreign arms supplies and increasing the burden of debt, will usually affect that state's international alignment. Both the perennial and unquenchable rebellion in the southern Sudan, and the revolt of East Pakistan, culminating – with the help of Indian armed intervention – in the independence of Bangladesh resulted from the attempts of military governments to impose military solutions upon situations requiring the exercise of statesmanship of the highest order. Such attempts, unless accompanied by the mass expulsion of populations, or by genocide, are usually destined to fail, which is not to say that a 'solution' by those barbarities may not be the intent, or tried in part, as witness the use by Iraq in 1988 of poison gas on some scores of Kurdish villages.

Compared with foreign offices and defence departments, intelligence agencies are newcomers among institutions influencing foreign policy, although intelligence itself is as old as diplomacy, to which it stands as a sort of murky companion. The aim of intelligence is to discover the 'real mind' of other powers, in particular of potential enemies; to detect those withheld and guarded facts which it is necessary to appraise before sound policy can be formulated; and to counter the like activities directed against oneself. Diplomacy is similarly employed, but overtly. It is the covert nature of intelligence which can create difficulties for the executives whose needs it exists primarily to serve. Because those engaged in this work live in a world with its own ethics – or lack of them – and its own peculiar psychology and dangers, there is always the risk of seeing 'through a glass darkly', of distorted judgements, of becoming bemused, not, as with the military, by the 'machismo' of one's profession, but by, in this case, its cleverness and cunning. Thus, to have surveyed the bottom of the cruiser which had brought the Soviet leadership to Portsmouth in 1956 might have appeared smart – had it been done without discovery – in a lecture on Soviet warship design delivered to Admiralty experts, but politically it was crass: comparable, as it turned out, and as one commentator put it, to getting caught while going through a house-guest's suitcase. Eden quite properly disclaimed responsibility for Commander Crabb's ill-conceived and personally fatal exploit, which, it later transpired, had been authorized at a relatively low level and in disregard of his express orders. The U-2 incident, the shooting down of an American spy-plane over central Russia on the eve of the Paris summit conference of 1960, had more serious diplomatic consequences because Eisenhower, instead of disowning the action, took full responsibility for it, and Khrushchev, feigning outrage, brought the conference to an untimely and sterile end. In such ways can intelligence missions sometimes harm the delicate processes of interstate relations.

These occasional incidents and embarrassments are symptomatic of a much wider problem: the difficulty, in large modern states, of achieving central direction and cohesion in the field of foreign policy and defence. For the bodies concerned, massive and complex, and each with its corporate character and momentum, are prone to identify the national with their own institutional interest. They are, in effect, the new medieval barons, jockeying for position at court. It is desirable in these circumstances for the ruler to impose his will, or at least 'hold the ring', but in the case of the USA, for example, this is something which it is increasingly difficult to do. Presidents have to fulfil the functions of head of state as well as chief executive, and also continually cajole Congress to do their bidding. It is too much. Small wonder that some virtually 'opt out', or, like Jimmy Carter, in attempting to read and master everything, become overwhelmed by the detail. Truman, perhaps the most outstanding of post-war presidents, in seeking to establish cohesion in policy making, set up the National Security Council to co-ordinate the work of the presidential office, the State Department and the Department of Defence, to be served by the newly created Central Intelligence Agency, but institutional dynamics in time prevailed and the Council and the Agency became yet other 'barons' with their own concerns to promote and with their own ideas of what the national interest required. In the 'Irangate' affair, two of the Council's officials, advisers to the president – perhaps without, but more likely with, the connivance of their superiors – devised a secret and illegal scheme to sell arms to Iran in order illicitly to finance the anti-government guerrillas in Nicaragua. For this they were tried and found guilty, but as their move was clearly designed to further the president's own political aims in the region, and as these aims were approved of by much of 'middle America', the delinquent pair were hailed as patriotic heroes by a sizeable section of the American public.

'Irangate' is really illustrative of the difficulties which can be encountered by the makers of American foreign policy in consequence of the essential nature of the Constitution and structure of the government. Thus, whereas the president is primarily responsible for the country's foreign relations and defence, the Senate has the constitutional role of declaring war and ratifying treaties, and Congressional approval is required for the financing of America's huge overseas commitments. Congress, too, makes the laws, and sometimes laws that are frustrating to the executive. The president, on the other hand, keeps some things from Congress – as did Roosevelt and Truman with the clauses of the Quebec Agreement of 1943 for exchanging atomic information – for fear of raising a political storm. This dichotomy, reinforced by the post-Vietnam reassertion of Congressional authority alluded to earlier, and compounded by the growing tendency of the American electorate to choose their presidents and their Congresses from rival parties, can result only in uncertainty and instability in the long-term conduct of the country's international relations. Foreign issues risk getting caught up in domestic political battles, with the officials involved, their loyalties in conflict, placed in an invidious and possibly illegal position. Nothing comparable has occurred in England since the reign of Charles II, when Court and Commons were at odds over the Catholic issue and much else. An executive so hamstrung by the legislature will resort to subterfuge, and 'Irangate' recalls the notorious Treaty of Dover by which the King of England, to avoid dependence on the Commons, received a secret annual subvention from the King of France.

In parliamentary systems, government and legislature are interdependent and, although in Britain the former may be held to exercise undue influence over the latter, it must nevertheless command a majority in order to survive. An American president and his administration can expect power for four years; a British prime minister and cabinet can be turned out at a moment's notice. This means that even though it may enjoy a large majority, the government will need, especially when some great issue is involved, to heed the mood of the House. When Hitler attacked Poland in 1939, the question was, should Britain go to war? Chamberlain and Halifax dithered. It seemed no more in the country's best interests then than it did at the time of Munich. But there was the guarantee to Poland, the national honour was at stake, and Chamberlain was told that unless war was declared promptly, 'it would be impossible to hold the House'.[12] Thus the Second World War – for a German–Polish war would hardly have been that – was begun by the House of Commons. At such moments a legislature, by expressing some deep-rooted national instinct or feeling, will transcend that hard-headed calculation of political or economic advantage which is normally the policy-maker's approach to a decision.

The way in which a parliament reflects divisions of opinion within society will determine not only the political complexion of the government, but also its scope for acting decisively over controversial issues. The Israeli Knesset provides a classic case of the tail wagging the dog. The Labour Party and the ultra-nationalist Likud Party each hold around 40 per cent of the seats. But in a system of pure proportional representation, 1 per cent of the popular vote will secure one Knesset seat (out of 120). The result is that the slight edge one of the main parties normally has over the other is exceeded by the voting strength of a number of very small religious parties. Every government has to be a coalition and every coalition depends for its existence upon satisfying an extreme religious viewpoint. The consequences for foreign as well as for domestic questions are considerable, including the most important one: in whatever way the pieces are assembled, the parliamentary kaleidoscope cannot produce a majority for movement on the issue of peace for the West Bank. For similar reasons, no Sudanese parliament, whenever the Sudan has returned to democratic government, has been able to agree to an equitable settlement with the rebellious South.

Parliaments have historically been the sounding boards for opinion in the country. When, in the Middle Ages, the knights of the shires and burghers met in Westminster Hall, the object was not only that they should hear what the king required of them, but also that his officials should learn of any regional discontents from them. Today the intense and continual lobbying of legislators by the public and by specialized groups and bodies is an integral part of democratic government. It is indicative both of the ever-increasing professionalism of the politician's calling and of the vast and growing range of matters with which the state now concerns itself. And whenever policies are unpopular, those initiating or supporting them will soon be made aware, whether by public opinion polls or by reports from party officials, that they are drawing upon their political credit. On foreign policy issues, governments are usually aware of what they can, and what they cannot, commit themselves to. Thus in 1914, Grey knew – such was the mood of the nation – that publicly to bind the country to any firm line of action in the event of war would have been to risk the break-up of the government. Roosevelt was similarly placed, and similarly affected, on the eve of the later conflict. Baldwin, in a confession that was to become notorious, stated that had he, in 1934, appealed to the country to re-arm, he would have lost the ensuing general election. And in 1968, Lyndon Johnson, realizing that a deep revulsion towards the war in Vietnam was abroad and growing among the American people, declared that he would not run for a second term as president.

By the 1960s, however, a new and potent factor had entered upon the scene and one whose full effects upon international relations are only now, a generation later, being experienced. Mass television for the first time brought the horrors of war into everyone's home. It also brought the harrowing scenes of famines, floods and earthquakes. Not least it brought to millions the unprecedented visual knowledge of how well 'the other half lived'. If the nationalist ferment which swept the Middle East and elsewhere during the 1950s and 1960s might be described as 'the transistor revolution', then the social and political break-up of the old communist order in 1989–90 might equally be termed 'the television revolution'. Stalin could build his empire by forbidding travel and shutting off any real knowledge of other lands and systems. This is no longer possible in McLuhan's 'global village' where people are beginning to vote not only with their feet but also with their shopping baskets.

Understanding the system

The foregoing analysis has attempted to show how international politics, and the foreign policies of states, may be affected by the political cultures of states, their constitutional structures, and the opinions and concerns of their peoples. In nearly every state, the political class has expanded, and in some must approach the total adult population. Except that the threat of general war seems to have receded, the international world, particularly in the economic realm, impinges on most people's lives at many more points than once it did. It is therefore inevitable that there are many who take an interest because their interests are seen to be involved. The question however arises: is the required sophistication present? Have the new participants as good an understanding of the workings of the international system as the much smaller political class of earlier times?

Part of the art of statecraft is to steer a nicely judged course between the 'outer imperatives' and the 'inner imperatives' of states. Too much steerage towards the Scylla of the former and those directing the state risk losing the support of their domestic power-base; too much towards the Charybdis of the latter may well produce a foreign policy which, while expressing domestic needs, desires or rivalries, ignores the state's power-political or economic position within the system. Either way the outcome can be unfortunate, or even disastrous. Woodrow Wilson, Lloyd George and Lyndon Johnson all eventually paid the penalty of sailing too close to Scylla, while Galtieri and Saddam Hussein fell classic victims to Charybdis. Eden, over Suez, achieved the unusual feat of running foul of both together. The supreme masters of the balanced course were Bismarck and Roosevelt, although even Bismarck ultimately foundered on an unforeseen Scylla when, adroit in his foreign policy to the last, he yet failed to ensure the confidence of the Kaiser and his circle which in the end was essential to it.

If leaders cannot always maintain the right balance, it is scarcely to be wondered at that peoples, once they have achieved influence, will find difficulty in doing so, especially when they have been cushioned against international political and economic realities either by the size, wealth or remoteness of their countries, or by their being so cocooned within an ideology or religion as to give them a restricted or distorted view of the world. Such disorientation is always liable to occur when an international system expands beyond the culture, or even the continent, which gave it birth. If, in contrast, the nineteenth-century European system worked reasonably well, it was because the élites which underpinned it for the most part shared similar values and were tolerably familiar with one another's countries and forms of government. Indeed, if Tenniel's cartoons are anything to go by, an acute appreciation of the international system, and of the actors within that system, must have been shared by the Victorian upper and middle classes and perhaps a wider circle still. If those perceptions were in part lost in the period following the First World War, it was because the horror and magnitude of that war, the threat posed by the Bolshevik Revolution to all accepted values, and the new dimension in international politics of ideological conflict, caused many people, even statesmen and scholars, to lose their bearings in this unfamiliar scene. There were many who simply 'did not want to know' and, if they were Americans, took refuge in isolationism. Others approached this new world with almost unbelievable naïvety and sentimental idealism. Yet others saw it from the perspective of their own professional calling, so that much of the thinking about international relations from Versailles to the rise of the dictators was suffused by Anglo-Saxon legalism, itself indicative of the growing prominence of the middle class, as well as of the expanding cultural and intellectual influence of the USA. It took another war, and the onset of a Cold War, to educate in the ways of the world that well-intentioned but hitherto unengaged section of Western opinion that now felt it had a right to be heard and heeded.

The lesson was, in the main, well learnt, but now, in the closing years of the twentieth century, the picture is changing once again, with ancient ethnic and religious enmities standing out like reefs as the tide of power ebbs, and with welfare and environmental issues adding dimensions with which statecraft did not formerly have to deal. Moreover, the interpenetration of economic systems, the rise of great multinational companies, and the incidence of international terrorism and other political activities and movements, have noticeably shifted the emphasis away from individual states, their foreign policies and alignments. Those symbols of national statehood, the goddesses and animals – Britannia and Marianne, British lion and Russian bear – have virtually vanished from the cartoons: people no longer think in those terms. Yet, despite the many new things to be considered, public opinion in most countries is probably better informed about international political realities, and more sophisticated in its approach to them, than ever before. In this, there lies hope, for if nationalism has turned peoples into princes, and they are to bear the responsibilities of princes, then it is right that they should cultivate the 'enlightened realism' of princes. In the task of helping them do this, a great trust and duty falls not only upon the universities, but upon the schools and the media. They alone can equip the generality of people for the new 'foreign policy' of useful participation in a world growing ever more complex and interdependent.

Notes

1 J.J. Saunders *The Age of Revolution* (Hutchinson, 1947) p. 158.
2 Alan Bullock *Hitler: A Study in Tyranny* (Odhams, 1952) p. 450.
3 The writer is indebted to Professor Inis L. Claude Jr of the University of Virginia for acquainting him with this comparison of Truman with Roosevelt.

4 Winston S. Churchill *Triumph and Tragedy* (Cassell, 1954) Ch. XXVII 'Western Strategic Divergencies'.

5 Harry S. Truman *Years of Trial and Hope 1946–53* (Hodder and Stoughton, 1955) p. 96.

6 A striking example of this morally superior attitude, quoted by Professor C.A.W. Manning, was of when he encountered a corseted Bostonian lady of local quality in 1926. 'Will your country', he had innocently asked, 'soon be accepting membership in the League?' 'NOT', she magnificently replied, 'until they come up to OUR standards!' 'And', he comments, 'she said this as if it were the most inevitable, axiomatic, and accepted thing to say': C.A.W. Manning 'The Legal Framework in a World of Change' in Brian Porter ed. *The Aberystwyth Papers* (Oxford University, 1972) p. 313.

7 R.C.K. Ensor *England 1870–1914* (Oxford, Clarendon, 1936) pp. 496–7; see also Appendix C, Section 3 'Grey and the Liberals'.

8 In response to a memorandum that Britain should cede Cyprus to Greece, Bevin told its author (John Colville) to ' 'ave a 'oliday'. For the whole amusing incident, see John Colville *Footprints in Time* (Collins, 1976) pp. 213–14.

9 Gordon A. Craig *Germany 1866–1945* (Oxford, Clarendon, 1978) p. 134.

10 George S. Patton Jr *War as I Knew It* (W.H. Allen, 1948) p. 327.

11 Fisher, the First Sea Lord, in fact resigned (over Churchill's Dardanelles policy), but in a way designed to force the government's hand. When he went on to demand dictatorial control of the navy and the war at sea, and Churchill's removal from the Cabinet, his resignation was curtly accepted. This was the nearest thing to an attempt by a service chief in Britain to dominate the government, as was already happening with the generals in Germany. It stood no chance of success.

12 L.S. Amery *My Political Life, Vol. III: The Unforgiving Years, 1929–1940* (Hutchinson, 1955) p. 324.

5

Diplomacy and the Modern State

Christopher Hill

Diplomacy is usually tackled by those interested in international relations in one of three ways: as an institution of international society; as an instrument of foreign policy; as a way into the nature of policy formulation.[1] The concern here is different from all three. It is the impact of diplomacy on the modern state, and vice versa, in contemporary conditions, and the question of what is expected of diplomacy by a modern state. Up to a point, the nation-state has produced a diplomacy to match its own character, and perhaps conversely. It is not clear, however, that changes in the nature of the state have gone hand in hand with changes in the nature of diplomacy, in such a way as mutually to reinforce one another. On the contrary, potential strains and fault-lines exist between the two institutions, raising questions about the nature and purpose of each.

Changes in the state: the impact on diplomacy

Democratization and the widening of the suffrage ought to have had the widest impact on diplomacy. Certainly, their advocates often defended political liberalization precisely on the grounds of the likely consequences – both dramatic and beneficial – for the conduct of relations between states. Democracy, it was argued, would produce less war and bellicosity, closer links between peoples and governments and greater stability. In the event, its consequences have been less clear-cut. On the one hand, we have seen open covenants, secretly arrived at, as governments have successfully argued that the process of negotiations should be conducted away from the public gaze, even if the comings and goings of diplomats may occur in a blaze of publicity and are conducted in the interests of 'national security' rather than *raison d'État*. Foreign policy has been the least affected by democratization of all the areas of public policy.

Equally, however, the demand that diplomacy serve the 'whole people' has clearly affected diplomatists' perceptions of their role, at least in those societies where the process of democratization has begun. There is regular forelock tugging in the direction of the masses, and the associated anticipatory trimming of foreign policy positions according to fears of domestic opposition. Governments have learned to fear peoples. This has scarcely given rise to stability of foreign policy, however. On the contrary, it has created great problems for continuity. Just when leaders become accustomed to the notion that it is safe to test the waters of openness, a surge of domestic protest is capable of disrupting their best-laid plans – a fact most dramatically demonstrated by the humiliation of the Chinese leadership at the hands of protesting students during the path-breaking visit of Mikhail Gorbachev in June 1989. The subsequent crushing of dissent in Tiananmen Square has altered the calculus of great power relations.

The modern state is also, very often, the ideologically specific state. Governments seem to need constant broad statements of principle, in order to win and hold broad coalitions of domestic backing; and diplomacy, at least *public diplomacy*, also increasingly uses ideological language to defend and secure the state's purposes, where formerly the language of interests would have sufficed. This has most obviously been true in post-revolutionary Iran, where those who took over the US embassy in 1979 have not wholly given ground to, calculating professionals, and in Ghaddafi's Libya, whose People's Bureaux (deliberately distinguished from embassies) have been used as bases for acts of violence on the streets of host states.

Thus diplomacy may find its values disregarded, particularly in the less wealthy states where scarcity of qualified diplomatic personnel and the suspicions engendered by decades of subordination to outside powers, have led to some rude intrusions into diplomacy by leaders such as Galtieri, Noriega and Master-Sergeant Doe. On the other hand, as Peter Boyce's work shows, most developing states are struggling, less spectacularly, to come to terms with conventional diplomacy, to develop an expertise therein, and also to modify it to reflect their own concerns.[2] If they do not succeed, the general institution of diplomacy may, indeed, be degraded.

The use of embassies as spy-nests or propagandist megaphones inside other states – with the natural consequence of encouraging siege-states in response, mobilized for social control and external conflict – has the potential to destroy the function of diplomacy as an institution in international society.[3] In the event, the persistence of continued abuse in this respect has not managed seriously to damage diplomacy's wider importance, in part because of its minority character, but also because diplomacy has become enhanced by the very contrast with such attempts as manipulation. But it certainly risks damaging the idea of the sovereign state, the siamese twin of diplomacy, in the very process of bolstering particular states over others.

Equal to the impact of ideology, democratic or otherwise, as a major development in the twentieth-century state, is the vast expansion which has taken place in the role of the state in society (though it should be noted that interventionism has taken a rather different role in the developed capitalist states from that in one-party systems and in Third World systems of all political complexions). In developed countries, the extended complexity of the state apparatus (perhaps paralleled by the apparatus of a party) has undoubtedly led* to the weakening of a specialist diplomatic corps. Intermediaries of all kinds, from Armand Hammer to Lord Hugh Thomas to Georgi Arbatov, now regularly operate round, through and over the top of regular diplomatic personnel, while for every envoy who becomes publicly known there are ten who bask in the coves of secrecy.[4] However, the utility of diplomatic behaviour as such has in no way been diminished by the proliferation of its practitioners. On the contrary, while societies have engaged with each other with more and more tentacles, most still behave diplomatically, in the sense commonly identified as involving tact, discretion, toleration and a concentration on negotiations. François de Callières' 'freemasonry of diplomacy' has simply undergone a vast expansion of membership.[5]

Accompanying interventionism has been the administrative dispersal of external relations and the increased involvement in foreign policy of ministries other than that formally designated the foreign ministry. Treasuries, defence ministries, trade ministries, health ministries *et al.* are all now actively and extensively concerned with conducting their own external relations, as well as (sometimes nominally) participating in the attempt to weld together a single external strategy. The prescription of Kuo Sung T'ao (China's first ambassador to the West) – that 'all officials should pay attention to the understanding of foreign affairs, and then almost anyone could be sent as an ambassador'[6] – has nearly come true. The specialist foreign ministry and diplomatic service may well be on the way out, to be replaced by a multi-component 'foreign service group' à la Berrill.[7] This may not matter; the functions of representation, expertise and accountability may all be served better by such a change. On the other hand, the allied development of the forging of trans-national and trans-governmental coalitions of experts (such as that well-established betweeen the UK Ministry of Defence and the Pentagon) raises serious questions about for whom and to what end policy is being constructed. It may not go so far as a *trahison des fonctionnaires*, but it will certainly redraw the boundaries of political argument, while obscuring the question of the legitimacy of interventions in that debate.

The administrative disperal of the modern state has everywhere been accompanied by the enhanced role of chief executives, who provide the visibility, co-ordinating capacity, and at times populist leadership, which otherwise cumbersome modern systems require. This has been particularly important in foreign policy, where heads of government have come to replace royal dynasties as embodiments of their countries and to negotiate at the highest levels when trade-offs are required between the various strands of 'domestic policy'. It has been noteworthy in the European Community how disagreements have been referred increasingly upwards from the Council of Ministers to the European Council, where the heads of government sit.

The consequence for diplomacy of the concentration of power at the apex, even in democracies, has been the accentuation of summitry as a means of conducting business. Summitry is hardly an innovation, but it clearly serves a number of important political and symbolic functions in international politics. The pseudo-pageantry of meetings between the leaders of the superpowers, or of the 'G7' meetings between the principal Western industrialized states, is the best example of the personalization of diplomacy, which runs as an equal and opposite trend to that implied by multilateralism. Wherever 'complex interdependence' seems to have reduced international differences to those negotiable by technocrats, the primitive need to understand politics in terms of personality or culture leads to a renewed interest in the dealings of eminent individuals meeting in historic palaces and chateaux. Of course there are considerable dangers attached to such an emphasis on image. Those who expected Henry Kissinger to be able to act with the freedom of a Metternich or Bismarck were doomed to disappointment, and even creative breakthroughs like Anwar Sadat's trip to meet Menachem Begin risk distorting difficult issues in the interests of personal deal-making.

So far we have been discussing evolutionary changes in the state and their impact upon diplomacy. But there are also two continuing kinds of overt challenge to the nature of the state which should be considered. Of these the first is the conservative attack on the idea of an over-weening state which has been mounted in the West over the last two decades, in reaction to the welfarist philosophy spawned by the Depression of the 1930s. On the surface, these neo-liberal attempts to push back the frontiers of the state have tended to leave diplomacy relatively unscathed. This is partly because diplomats do not make up a very large portion of the well-fed civil servants so irritating to the followers of F.A. Hayek[8] (and personal observation suggests that the modern diplomat, perhaps under new strains and dangers in the job, tends to wear a lean and hungry look). But it is also because of the familiar paradox that the opponents of the state at home can be its most fervent defenders in international relations. In the crudest form this means, of course, that their patriotism leads them to view diplomacy as mere cobwebs on the mouth of the cannon, and diplomats as natural friends of foreigners, but more sophisticated conservatives are likely to avoid the error of equating diplomacy with appeasement, and will be agnostic about the institution as such. Indeed, they may be in the forefront of those who would like embassies abroad to be opening up opportunities for private export drives, and scouting a path through the thickets of other states' non-tariff barriers. In this they may tacitly join forces with Edmund Dell's 'liberal mercantilists' of a more social democratic persuasion, who see diplomacy as an essential instrument in the partnership between the state and private enterprise which has seemed the best guarantee of prosperity to those admiring the record of Japan, West Germany and France.[9]

The second overt challenge to the role of the state which has reverberated around the world of diplomacy, has been constituted by the various separatist movements which continue to thrive, particularly in new states, but also in such relatively well-established states as Spain and now the Soviet Union. Separatism, almost by definition, is the product of intercommunal disputes, which are among the most serious of all the threats to the fabric of a state. They immediately pose serious problems for diplomats over matters of recognition, immunity and membership of international organizations. In the last decade, these have been particularly evident and sensitive in relation to the self-proclaimed Turkish Cypriot Federated State, and the Heng Samrin regime in Cambodia. Just as with the short-lived Biafran state in Nigeria, and the claims of the Polisario guerrillas (both of which fractured the Organization of African Unity), such developments have tested the ingenuity of the international diplomatic community to the full. The studied indifference of most governments to the recent claims of the Baltic republics for independence from the Soviet Union is evidence of the severe embarrassment which those who work in the service of a state feel in the face of demands to break one up. Indeed, handling the Lithuanian issue with delicacy so as not to endanger the stability of Europe or to set dangerous precedents, while at the same time not offending public opinion by too brutal a dismissal of Baltic aspirations, was undoubtedly one of the highest priorities of Western governments in the first half of 1990.

Despite dilemmas of this type, however, it remains clear that separatism in the end reinforces the concept and importance of the state (since each independence movement holds up the notion of the separate state as its goal and ideal). By extension, it also fosters the need for regularized, legitimate, diplomatic relations between the units concerned, rather than interference and claims of supremacy by one over the other. If all states in the world were to split into four, the institution of diplomacy would be boosted in spectacular fashion, as a far greater proportion of political transactions would take place at the diplomatic level of sovereign equality rather than that of an authoritatively–allocated value-structure. Conversely, if amalgamation were to take place on the kind of regional basis represented by the European Community and its enthusiasts for integration, the importance of diplomacy in the classical sense would be proportionally far less.

One of the most dramatic developments with relevance to our subject has taken place not *in* the state or *in* diplomacy, but at the point of intersection between the two. The tripling in size of the international system through the creation of over 100 new states since 1945 has vastly increased the number of diplomats in the world and spawned a great growth in inter-governmental organizations. On the other hand, it is worth noting the conclusions of Chad Alger and Steven Brams that the increase in numbers of missions has fallen well behind the increase in the number of states and potential dyadic links – that is, the percentage of actual to needed links has dropped from 45% in 1920 to 26% in 1963–4. The cobweb, therefore, may have become more extensive but also more thinly stretched.[10]

The expansion of the international system has certainly produced a much greater variety of states, from China to Tuvalu and Indonesia to Belize. In many respects, it is striking how these states have all necessarily adapted to the institutions of international society, and vice versa, but it is also true that about 20 mini- and micro-states have been created which have little hope of being able to represent themselves effectively on a global scale, let alone contribute to the shaping of the system as a whole. Moreover, there are many more states which are inherently unstable or turned in upon themselves. Lebanon is the most extreme example, but others such as Cambodia, Nicaragua, Haiti and Mozambique spring readily to mind. In a diplomatic sense, at least, these states are *hors de combat*. In fact, out of around 170 states in the world, only about one-third can be regarded as significant players in even the international politics of their regions.

This is, of course, very far from arguing that such states are non-viable entities from the viewpoint of their own peoples. On the contrary, the changing scope of international diplomacy has led to a revolution of rising expectations in respect to the state's external performance. Diplomacy is expected to produce goods, both for the individual state and the inter-national system as a whole, and both literal and symbolic, which it cannot actually provide. Some states, therefore, particularly new ones, may become dangerously over-externalized, even over-extended in their diplomatic activities, while at the same time being unable to cope with penetrations of their own society from outside. They will have to rely upon diplomacy as a resource against external penetration, yet diplomacy is hardly the most effective way of dealing with such interventions. Frustrations with diplo-macy as an institution of international society and a sensible instrument of national policy, therefore, inexorably follow.

Changes in diplomacy: the impact on the state

The steady development of multilateralism, from at least the Congress of Vienna through the Hague Conferences to the League of Nations and the UN system which has superseded it, has been the most striking line of evolution in diplomacy. It has been paralleled by a decline in traditional diplomatic agreements: treaties of alliance, non-aggression pacts, ententes and guarantees – even though problems of military security have hardly been eradicated for most states. These bilateral diplomatic deals, common in the nineteenth and early twentieth centuries, have been supplanted by multilateral and often institutionalized frameworks which tend to discount dramatic gestures of friendship or enmity, particularly when they involve sudden changes in alignment. The pulling out of the hat of Reinsurance treaties or the equivalents of the Nazi–Soviet Pact would be regarded as in less than good taste today (as the latter was even in 1939 – although it was not such a shocking event as people tend to suppose today). The pure interests of *state*, narrowly defined, are becoming more and more difficult to assert over and above the intertwined complexities of ideological, ethnic and systemic considerations.

What then are the consequences of all this for the state itself, in so far as we can separate its internal and its external lives? The implications are two-fold. First, the state is likely to become more bureaucratized, and more of its bureaucracy externally directed, as the requirements of the international system lead to the setting up of patterns of cooperation in many more functional areas. There was, after all, a conscious decision made in the political intelligentsia of the Western victors towards the end of the Second World War, that international cooperation would now have to extend to the regional, economic and cultural areas, so as to underpin obligations of a more formal, legal kind. This inevitably meant developing national cadres capable of contributing to the Organization for European Economic Cooperation (OEEC), the Council of Europe, the General Agreement on Tariffs and Trade (GATT), the International Civil Aviation Organization (ICAO), and so on. In this respect, the permanent secretariats were less significant than the civil servants, increasingly from outside foreign ministries, who oriented their activities towards the processes of international co-ordination.[11]

The second consequence of multilateralism is more two-edged. Where the institution concerned is a broad church, and represents in its own procedures the values of free exchange and adherence to certain rights and freedoms (whether political or economic), it is possible that some of the intrinsic pluralism of the organization might slowly transfer itself into the state. The Lomé process may be slowly affecting some of the African, Caribbean and Pacific countries in this way. Conversely, adherence to more pluralist norms can – and often is – made a condition of entry into a particular organization, as with the European Community itself, and in the GATT. World Bank conditionality in respect of loans to developing countries is another facet of the same thing.

The other edge of this process is that membership of a multilateral system need not always transfer pluralism, even where the aims of the organization are avowedly democratic. Rather the reverse: the institutionalization of a military alliance may over time be a way in which the dominant power in the alliance increases its ability to intervene in other members of the alliance, and the proliferation of bases, arms industries, sophisticated communications networks can encourage the pathology of the 'security state', where the freedoms of citizens within the state may actually prove to have been curtailed by the very set of international arrangements intended to defend them. *Mutatis mutandi*, this can be applied to certain aspects of life under both the North Atlantic Treaty Organization (NATO) and the Warsaw Pact in the Cold War era. It counterbalances the dilution of the power and emotional significance of the state which has resulted from the fall from grace of the values of *raison d'État*.

A further change at the level of international diplomacy – although hardly confined to diplomacy – has been the communications revolution. It does not need spelling out how changes in the technology of information have affected the daily lives of diplomats and foreign ministries. So far as the state is concerned, this may have had the effect of turning states outward, and involving them more directly with each other, providing less opportunity for diplomacy to act as a buffer between the barely compatible idiosyncrasies of separate societies. Equally, it may mean that diplomacy and a layer of deception has been thinned down and the possibilities of truthful understanding thereby heightened. But just as actions can bring forth equal and opposite reactions, so the state has responded to freedom of information in the technical sense by increasing the sophistication of its own efforts at news management in order to remind news media – which often wallow in nationalistic excess without any encouragement – of the requirements of security and the 'national interest'.

None the less, instant and multi-channelled communications have made possible many more 'private foreign policies' than have occurred in the past, when they were limited to the activities of individual intermediaries such as Birger Dahlerus in 1939, who focused on, and were manipulated by, governments more than peoples as a whole. It is true that there have been for at least the last century organized groups pursuing their own ends on the international stage, such as the Socialist Internationals, but the previous exception has now become virtually the contemporary rule – witness the activities of groups such as trades unions, human rights groups and the European Nuclear Disarmament Movement. A state cannot hope now to monopolize its society's external relations, unless it is prepared to adopt the isolationist mode of a Burma or an Albania. Among other things, the increase in the surplus wealth of most individuals in developed societies since the Second World War has produced more independent travel, telephone usage and the power to purchase imports, all of which have weakened the gatekeeper function of the state.

The extensive spread of both acts of private diplomacy and the perception of a right to pursue ends in international society unrelated to the needs of a mere nation-state, entail wider consequences. These can be seen from a functionalist point of view as actually binding together, despite themselves, separate societies, or they can be viewed from the perspective of their disintegrative effect on states, and by extension on international society, because of their chaotic and subversive nature, and their intrinsic inability to offer an alternative structure of political responsibility. Of course, all this may only be of real relevance to democratic states, who are in any case those resilient enough to withstand it, but because the last few years have witnessed the expression of democratic yearnings in many different types of society, it is not a marginal consideration.

Moreover, transnational actors can sometimes constitute a serious challenge to state authority. How they do so is somewhat paradoxical. On the face of things, the operations of multinational corporations and terrorists do tend to leave diplomacy and diplomats beached. It is very difficult for governments to negotiate with private organizations about the issue of fundamental authority, without conceding their own basic rationale. Britain's refusal to recognize the political status of the Irish Republican Army (IRA), Israel's to recognize that of the Palestine Liberation Organization (PLO), and the USA's futile attempt to control the European subsidiaries of US firms in their campaign of sanctions against the USSR, all illustrate the point. Diplomats have very little to say or do in such affairs, except to push the conventional line to both sides about the inviolability of the state and the supremacy of the law. Beyond that, the basic initiatives and actions have to be political.

Behind the scenes, however, diplomacy may be more active, particularly when events seem compelling; then diplomats take on a curious role: that of both state actor *and* mediator between proscribed organizations and the state. To the challenger they stress that it is necessary to recognize the realities of states' power, and to the rest of the state apparatus they point out the necessity of talking to those who might have effectively annexed some of that power. Much of this kind of activity will be necessarily secret and limited to a small number of people.

Most transnational activities do not, however, take place in issue-areas which become subject to the 'high-policy' definitions unavoidable when security or sovereignty is perceived to be at stake. Rather, they quietly rearrange the political furniture so that more and more of what the state is, is directly represented abroad and a large number of groups actively make external relations. This not only strengthens the groups and institutions in question but also enhances their role inside the state. Amnesty International and Friends of the Earth, for example, have achieved legitimate monitoring rights in and through international organizations and this has increased their status and influence with their various domestic constituencies.

The other side of the coin of the spread of democratization within the state, is the increased importance of external relations for the ordinary citizen and the consequent slow growth of interest and concern about the consequences of what happens 'abroad'. Greater accountability by itself (and there are still not many manifestations of it in foreign policy) has only meant (we must assume) fewer secret clauses to partition Poland. But in principle the evident impact of international developments within the state could prove a powerful lever for obtaining more democratic procedures across the board. The bandwagon effects which have been obvious in Eastern Europe, and even South Africa, over the last year are certainly evidence in favour of the hypothesis. On the other hand, a longer historical perspective produces more pessimistic conclusions; states have proved adept at exploiting the symbols of unity in their demands that the nation speak with one voice. Even now the Chinese Government has been able to isolate its student critics without too much difficulty by playing on their very association with foreign values, while powerful forces in the Soviet Union would like Moscow to take a similar stand against the international trends which threaten to dissolve the cement holding the Soviet state together.

There are more prosaic ways, of course, in which diplomats are affected by the narrowing of the gap between world affairs and the people stuck listening to car radios in traffic jams the world over. They have come to be at once more in touch with the societies they are representing and more insulated from them: in touch, because more of the business of diplomacy is commercial or cultural, helping business people or youth orchestras on their travels, and needing to know much more about the domestic environment from which they spring (although pure consular work, such as that with stranded tourists, is still kept at arm's length); insulated, because the physical threats from terrorists have produced a way of life in which metal detectors, security fences, and in some cases diplomatic compounds reminiscent of that which failed in 1900 to hold back the Boxers in Peking, are routinely accepted. Such dualism, unsurprisingly, serves to perpetuate the popular view of diplomacy as a rarified activity of little benefit to the citizens who pay its way.

The most important single development in modern diplomacy is unlikely to disturb such stereotypes, as it has so far served only to widen the gap between the discourses of international negotiation and national politics. This is the emergence of pure foreign policy integration, to be observed in such phenomena as European Political Cooperation, and the development of an Association of South-East Asian Nations (ASEAN) position on Cambodia. These are examples of states binding together in diplomatic stances and procedures, without being fully integrated at the economic, social and constitutional levels. Such developments have their important effects for the pattern of international relations, but they also rebound into the states concerned. Most obviously, this is by opening up an inconvenient contrast between the intentions of the state at the level of external strategy, and its intentions at the level of identity and community. The subsequent credibility gap could either undermine the foreign policy strategies produced, or equally have a motor effect on otherwise stagnant processes of integration. It used to be taken for granted in the literature of European integration, that the development of European unity in diplomacy could only follow on from the prior achievement of a single industrial and economic policy, for instance. Since 1976, however, speculation has gradually hardened into conventional wisdom to the effect that new perceptions of European identity, and tangible pressures for cooperation, are being generated by the systemic pulls of diplomatic activity.

The act of diplomatic solidarity alone – leading to what Michael Leifer has termed a 'diplomatic community'[12] – is probably not enough by itself to create major changes in the state (although some might argue that NATO has effectively changed the nature of the states which are members of its military command structure). However, diplomatic integration certainly raises major questions of purpose for the states involved, to do with their definition of community, the aims of cooperation, the nature of their constituency, and the dividing line between insiders and outsiders. It also certainly demonstrates that the great questions about the nature of the state, and its changing status, come not just from within, from developments at the level of class or bureaucracy, nor even from those factors able to 'transcend sovereignty' by bypassing it; they come also from the very nature of formal inter-governmental relations themselves. That is, the pattern of foreign policy commitments into which a state enters can, according to the nature of the commitment and its institutional consequences, lead the state and its citizens into a fundamental reconsideration of who they are and what they are about. This is as true for the Arab League considering joint measures against Israel, the Commonwealth arguing about sanctions against South Africa, and the European Twelve deciding on the appropriate foreign policy actions of a 'civilian power'. Diplomacy in this sense is far from being merely superstructural to the state or to grand strategy. It can be an important source of choices about the future character and autonomy of the state.

Conclusions

It seems clear that the state is moving in several directions simultaneously in world society, some undermining and some reinforcing what it is and stands for. In this climate of contradictions, the institution of diplomacy appears to be surviving reasonably well, at least to the extent that the community of states as a whole is surviving. States of most kinds continue to set considerable store by diplomacy, and both the very weak and the very strong have excellent reasons for wishing to ensure that international relations pass largely through a diplomatic funnel, avoiding military force and its escalations. Diplomacy is a crucial buffer between different types of state.

Yet the specialized diplomatic profession has undoubtedly been undergoing some sea changes. If these have mostly been at the level of process, procedural change in itself can easily spill over into questions of purpose, as the Swiss people recognized (albeit hypersensitively) when they rejected in a referendum the proposal that Switzerland join the United Nations. Whatever the changes in scope and personnel, however, diplomacy remains well established as one of the main pillars of international society. It thus acts to reinforce the society as it is, centred on states and their inter-relationships, rather than to undermine that order in favour of some alternative schema. The institution of diplomacy itself, rather than the always fragile status of diplomats, would have to enter a decline before the state could be seriously damaged by developments at the diplomatic level.

The corollary of this is that only if transnational relations and trans-governmental alliances between them threaten the identity and usefulness of the state, will diplomacy as an institution also suffer. Even here the position is complicated by the fact that trans-governmental alliances derive from traditional diplomatic activity and its interpenetration with defence and political economy. Thus again diplomacy is as much promoting change in the state as reflecting it.

As has been suggested above, there is evidence to suggest that some damage is being inflicted upon the institution of diplomacy. However, it is also true that at present states still perceive themselves as autonomous decision-making communities which need to engage in *systematic* relations with each other (positing separateness) precisely because they have not the option of proper *constitutional* relations among themselves. Diplomacy provides these systematic relations.

The possibility of constitutional relations is raised by the diplomatic alliances whose emergence we have noted, but there are still *sauts qualitatifs* to be made before the issue is fully joined. It is possible that the European Community is teetering on the edge of such a leap in its pursuit of integration at the levels of both monetary and political union in the early 1990s, but there are still formidable obstacles in the way of even the Twelve. For the present, we have to assume that the systematic relations provided by diplomacy are going to remain of central importance to the international system.

From that starting point, three broad themes suggest themselves by way of conclusions. The first is the relationship which can be observed between the structure of the diplomatic system and the nature of the modern state. The current diplomatic system is a mixture of egalitarianism and privilege, but it only very dimly mirrors the huge variety of states and powers which exists in the world. To the extent that the institution of diplomacy is a restraining and homogenizing force, then various kinds of states may come under pressure to adhere to the mean. But it depends on what exactly the price of an entry ticket to the club is: mere acceptance of reciprocal embassy facilities, plus recognition? Or acceptance of common standards of civilized behaviour on a wider basis – what *should* we expect of Libya?

Conversely, the perpetuation of deep cleavages between differing types of state may bring the diplomatic structure under severe pressure. While we should not carelessly elevate short-term developments into harbingers of system-transformation (as did Carter Mark I with 'the interdependence agenda'), it would be equally short-sighted to overlook the fact that where states are frustrated in finding international assistance for their often externally exacerbated problems, they may (as in the 1930s) suffer nationalist spasms in a backlash that can only weaken the evolving set of compromises that is the states-system.

Another aspect of the uneven isomorphism which exists between the state and the diplomatic system is the weakening effect which the complex interchange between bilateral and multilateral activity has on the relationship between the two. For the modern diplomat hardly represents or 'stands for' his or her country. As often as not, it is impossible to know both what is distinctive about his or her country's position on any given issue and what values he or she is supposed to be representing on behalf of it. The diplomat is perhaps better viewed as a plain negotiator or bureaucrat, working to specific mandates from his or her government, but often stranded between different constituencies, than as an embodiment of a particular society.

The state and the diplomatic system, then, are in an uneasy relationship with each other, neither wholly distinct nor changing in parallel, which brings us to the second concluding theme: the paradox that diplomacy continues to be consolidated even though it is ever more apparent that it cannot cope with more than a small proportion of the problems on its agenda. For as the rules of diplomacy have become accepted, so the expectations have become heavier: diplomacy should be able to engineer peace, conflict-resolution, the co-ordination of disparate policies, the identification of common interests. But as realists often observe, the spirit of compromise represented by diplomacy is not always enough – merely splitting the difference rarely copes with major challenges to structures. At certain crucial junctions creative initiatives are required, and it is revealing that these have often tended to come from non-official or at best semi-official sources – Monnet, Baruch, Brandt and Spinelli are all good examples.

This is partly because diplomats increasingly have to cope with not just inter-governmental relations but also the consequences of the domestic entrails of states spilling out onto international relations. They have to know and deal with the most intimate aspects of a state's inner life in order to understand its external behaviour. This was true, of course, for both the French and Russian revolutions (although honoured by diplomats of the time more in the breach than the observance), but it is now the general rule, and the scale of necessary comparative knowledge is global. The Americans, for all their resources, are supposed to have had only 'a handful' of Farsi-speaking Iranian experts in the government machine in 1978, and to have suffered accordingly.[13]

Equally, as foreign policy becomes more susceptible to competing demands in most societies, so the continuity on which diplomacy depends for success begins to disappear. As a result, diplomats need more and more to explain and defend the needs of the international environment to their own domestic constituency, which risks the charge of international clientelism even from their home-based colleagues in the bureaucracy.

More importantly, the demands of complex interdependence tend to produce a division among diplomats, between the specialists and the 'policy managers'. The latter identify with their state, and try to put together packages of positions which are geared to the perceived needs of the community which they serve. Theirs is the more obvious political imperative. The former, however, also have a political criterion, although they may be barely aware of it. Theirs is a more functional perspective, and they are likely to make alliances with the equivalent specialists in other states' bureaucracies. Thus if the Oceans section of the State Department had been better staffed, it might have been able to press the internationalist arguments for the Law of the Sea Treaty over the American business interests which eventually prevailed.[14] As with the British Intelligence officers who are supposed to have dished Eden with the Americans over Suez,[15] it would be a question of looking at a problem from a very different stance and being convinced that their solution was genuinely preferable, even if in so doing they were actually smuggling in different criteria (even interests) from those of the national government, which usually will hold a political if not electoral mandate for its actions. In other words, the nature of changing international relations is reflected in changing diplomatic practices, which in turn can stretch and even subvert the loyalties which the state demands of its diplomats.

The last of our concluding themes returns to the fundamental question about both diplomacy and the states which lie behind it: what should diplomacy be about? States are in principle devices for autonomous decision making. And yet they routinely enter into diplomatic arrangements which at the least identify them in common cause with 'like-minded' states over long periods of time, and at most promote integration and the blurring of separate identities. This – as has been stressed here – can be as true of informal, evolving, 'diplomatic communities' as of formal derogations of sovereignty.

In practice, states rarely have the capacity to confront the difficult questions which such arrangements ought to provoke. The British, for example, have consistently avoided the issues of how truly independent their nuclear deterrent is, and what consultation they would be entitled to in the event of the US wishing to use those of its nuclear weapons based on British soil. This is because diplomats generally wish to avoid the kind of public arguments that New Zealand stirred up in the 1980s, when it raised the issue with Washington of visits from nuclear-armed ships. But, in the event of a crisis, the lack of clear understandings and agreed procedures might turn out disastrously for the less powerful states in an alliance – as it did for France in 1940, when Reynaud found that he could not depend on British fighter squadrons being sent to the front, and for Hungary in 1956, when Imre Nagy discovered that the very last freedom Hungary enjoyed was that to withdraw from the newly formed Warsaw Pact.

The point here is that diplomacy can reach down to the very foundations of the state both because it raises the question of which other societies you wish to identify closely with, and because it can construct a spider's web that is difficult to escape from at some later date. It is no accident that Americans have feared 'entangling alliances' from the very beginning of the Republic, and the British have emphasized (increasingly vainly) that a Parliament can change any international agreement entered into by a previous government. Conversely, in the Sino-Soviet split, it was difficult to disentangle the elements of ideological or social divergence from the two states' foreign policy quarrels.

Ultimately, it is necessary to decide how much of what we require and expect of diplomacy is derived from our picture of it as a central institution of international society, and how much from our hopes for the state as a vehicle for prosperity, safety and self-realization. This goes beyond the truism that in making possible an orderly international system, diplomacy is also upholding the state itself. The paradox of the modern condition of the state is that it leads us both to see diplomacy instrumentally, as a way of promoting our solipsistic sense of national community, and open-endedly, as a way of trying out new possibilities for coping with problems whose scope goes far beyond the capability of the individual state. This creates tensions which may prove irreconcilable.

Certainly, it demands that we try to strike a balance between diplomacy as a means of identifying and fostering 'us' and diplomacy as a means of fostering the latent community of mankind. In decisions about the whole range of issues attaching to diplomacy, governments and peoples have to think about how far their conception of community extends. This inherently involves confronting the issue of how attached they are to the particular states they inhabit, but more importantly also to the very idea of the state. At present, the idea of the state, not least in the context of diplomacy, arouses such passionate ambivalence that for most the temptation is overwhelming to duck the issue altogether.

Notes

1 For two examples of the first, see Adam Watson *Diplomacy: The Dialogue between States* (Eyre Methuen, 1982), and Alan James 'Diplomacy and International Society' *International Relations* VI, 6 (1980) pp. 931–48; an example of the second is Robert Jervis *The Logic of Images in International Relations* (Princeton University, 1970); and of the third, Ronald Barston *Modern Diplomacy* (Longman, 1988).

2 P.J. Boyce *Foreign Affairs for New States: Some Questions of Credentials* (St Lucia, University of Queensland, 1977).

3 Although it is important to keep a sense of historical perspective. The writer's home institution, the London School of Economics, is sited on Portugal Street, where the Portuguese Embassy Chapel was sited until it was burnt down by an anti-Catholic mob in December 1688. Anglo-Portuguese relations survived. See Peter Barber *Diplomacy: the World of the Honest Spy* (The British Library, 1979) p. 31.

4 For examples of the more benign, if perhaps less effective, type of intermediary, see Maureen R. Berman and Joseph E. Johnson eds *Unofficial Diplomats* (New York, Columbia University, 1977).

5 François de Callières *De la manière de négocier avec les Souverains* (Brussels, 1716). English edition *The Art of Diplomacy* edited by Maurice Keen-Soper and Karl W. Schweizer (Leicester University, 1983).

6 See J. Frodsham ed. *The First Chinese Embassy to the West: The Journals of Kuo Sung Tao, Liñ Hsi-Hung and Chang Te-Yi* (Oxford, Clarendon, 1974).

7 Sir Kenneth Berrill was the head of the British Government's Central Policy Review Staff which in a 1977 report recommended the abolition of a separate foreign service, and its merging on a flexible basis with the home civil service. *Review of Overseas Representation* (London, HMSO, 1977).

8 Irritation at the luxuries of diplomatic life is, of course, hardly confined to the Right. Just after the Berrill Report, Simon Winchester's 'Third World Commentary' in the *Guardian* of 11 August 1978 was by-lined 'Why should a flock of privileged foreigners be permitted to display wealth undreamed of . . . in India?'

9 Edmund Dell 'Trade Policy: Retrospect and Prospect', *International Affairs* 60, 2 (1984) pp. 193–205. See also Dell's *The Politics of Economic Interdependence* (Macmillan, 1987).

10 Cited and adapted in George Modelski *Principles of World Politics* (New York, Free Press, 1972) p. 188.

11 The complexities behind this generalization are discussed in Max Beloff *New Dimensions in Foreign Policy* (George Allen and Unwin, 1961). Multilateralism is considered more generally in a recent survey by Sir Michael Palliser 'Diplomacy Today' in Hedley Bull and Adam Watson eds *The Expansion of International Society* (Oxford, Clarendon, 1985) pp. 371–85.

12 Michael Leifer *ASEAN and the Security of South-East Asia* (Routledge, 1989).

13 Gary Sick *All Fall Down* (Tauris, 1985) p. 281.

14 William I. Bacchus *Staffing for Foreign Affairs: Personnel Systems for the 1980s and 1990s* (Princeton University, 1983) pp. 50–2.

15 According to the unverifiable account of Anthony Verrier, in *Through the Looking Glass: British Foreign Policy in an Age of Illusions* (Jonathan Cape, 1983) pp. 151–2.

6

The State and Integration

John Baker and Martin Kolinsky

Aspirations for European unity were widespread at the end of the Second World War. There was deep revulsion against aggressive nationalism, and a new awareness of the limitations of the nation-state as an ultimate frame of reference. A higher level of transnational European cooperation was seen as necessary for the resolution of post-war political and economic problems. Unity was seen as the means of supporting and reinforcing internal democratic and social renewal, and safeguarding against the possibility of another war. The new constitutions of France, Italy and West Germany included statements indicating a willingness to accept limitations of national sovereignty for the goal of an international order of peace and justice.

However, ideas about the nature and scope of unity varied. The federalists sought to create a European nation on the model of the USA, and exercised considerable influence in the non-communist Resistance; after the war they attracted some support among Christian Democrats, Liberals and Socialists. But at government level, a less ambitious approach to European unity prevailed for some time. The major institutions of the first decade after the war – the Organization for European Co-operation (OEEC), the Brussels Treaty Organization, the Council of Europe and the North Atlantic Treaty Organization (NATO) – were all associations of states which placed no formal limitations on the exercise of national sovereignty. They provided permanent machinery for multilateral cooperation and consultation on vital military and economic issues, but were strictly inter-governmental in character.

In these circumstances, the advocates of federalism adopted a strategy of piecemeal measures. The main inspiration was provided by Jean Monnet, the architect of French economic planning. His tenacious commitment to the gradual creation of a new set of interrelationships was readily accepted in Belgium, Holland and Luxembourg, and became increasingly influential in the larger countries. In Italy, the Foreign Minister, Count Sforza, was a convinced European and influenced Prime Minister de Gasperi. In Western Germany, Monnet's views found a sympathetic response among Christian Democrats, and at a later stage, among the post-Schumacher Social Democratic leaders. In France, Monnet's approach became official policy at the beginning of the 1950s, a decisive breakthrough which led to the establishment of three transnational communities: the European Coal and Steel Community (ECSC), the European Atomic Energy Community (EURATOM) and the European Economic Community (EEC).[1]

Membership in these communities involved a transfer of some powers of law-making from the state to transnational institutions. By definition, it implied a limitation of sovereignty on the part of the individual member states; but the question to be considered in this chapter is to what extent did it represent a loss of *political* sovereignty? An answer to this question will entail an examination of ideas of the state prevalent in Europe, the relationship between the state and the institutions of the European Community (EC), in particular the Commission and the Council of Ministers, and the ways in which common interests are articulated or, as often happens, blocked.

Ideas about the state held by protagonists of European integration

The idea of European integration did not suddenly appear after the Second World War. In the aftermath of the First World War, Count Coudenhove Kalergi and the Pan-European Union had attracted support in several countries including the UK, France and Germany, largely by aiming at the intellectual and political élites. This approach produced the tabling of a plan for European union, under the auspices of the League of Nations, by the French Foreign Minister Aristide Briand on 5 September 1929. Yet it failed, because, according to some 'federalists', it had ignored the need to gain the support of the peoples of Europe. This view was promoted by Jean Monnet, whose Action Committee campaigned for the Treaty of Rome in 1956. According to the Action Committee, 'we will not build another coalition of Governments, we shall unite human beings'.[2] Such a conception of integration, from below as well as from above, through creating a community of peoples, meant a broadening of potential support for the aim of European integration. If successful, it would have had grave implications for the state: it implied the possible transfer of loyalty across national boundaries to a greater European entity.

The declarations of the Resistance movements in German-occupied

Europe and the inclusion of European integration in the platforms of some free political parties reinforced the demand for limitations of sovereignty and a new unity.[3] Largely of socialist origin, the movements argued that social reform required co-ordinated action among states, and that state 'egotism' endangered it. Their influence on ideas of the state can be seen in the new constitutions of the Italian Republic, the French Fourth Republic and the Basic Law of the Federal Republic of Germany.[4] These all provided for the limitation of national sovereignty on conditions of parity with other countries in future international organizations.

However, Britain saw integration in a far more limited way than the European Movement – a transition to normality, to be backed by a defence arrangement with the USA. The British concern was continental Europe's defence capability. Winston Churchill, the British wartime leader in Opposition, voiced support in Zurich in 1946 for a form of a United States of Europe to strengthen Europe so that it might resist becoming demoralized in the face of Soviet expansion. But it later emerged that he meant Britain to be a friendly outsider and not a participant in such a scheme. Britain, as one of the 'Big Three', was still a Great Power. Although greatly weakened by the war, its prestige, the Empire and its 'special' relationship with the USA, made it, still, a major actor on the world stage. In 1950, it produced more iron and steel than the 'six' and was technologically more advanced;[5] hence, it was in a far stronger position in its own right than any other European power. Largely in consequence, Britain avoided the plans for more extensive integration in the form of the European Defence Community (EDC) or the ECSC.[6] Indeed, the formation of the 'little' Europe of the ECSC, rather than a wider integration including Britain and its Nordic supporters, was due to a realization by the Belgium Foreign Minister, Paul-Henri Spaak, that integration was only possible without Britain.

The USA was above all concerned with reconstruction. Marshall Aid was made dependent on European planning rather than grants of aid to individual nations; and the OEEC was intended as an engine of regeneration. American encouragement of integration in post-war reconstruction was aimed in part against the supposed danger of communist takeovers in France and Italy, and was concerned to create a viable context for the economic and strategic absorption of West Germany.[7]

The emergence of the superpowers had divided Europe into two camps, and led to the belief that European states were far too weak individually to act with the full sovereignty of earlier years. The East–West divide, together with the rapid withdrawal of American troops after the Second World War, also made European collective security essential to face the perceived military threat of the Soviet Union. This led to the Brussels Pact of 1948, the abortive EDC of 1954 and the West European Union of the same year. The establishment of NATO, to which West Germany adhered in 1955, provided the framework for the defence of Western Europe in close association with the USA. Moreover, to compete economically with the USA, the Europeans had to unite to create larger markets. Further, it was thought that only a united Europe would be large enough to gain a hearing in the new bipolar international system. This form of argument, in light of the remarkable speed of economic recovery since 1945, has led later supporters of full integration to see Europe as a potential superpower in the making.

Another cluster of arguments focused on the practical implications of a united Europe for inner European relations. It was recognized that the continent could not afford another conflict on the scale of the Second World War, especially in a nuclear age. Integration, it was argued in the European Resistance Movement, was the best means to achieve peace. The uniting of the European states would remove the means of making war, because full integration would necessitate total interdependence of war-making capacity. It would also create a new loyalty to a new political entity superseding the national loyalties which had previously disturbed the peace of Europe. Finally, and by no means unrelated, was the belief that an integrated Europe would prove an ideal vehicle for rehabilitating the defeated powers of Germany and Italy. Within a united Europe, these powers could be integrated into the world community while reassuring their neighbours who had recently suffered from occupation and defeat.

Thus, generally, European 'federalists' of all sorts believed that the old European states were too small and weak in a post-war world dominated by the superpowers. In effect, they believed that the nation-state, at least in Europe, was becoming obsolete and that only by the integration of resources and markets in a united Europe could the continent hope to be a force in the post-war period.

In terms of sectoral integration, this assumption can be clearly seen in EURATOM. Only through the integration of the 'Six' could Europe hope to compete with the superpowers in the nuclear industry since, it was believed, the expenditure required was beyond the capacity of any single member of the Community. This was the argument stated in 'A Target for EURATOM', which was put forward in May 1957.

Yet in 1957, the French Second Five Year Plan of the Commissariat à l'Energie Atomique (CEA) had come to the conclusion that France alone could afford its own programme. The West Germans also found it was possible to run their own programme, and Monnet's view of EURATOM as 'the spearhead for the unification of Europe'[8] proved wrong. Both France and West Germany developed independent programmes to the detriment of financing a European venture, a venture moreover which would have benefited the weaker states in this field. Integration has, in fact, produced conflicts of interest between countries which are strong or weak in any field. The weaker states were, as the federalists assumed, those who most favoured integration. Conversely, a state which could afford a major national effort preferred independence.

Equally, by the time it was clear that Britain would not go far down the road of integration, Marshall Aid had started to facilitate reconstruction and recovery. In consequence, recovery proved to be more rapid than the assumptions of the federalists. By the time of the Treaty of Rome in 1957, full economic capacity was well on the way to restoration, and some of the impetus towards integration had been dissipated.

On the other hand, in the field of defence, the very weakness of Europe made the Europeans, including Britain, attempt to get the Americans more fully involved with their defence. Britain participated in the Treaties of Dunkerque and Brussels, but declined to join the EDC. The EDC, with a European Army, would certainly have been a far more extensive step towards integration than was the later EC. The NATO Council announced at the Lisbon Meeting in 1954 a scheme that was to create an army of 43 divisions, growing 'to ninety-six divisions, thirty-five or forty of which would always be in combat readiness (twenty-five to thirty of them for the central front)'.[9] With Britain and France needing troops for their colonial empires, to achieve anywhere near this level of troops would have meant a larger German contribution and potential German domination. Even NATO, including the USA, was unable to obtain this level of manpower without putting European recovery at risk. The Lisbon estimates of force levels required for the conventional defence of Europe were clearly unrealistic, but they led to an Atlantic solution for defence problems, not a European solution.

Through the 1980s, despite European economic recovery to a level where the EC's GNP is on a par with the USA, despite the French and British withdrawal from their empires, and the fact that the Community has a larger population than the USSR, Europe has continued to rely on substantial US inputs in defence. Nor has there been any real pressure, at least by governments, to push integration forward into defence at the expense of NATO and the US presence in Europe, partly because this would mean a substantial increase in defence expenditure. However, the EC, without a security element, is clearly far from being a new super state.

In the Single European Act, there is an article which allows for security to be a possible future field of cooperation.[10] Yet even this is limited by a section stating:

> Nothing in this Title shall impede closer cooperation in the field of security between certain of the High Contracting Parties within the framework of the Western European Union or the Atlantic Alliance.[11]

And the Act, despite its caution, ran up against the neutrality clause in the Constitution of the Republic of Ireland. A referendum was necessary in 1987 to ratify it.

The claim that it is integration which prevents war among the member states is certainly overstated. The threat of war has been inhibited by the security arrangements of NATO; and the maintenance of the US presence in Europe has been the key stabilizing factor. The removal of the Soviet threat by events in Eastern Europe has precipitated a crisis of reorientation, but the problem is for NATO to resolve, much more than for the EC.

The division of Germany was a contributory factor to the successful integration of the Federal Republic of Germany (FRG) into Western Europe and the lack of conflict in the region. The FRG, being only part of pre-war Germany, was a lesser threat and thus easier to integrate than a united Germany would have been. The West German state under the leadership of Konrad Adenauer, although paying lip-service to reunification, was dedicated to full integration of the new state into the West. All of his successors have realized the crucial importance of this orientation, and continue to do so. Indeed, the EC has been a major factor in the successful gaining of legitimacy by the new smaller German state, the ECSC in particular laying the basis of France-German reconciliation and partnership.

The impact upon the EC of a united Germany, resulting from the dramatic events of November 1989, is still unclear at the time of writing. The free East German elections held on 18 March 1990 showed that unification was likely to happen far more quickly than had been envisaged previously. East Germany was formally absorbed into West Germany in two stages – monetary union in July 1990 and formal political union in October 1990. Two months later, the first elections of the new united Germany were held. But the tasks of bringing the environment, industry and economy of the former Democratic Republic of Germany (DDR) up to the standards of the West is expected to take a decade or more. The doubts raised about Germany's preoccupation with the question of unification and about the rapidly changing situation in Eastern Europe has created anxieties that Germany might turn its back on the West. But Chancellor Kohl remains as committed to the Community as his predecessors. There appears to be no fundamental contradiction in the minds of the German leaders, or among the German public, between a new unified German state and European integration. Indeed, in April 1990, jointly with President Mitterrand of France, Kohl raised the goal of 'political unity' in the EC after the completion of the single market in 1992. Although it had a cool reception from the British Government, the objective was endorsed at the Dublin summit of EC leaders at the end of April 1990.

Whatever the eventual form of 'political unity', the role of a united Germany within the EC is likely to be greater than ever, given its economic strength and size (with a population of over 78 million, a united Germany is significantly larger than Britain or France). Moreover, the 'Two plus Four' talks in 1990 between the two German states and the wartime allied powers of the USA, USSR, UK and France removed the remaining occupation powers, and the special status of Berlin. This has enabled the new Germany to emerge with almost full equality in international political status.

Idealism and national interest in the Treaties of Paris and Rome

The Treaty of Paris, which set up the ECSC, and the Treaty of Rome, setting up the EEC and EURATOM, are the basis of the development of the EC. The ECSC was the prototype for the functionalist conception of European integration. Its aims were the harmonization of coal and steel policies of the Six and the political attempt

> to substitute for age-old rivalries the merging of their essential interests; to create, by establishing an economic community, the basis for a broader and deeper community among peoples long divided by bloody conflicts; and to lay the foundations for institutions which will give direction to a destiny henceforward shared.[12]

The EEC and EURATOM continued the process of integration. EURATOM provided for cooperation in the field of peaceful nuclear development. The development was to be a means of European modernization under safety regulations which would ensure its safe exploitation for the 'prosperity of their peoples'.[13] Finally, the most ambitious of the communities, the EEC, aimed at creating a Common European Market by a common tariff barrier. This was to be achieved by the harmonization of tariff policy, the raising of internal tariffs and the encouragement of links between European peoples. The treaty included agriculture, transport, economic and social policies in its provisions. It aimed at the free movement of goods, persons, services and capital. All the communities aimed at the improvement of the conditions of life for the citizens of its members and the desire for economic and social harmonization.

In terms of political philosophy, the communities represent the functionalist approach over the more ambitious method of the federators. The federators had aimed at a United States of Europe in fairly rapid stages by inter-governmental agreement. The functionalists took a more gradualist view of integration through gaining sectoral harmonization. The choice of coal and steel as the first community in the Schuman Plan was essentially political despite its technical nature.[14] It was the first step to a more comprehensive Community, yet it offered the 'Six' a means of gaining security by integrating the vital field of iron and steel, and at the same time offering a solution to the larger issue of reintegrating Germany into the European system.

This first step at functional integration was to be furthered by the 'Community Method', a process whereby the High Authority (or the later Commissions), as the 'European' element of the executive, could identify sectors for inclusion in integration. Thus while the ECSC was limited in scope to coal and steel, it had overlaps with other sectors such as transport. The High Authority or Commission could use such overlaps to widen the scope of integration to other related sectors, widening its powers as the process gathered momentum ending in full European union. Hence Jean Monnet's Action Committee for the United States of Europe, in its founding resolution of 18 January 1956, said, 'The Committee shall guarantee the concerted action of those organisations numbered among its members, in order to arrive at the United States of Europe by concrete and gradual steps.'[15] The Committee provided the justification, and idealism necessary to promote the Treaty, and the EAEC and EEC can be seen as a vindication of the Community Method in expanding the Community.

Apart from the idealism that fired men like Jean Monnet, however, it cannot be forgotten that more narrow national self-interest played a major role in both sets of treaty negotiations.

The Treaty of Paris dealt with the vital subject of coal and steel. The integration of these commodities was economically logical; there was the danger of a glut of steel in Europe in the late 1940s and the early 1950s due to the success of reconstruction. The integration of coal and steel under the rigid rules of the ECSC was especially of benefit to the Benelux states, France and the FRG. To the FRG, which did not exercise control of its foreign relations until 1951, the ECSC provided a chance to 'regain' its coal and steel industries. At the same time, it gave reassurance to Germany's neighbours, as the surrender of power in this field made it safer to allow the FRG sovereignty. The Paris Treaty, negotiated on the grounds of equality, also signalled acceptance of the new state, and the FRG gained on the path to full sovereignty. The ECSC did not involve the FRG in any surrender of sovereignty at all. In effect, it was giving up a potential power in order to gain the greater prize of full sovereignty and acceptance in the West. For the French, it helped give a sense of security against their stronger neighbour which was moving towards independence with the support of the UK and USA. This was true for the Benelux countries as well, who also feared a possible resurgent Germany. There was also the economic threat from Germany that the French feared, because in a European steel glut it would be threatened by more efficient FRG production. The Schuman Plan and the ECSC, providing for a common market in coal and steel, would aid its ability to modernize. Similarly, the many powers given to the High Authority were those that the French Government itself had failed to achieve over its own industry. Thus, even for France, the ECSC involved no loss of sovereignty but a gain in powers, exercised indirectly via the Community. The supporters of functional integration were, in fact, very shrewd in their choice of coal and steel, and in their preference for functionalism over the more ambitious federalism. It offered the first step to integration at a small cost of sovereignty while offering a range of national policy benefits to the two largest members of the 'Six'.

The Messina Conference of the ECSC powers in 1955, which discussed the expansion of integration into new sectors, fixed on nuclear power and the formation of a European Common Market as the next step, a step encouraged and campaigned for by Jean Monnet and the Action Committee. The Action Committee saw both communities as vital steps to integration. But this was not a view shared by the leading state protagonists. The idea of EURATOM was essentially a French initiative and the rationale was far from altruistic. Because the French believed that they could not compete with the British nuclear programme, which had US aid, they wished to harness the rest of the 'Six' to their own programme. EURATOM, in the French view, was to spread the research costs to its partners, who would provide expertise and a market for a new French nuclear industry. Conversely, the other ECSC states far preferred the common market as the next step in European integration.

The Benelux countries and the FRG were keen on an EEC because Germany in particular was generally more competitive than France. The common market, a large internal market with an external common tariff, would allow economic recovery to continue at a faster rate. The FRG and the Benelux countries also saw a common market as a more equitable development than the original French conception of EURATOM. France's partners realized that the purpose of the proposed nuclear common market was to perpetuate France's lead in the field, at their expense. Thus they ensured the eventual treaty had American input via the 'Atoms for Peace' programme which countered the threat of French dominance. The French, for their part, saw the EEC as dangerous, given a less efficient industry than its partners, especially the FRG. France's modernization was protected by high tariff barriers and it was far more dirigiste in tradition than most of its partners. The FRG in the post-war period followed a far more *laissez-faire* policy in industry. The achievement of both the proposed communities can be seen as a *quid pro quo* between France and the 'Five'. France gained a nuclear power community and a common agriculture policy, while the others gained the EEC and the common market. These reservations about the treaties were vital in determining the final shape of both communities.

Attitudes towards integration

The Benelux states were clearly among the leaders of the movement towards integration. The Benelux Customs Union of 1948 was seen as a first step, with closer economic union anticipated. When other European states started to move in the same direction, they willingly participated.[16] Because of their small size and weakness, they also favoured integration on the assumptions of the idealists, partly because they would gain prestige and power from union with their more powerful neighbours. These countries, situated between the FRG and France, also had a strong interest in resolving Franco-German rivalry. Belgium had been a victim of this rivalry in both world wars and could avoid a recurrence only by ensuring peace on the Continent.

The Italians saw integration as a means of underpinning their new democracy. There was also Italy's lack of industrial strength, despite its status as a pre-war Great Power. Even more than France, Italy's post-war aim was modernization. Its lack of coal and steel industries could be remedied by closer cooperation with the Northern European countries. Thus, rehabilitation and modernization gave Italy good reasons for support of integration. As with the Benelux states, the putative loss of sovereignty could be balanced by strengthening the social fabric of the nation.

Before 1939, France and Germany had been Great Powers in a real sense, and even after the war their size and strength set them apart from the other four, and increasingly so as reconstruction made them economically important in the OECD. For the FRG, post-war aims were clear, desiring to gain full sovereignty and full integration into the Western world. Participation in the communities offered rehabilitation and support for the new democracy, and was an ideal vehicle for Adenaur's concept of the new German state. The FRG's position as the front line of NATO, however, also made it especially reliant on the USA. It was willing to play a major role in European integration only so long as such a role did not put its defence relationship with the USA at risk. Hence, it was not prepared to put Franco-German relations above its Nato commitment, when de Gaulle was trying to build a Europe 'from the Atlantic to the Urals'. France, for its part, can be seen as the least enthusiastic of the 'Six' about full integration. At the end of the Second World War, France was accorded status as one of the Big Four and gained a permanent seat on the UN Security Council, although on the sufferance of the British and Americans rather than on any objective power position, given its defeat and occupation in 1940. None the less, the French still had far more to lose than the others in terms of sovereignty. The small Benelux states recognized their own weakness, and their Customs Unions aimed at enhancing their combined position. For these countries, and Italy, integration was likely to bring net gains and prestige in a united Europe. For France, with its Empire and status as one of the 'Big Four', this was less evident; in any case a massive programme of reconstruction and modernization was undertaken, which de Gaulle later accelerated. The French aims were to ensure that the Germans could never again wage war on France; here, integration was perceived to offer solutions. And, as de Gaulle saw when he came to power in France in 1958 and despite his earlier misgivings, integration provided an opportunity to use the communities to enhance France's foreign policy stance. In the absence of the UK and with the FRG in no position to take up leadership of the 'Six', France was the natural leader. (It is worthwhile noting, however, that in 1952 and 1957, Britain would have been a stronger leader, able to integrate from within; France did not enjoy such a commanding superiority in strength over its partners as the UK would have in this period.)

From this brief survey, it is clear that the weakness of a state in the

Community either through size, lack of economic development or due to restrictions on the status of defeated powers, encouraged integration; and integration was seen as a way of regaining state power. Only in France, a victorious power of some strength, did the serious fear of loss of sovereignty present itself; and French fears were contained by the functionalist approach, an approach which precisely limited the loss of real sovereignty while offering valuable prizes in the field of national self-interest.

The institutions of the communities

The three communities were merged into the European Community in 1967, by a treaty which revised the Paris and Rome Treaties and merged certain of their institutions. These are the Council of Ministers, the Commissions (the High Authority in the case of ECSC) and the European Parliament (earlier Assembly). The Council of Ministers is part of both the legislative and executive branches of the communities. It is made up of the ministers of member governments, relevant to the topic of discussion. This body is the main representative of the 'state' in the Community structure. For this reason, merger of the communities did not produce any major alteration in its make-up or function. In the case of the ECSC, that function was 'to harmonise the action of the High Authority and that of the Governments'.[17] In the case of the EEC, it was to 'exercise a power of decision'.

In the initial treaties, the Council could act in most cases on the basis of qualified majority voting, based on weighted votes depending on the size of country. The FRG, France and Italy had 10 votes, 5 votes were given to Belgium and the Netherlands, while Luxembourg had 2. With later expansion, the principle was continued; the UK has 10 votes, Greece has 5 and Denmark 3.[18] (The shift to unanimous voting and a national veto will be considered later.) A decision can be couched as either a regulation or a directive. A regulation has the force of law and must be incorporated into national law, while directives express general aims and are to be enforced as the national governments or legislatives see fit. The Council can also 'request the Commission to undertake any studies which the Council considers desirable for the attainment of common objectives'.[19]

The Council works with the Commission, the European element in the Executive; in the early years, it saw itself as the motive force of integration through the Community Method, a self-image which often led to conflict. (The two commissions of the Rome Treaty and the ECSC's High Authority were merged as part of the establishment of the EC in 1967.) The Commission consists of at least one national of the member-states; the five largest states have two each, making 17 in all. The members of the Commission, together with the rest of the Secretariat, must undertake to serve the Community alone and not seek or take instructions from the governments of the members,[20] so as to ensure the independence of the Commission in the fulfilment of its work. In the early years, in line with the Community Method, it attracted committed Europeans like Jean Monnet and Walter Hallstein who saw the Commission not merely as a European secretariat drafting legislation and overseeing the community's operation; it was also to push forward integration into new fields and strengthen its own powers and those of the Assembly. Before 1965, the Commission's powers lay in drawing up proposals for the Council and the ability to lobby in their favour before they reached the Council of Ministers. The Commission was an equal in its relationship with the Council, consulting with it and providing inputs for discussion, although it was the Council that had the final say. The crisis in the Community in 1965–6, however, severely limited its powers.

The Consultative Assembly (later the European Parliament) acts as the popular element in the EC. Until 1978, the Assembly was made up of delegates from the national parliaments, the size of delegations dependent on size of the state. The UK, FRG, France and Italy had 81 seats, while Belgium and Greece had 24 and Luxembourg only 6.[21] The parties in the Parliament do not sit in national groups but along political lines – Socialists, Christian Democrats and Liberals. In 1979, there was the first of the direct elections to the Parliament, the MEP's serving fixed 5-year terms, but there was no standard electoral system. The voting system used for European elections are decided by national parliaments, the UK alone not using a form of proportional representation.

The Parliament is the weaker of the European institutions, less influential than the Commission with its direct relationship to the Council of Ministers. It has little power over the Council, and the powers it does hold are too clumsy to be used. For example, the Parliament can remove the full Commission by a two-thirds majority vote but it cannot censure a specific commissioner. Also, if it did censure the Commission, it has no role in the selection of new commissioners, a power kept by the states. In the administrative control of the Council and Commission, its powers are weak, especially in the field of the budget. Budget expenditure is split into categories; the first includes 'expenses arising necessarily from the treaty or decisions taken by virtue of the treaty', and the second covers staff salaries, administrative costs and information services. The relative importance of these categories is 97% and 3% respectively, yet it is only in category II that the Parliament can exercise any control. The Council of Ministers can overrule Parliament's proposed modifications of category I expenditure.[22] In the field of legislation, the Parliament can only pass resolutions which bring issues to the attention of the Commission and Council of Ministers. On balance, Assembly seems a more accurate description of its function than Parliament. Ironically, its strongest sanction on the executive is the clumsy censure procedure against the Commission. Yet the Commission, like the Parliament, tries to get a wider reading of the treaties in order to widen its role. Finally, the element with most power, the Council of Ministers containing the executives of the states, has managed to avoid serious scrutiny both domestically and within the EC.

The European communities and the continuation of traditional diplomacy

The failure of the British to join, first, the ECSC and then the EEC and EAEC left France as the member best fitted for leadership of the 'Six'. On de Gaulle's return to power, he saw that 'Europe' had possibilities for furthering his ambitions for France, ambitions which explain his opposition to British entry: the UK would provide a serious rival to French leadership and a potential 'Trojan Horse' which would increase American influence in the communities. Britain, with its 'special relationship' with the USA, would encourage the Atlanticism of the FRG at the expense of the concept of a Europe from the Atlantic to the Urals. For de Gaulle, Europe stopped at the Channel. The other parties, however, hoped to bring in the British, since British membership would make the balance of power in the Community more stable. It would give an alternative to French leadership which Germany could not provide. The Benelux states, especially the Netherlands, had close trade and political ties with Britain and had gone ahead without the UK with regret. The Netherlands, in particular, saw British membership as beneficial, as it believed it would gain an ally in the Community with a similar outlook and save it from being perpetually caught between Franco-German interests. Indeed, it made any plan for political union dependent on Britain's entry. The subsequent unilateral French veto in 1963 of British entry did little to dispel the view that France desired to maintain its leading role in the Community. It made the 'Five' increasingly suspicious of France, suspicions enhanced by its stance in the mid-1960s towards NATO and the multilateral nuclear force (MLF), and caused them to postpone any development of the Community beyond the requirements of the Rome Treaty until after British entry.

The Commission was fully aware of the possibilities of, and indeed importance of, tensions between the states of the Community and their continuing national interests. Indeed, the Community Method functioned by the Commission acting in tandem with one of the strong members of the 'Six', usually either the FRG or France. This prevented the Commission from isolation and enhanced its chances of success.[23]

On the whole, until 1965, it was France which worked in tandem with the Commission. Newhouse has compared the relationship between France and the Commission to that between Holy Roman Emperor and the Pope, the Commission giving the blessing of the integration movement with France providing the state power.[24] Hence, in part, the lop-sided nature of the

Community with the vast majority of its expenditure on the Common Agriculture Policy (CAP). Agriculture was France's major interest, and the Commission encouraged that interest to further expand the integration process. The Germans, for their part, favoured integration on industrial and trade matters. Yet for the Germans, the maintenance of the new Franco-German relationship took precedence over issues like British entry or steel trade, preventing France from becoming totally isolated in 1963. Nothing, however, would make the Germans lose the US connection in NATO in favour of de Gaulle's policy. France's policies towards NATO between 1965 and 1966 also helps to explain why France found itself isolated in the 'Luxembourg' crisis.

The issues at stake in the 1965 crisis appeared to be relatively minor. It was sparked by the Commission tying three issues together, an increase in budgetary powers to the Parliament, finance of the Community via the proceeds of the common external tariff and the forwarding of the customs union to coincide with the onset of common agricultural prices in July 1967.[25] Qualified majority voting had been agreed to in the treaties, and the finance of the Community via central funds had been in Article 201 of the Rome Treaty. The increase in the budgetary powers of the European Parliament in the proposals was far from revolutionary. Also, parliamentarians in the national legislatives of member countries, especially in the Netherlands and Italy, saw an increase in the powers of the Parliament as necessary to gain accountability from the Council of Ministers. However, de Gaulle used this proposal to mount a campaign for recapturing the sovereignty of the state. He also brought in issues like qualified majority voting, which was due to be introduced. In effect, the crisis can be seen as an attempt to smother the Commission as an institutional integrator after France had gained most of its objectives, e.g. the CAP. It was now time to regain for the French state the concessions made to achieve the CAP.

In the dispute between France and its partners, the 'Five' maintained a united front, despite the 7-month walkout by the French. The 'Five' were not united for the same reasons, but unity was maintained with the Italians holding together the more aggressive FRG and Netherlands and the more conciliatory Belgium and Luxembourg.[26] The result of this major crisis was the merger of the commissions in 1966, but the commission's ability to lobby for measures before they reached the Council was circumscribed. The question of majority voting of the Council of Ministers was left open – in effect a victory for the French because unanimity of members in issues of vital national interest continued. Also, the original Commission proposals were dropped and the question of further institutional advance was shelved, as was France's aim of using the Community to push its view of Europe. It was not until after de Gaulle left government that Britain was able to gain entrance to the EC, in 1973, and institutional development could proceed.

This snub to the 'Community Method' did not mean progress on sectoral

cooperation stopped. New issues were tackled, notably foreign affairs and
the European Monetary System (EMS). These were essentially forms of
inter-governmental cooperation, however, in the fields of political and
monetary union. In 1972, the Davignon Committee made suggestions far
more limited than the earlier Fouchet Plan on political union. Political
cooperation has advanced by making meetings of state officials more
frequent and contacts between foreign offices more extensive. It has led to a
greater understanding of each others' positions, and consultation between
European foreign ministers has become the norm, but the overall results of
the EPC have not been particularly spectacular. The European Arab
Dialogue, initiated in 1974 after the oil crisis, yielded little. The dialogue
ended, after the Camp David Agreement on a peace treaty between Egypt
and Israel, split the Arab World. During the Falklands crisis of 1982, at the
initial diplomatic stage the UK's European parties held firm in support of
Britain. When armed hostilities broke out, however, this solidarity began to
break down over sanctions. The fact that many Argentinians were of Italian
descent made Italy reluctant to take measures, and the Irish stood by their
neutrality. Despite this, the general support to Britain in the crisis proved
useful in the diplomatic stage of the conflict.

The EMS was a scheme to keep the Community members' exchange rates
stable with respect to one another within a band of 2.25%, proposed after
the collapse of the Bretton Woods system of fixed parities in the early 1970s.
The result for Europe was first 'the Snake' and then the EMS. It was in effect
a regional Bretton Woods, underpinned by the strong Deutschmark rather
than the US dollar. There is no formal basis for the FRG Bundesbank to act
as a lender of last resort in the EMS, however. The function the Bundesbank
plays as the strongest currency is on a bilateral basis, to help an ailing
currency, e.g. the French franc in the early 1980s. From the very beginning
of the plan, the Italians have been given greater latitude for currency
fluctuations as a weak economy.

The advantages of EMS membership derive from the fact that a large
proportion of EC members' trade is within the Community. This pattern of
trade is aided by the maintenance of fairly stable exchange rates, which
makes industrial planning easier. The EMS can be seen as an island of
currency stability compared with the fluctuations in exchange rates of
floating currencies. Secondly, it helps governments to follow the 'sound'
economic policies favoured by the FRG, which often means unpopular
policies. Membership diffuses criticism of practices required to maintain
sound finance, which would not be the case if a government acted
unilaterally.

The degree of integration and amity between the EC states was put to the
test during the 1972–4 oil crisis. The Organization of Arab Petroleum
Exporting Countries (OAPEC) placed embargoes on those EC members
perceived to be pro-Israeli. At one end of the spectrum, the Dutch were

placed under a full embargo, while the UK and France, who were seen as sympathetic to the Arabs, escaped embargo entirely. Instead of European unity in support of the Dutch, however, there was a general scramble to gain as much oil as possible on the world market, forcing up prices. The Netherlands' appeals for help were in vain; indeed, the UK and France put pressure on their national oil companies to maximize their imports at the expense of others. This single-minded pursuit of national interest in the crisis made 1973 as the Year of Europe appear very hollow. The crisis also showed up other weaknesses. First, the EC, despite the merger of the three communities in 1966, had failed to integrate energy policy. Even after the 1973–4 crisis, it proved difficult to achieve an energy policy. The British and Dutch feared it might mean the sharing of their North Sea gas and oil reserves. The expansion of the Community in 1973, from six to nine, in the absence of majority voting, also made unanimity more difficult to achieve.

The effects of the second enlargement

Since 1980, Greece, Portugal and Spain have been admitted to the EC. This increases the difficulty of reaching unanimous decisions. Moreover, the new members are Mediterranean, southern European states that have shifted the balance of the Community. The treaties of Rome and Paris were negotiated by predominantly North European states; the subsequent amendments following 1973 further increased the northern bias. Because the new members are substantially poorer and more agricultural in nature, it clearly heralds a new era in the history of the EC.

With the entry of Spain, in particular, the EC has been seen increasingly as the European, economic element of NATO. Of the 14 European countries in NATO, 11 are members of the EC. The non-EC NATO countries are Iceland, Norway and Turkey. Norway rejected membership of EC by referendum in 1973, while Turkey applied for membership in 1987. In the case of Spain, without entry into the EC, the referendum about continued membership of NATO would have been in doubt. The increasing view that the EC is the economic arm of European NATO members makes the Republic of Ireland's neutrality appear problematic. It required a referendum on the Single European Act, because of its vague mention of defence as a possible field of integration. Secondly, the new members see it as a means of underpinning their democracies and as signalling full acceptance into the West, as with the FRG and Italy in 1952. This is a hurdle that Turkey must overcome if it is to enter the Community.

The problems of enlargement have been addressed by the Single European Act and the Final Act of 1986. Institutionally, parlimentary development has been encouraged; Article 6 Section 2 alters the EEC Treaty, replacing 'after consulting the Assembly' by 'in cooperation with the European Parliament' in Article 7. There are also moves towards qualified majority voting in the Council of Ministers, thought necessary to avoid chaos in decision making; if every decision required unanimity, it was believed, no progress could be made. To overcome the reduction of homogeneity caused by expansion into the Mediterranean, the Single European Act also addresses economic and social cohesion.[27] Hence the Community committed itself to 'develop and pursue its actions leading to the strengthening of its economic and social cohesion. In particular the Community shall aim at reducing disparities between the various regions and the backwardness of the least favoured regions'.[28] This would appear to envisage a shift away from agricultural expenditure to a fuller regional and social policy. However, the problem of the CAP must be solved first to avoid the continuation of persistent financial crises in the Community. This will be far from easy, considering the strength of the vested interests involved.

The 'revolutions' in Eastern Europe during 1989 and the transition of these countries into liberal democracies with market economies, raise the possibility that in the future there may be applications for membership from this area. Some commentators have likened the EC to a magnet attracting the newly free countries of the East, although most of these states will need to undergo considerable liberalization and modernization of their economies to be eligible for membership. It is significant that the EC is taking a leading role in the distribution of economic aid to Eastern Europe. In the shorter term, it has been suggested that countries like Hungary, Czechoslovakia and Poland might join EFTA as a transitional step towards eventual Community membership.

As a result of the changes in the East, including the agreements for the removal of Soviet troops from Czechoslovakia and Hungary, the perceived threat from the Soviet Union has receded. Therefore, it is possible that neutrality will be considered less of a barrier to membership by some potential applicants. Certainly under the spur of the single market, neutral states like Sweden and Austria might be more inclined to apply to join the EC. Because these countries have modern economies – indeed more advanced than some of the existing members – there would be few difficulties for them if they were admitted. They would help pull the balance back to the north and perhaps provide a link with countries like Poland, Czechoslovakia and Hungary.

Has the state lost sovereignty?

So far, much of the discussion has centred upon the location of power within the EC, between the Community and state institutions. It is now necessary to assess how much sovereignty has been lost by the States to the EC. The treaties of Paris and Rome have given the communities a competence to legislate on a wide range of issues, directives having the force of law. These Community powers vary; the CAP governs agricultural policy and the support prices for foodstuffs covered by it; regulations harmonizing the tariffs of the members towards the outside world while removing internal tariffs to create a common market are also significant. The nuclear installations of the member states are inspected by community inspectors; and the European Court of Justice exists to judge the actions of sovereign states who are parties to the treaty framework. The legislation from the EC would seem a threat to the sovereignty of parliaments, yet from our discussion of the significance of the Council of Ministers in the Community, it is clear that the problem is essentially one of the accountability of ministers.

The Council of Ministers is subject to very little scrutiny from the European Parliament and it is difficult for a national parliament to control the executive when it is in negotiation. Most national parliaments have committees to look at proposals from the Commission before they are discussed in the Council, but the committees cannot really control the various executives. If a national parliament laid down too strong positions which an executive was required to obey, then agreement in the Council might prove impossible. Similarly, even if a government agrees to a measure that is deeply unpopular in its home country, by the time of a vote of confidence the policy may already be law. Sovereignty has not been lost to the supranational Commission or Parliament but to the Council of Ministers, to the executive branch of each state.

Moreover, the diffuse nature of decision making in the Council gives governments a large degree of freedom. A prime minister can also pose as a guardian of the national interest against the demands of Europe, as de Gaulle did or more recently as did Mrs Thatcher in the struggle to get increased rebates for Britain from the CAP. A government is at one and the same time a part of 'European' decision making and also the protector of the state against Europe. Indeed, the EC can be seen as a centralizing force, increasing the power of the various executives. The ECSC, for example, brought indirect control of the coal and steel industries, which many governments did not previously regulate. The European elements of the Commission and Parliament only provide a screen that helps to obscure this process. The increased use of majority voting does provide a potential threat, but the other states are likely to be wary of using it against vital interests of any single state, lest it rebound on themselves. It is likely that the process of decision by consensus will remain the norm in the Council of Ministers.

If this is the institutional picture, of sovereignty moving towards the EC but being firmly held by the governments, there are other aspects which suggest traditional sovereignty is at risk. An important matter is the increasing interdependence in trade between the members of the Community due to the common market. After a long period of integration in trade, it would prove extremely difficult and risky to leave the Community. It may be hard to imagine a country which earnestly desired to leave the Community having punitive sanctions placed on it to remain; but even assuming an amicable withdrawal from the Community, it would seriously disturb the existing patterns of trade with adverse effects on both the seceding nation and its partners. The threat to national independence in the full sense is not obvious, and there is of course a danger inherent in traditional trade relationships based on reciprocal benefits. However, to the extent that common markets are created, the limitations and restraints on member countries are real, especially as European states are far more dependent on foreign trade than the USA.

The devotees of European integration continue to see the EC as a potential new superpower in the process of formation. Yet, as we have seen, the supranational elements remain weak, and the Council of Ministers plays a part in both the legislative and executive of the Community. The Community is, in effect, an association of nation-states who, although performing some functions in common, remain viable states with divergences of interest and policy. The EC has not become a new focus of loyalty likely to replace the state. Indeed, in the EC structures, citizens look to their governments to defend national interests, rather than pushing the process of integration forward.

On balance, the nation-state, although losing some sovereignty to the European communities, has not proved as weak as assumed by the founding fathers of the European Movement. As states, even the smaller members like Holland and Denmark are successful entities fulfilling a large range of functions. They are able to provide their citizens with law and order, social benefits and a stable business environment. The range of functions fulfilled by these states are formidable compared with a large proportion of the world's states. The idea of the state itself, originating in Europe, is firmly established there and accepted, unlike in many post-colonial countries of Africa, for example. The apparent paradox of these 'strong' states in such close supranational cooperation is partly explained by the security of the state idea in Europe. An area less secure about statehood has less confidence to step into EC-type cooperation. Indeed, community is the result of national self-interests being reconciled, with a net advantage to all states. The EC, although important to the policies of its members, has not precluded membership of wider international regimes, from the United Nations to the OECD, NATO and GATT. The attention of the partners is not fully focused on Europe; the relationship with the USA has been of parallel importance. When the French actions in favour of de Gaulle's Europe endangered relations with the USA, especially in the field of defence, its partners chose the Atlantic system. The EC is merely one of the inter-governmental groups in which the partners participate.

The defence of national interests by the member states has also undermined the belief that integration would automatically increase efficiency in economic fields. The predominance of CAP expenditure has warped the financial allocation of the EC, leaving insufficient funds for regional and industrial policy. The desires to expand these areas, expressed in the Single European Act and given impetus by the entry of Greece, Spain and Portugal, will come to nothing if the CAP is not reformed. The new members are likely to press for reform, since the goods covered by the CAP were those appropriate to the 'Six'. The concentration on Northern European agricultural production will appear increasingly irrelevant as the balance shifts south. Another inefficiency costing large sums annually is the failure to decide on one 'European' centre. The rivalry between Luxembourg, Strasbourg and Brussels further illustrates the European sin of national pride. All three cities, and their national governments, see the placing of EC institutions in their midst as signs of prestige which they refuse to forfeit.

While some powers of government are being transferred from the state to the EC, the state is far from 'withering'. Instead, paradoxically, European integration has helped to centralize power in the hands of the national executives. The diffuse nature of decision making has had effects on the state itself, to be sure. It requires governments in a fairly wide range of policy areas to think of their partners' views, in order to win consensus. This has helped, however, to maintain the importance of foreign ministries in some countries, and in others has led to European Community Ministries being established. Consensus can be seen as an indirect form of harmonization, required to make the system work when unanimity is required. The frequent crises of the Community in the field of finance, however, show that even this process is still very imperfect.

The Single European Act, finally ratified by all members in 1987, with its move to limit the exercise of the veto, gives more potential for integration. It is vital to prevent the whole system breaking down and leading to total paralysis. But the likelihood of integration advancing in any form which seriously threatens the state appears unlikely. It would require a new swell of popular support in all the member states and support for European integration via the supranational method. If this were the case, the structures of the EC could be adapted by transferring power from the Council to the Commission and Parliament, but such a move would require all 12 member States to agree to a more serious loss of sovereignty than has proved acceptable in the last 35 years. By 1990, the state appeared far from obsolete, despite the expansion of cooperation into new fields such as foreign policy. The nation-state has proved more durable and obstinate in the maintenance of the substance of its sovereignty. The assumptions that the West European states are becoming obsolete have proved premature. The concept of the nation-state in the popular mind of Europe has proved much stronger than that of a United States of Europe.

This was vividly illustrated during 1989–90 by the very strong resurgence of German nationalism around the theme of German unification. It was balanced by the desire of the West German Government, in conjunction with the French Government, to raise the prospect of the 'political unity' of the EC. Significantly, the Dublin summit of EC leaders on 28 April 1990, which was originally convened to discuss the issue of German unification, was dominated by a decision to proceed with discussions on the form political unity should take after 1992. Thus, the post-war history of West Germany in relation to European integration continues to move in the same direction. Integration into Europe was an important factor of legitimation for the post-Nazi German state. In 1990, legitimacy for German unity (essentially on West German terms), and solutions to the economic problems associated with it, were seen again to lie in the further progress of European Community integration.

But these two phenomena – German nationalism and European integration – may not remain as close in tandem in the future as in the past because of the ultimate limitations on the latter. The French political observer and sociologist, Raymond Aron, wrote in 1964:

> The old nations still live in the hearts of men, and love of the European nation is not yet born . . . one might ask: What would be the object of a European state? . . . A will to push Soviet Communism out of eastern Europe? But if this Soviet retreat is to be peaceful, is a European bloc something to be hoped for or something to be feared? A will to become a great power? But, in the nuclear world, do we want one or more Super power?[29]

It is a quarter of a century since Aron wrote these words, and the notion that a Western European political bloc could become another superpower remains unlikely. Most issues – defence, energy, finance and much of foreign affairs – stretch across the Atlantic, and often across the Pacific, too. In many spheres, bilateral relations have not, in the slightest degree, diminished in importance. That is why the EC is so very far from becoming a European government, which implies *one* executive authority, *one* army and, above all, *one* sense of political community. In fact, the diversity of international and regional organizations corresponds with the diversity of interests of the nation-states. What has changed since the Second World War is that in Western Europe the conflict of national interests, backed by armed force, no longer prevails. There is instead the acknowledgement that advantage can be only relative, and that it is better to seek advantage by some pooling of resources within co-ordinating organizations. The EC is unique juridically, but is essentially just one of many such organizations. This has changed the conditions in which national sovereignty is exercised, but political sovereignty remains rooted in the state in Western Europe.

Notes

1 The original six in the ECSC of 1952 were France, West Germany, Italy, Belgium, Luxembourg and the Netherlands. The UK, Republic of Ireland and Denmark joined in 1970.
2 Quoted by Roberto Ducci 'The Spirit of 1950' *New Europe* 5, 4 (1977) p. 17.
3 Arnold John Zurcher *The Struggle to Unite Europe 1940–58* (Greenwood Press, 1975) p. 19.
4 The Preamble of the Constitution of the French Fourth Republic, 27 October 1946, Article II; Constitution of the Italian Republic, 27 December 1947, Article 24; Basic Law of the Federal Republic of Germany, 8 May 1949.
5 Geoffrey Parker *A Political Geography of Community Europe* (Butterworths, 1983) p. 29.
6 It should be remembered that, apart from Churchill's offer of political union with France in 1940 (at the initiative of Jean Monnet), Britain had opposed integration before the Second World War. In 1932, it had opposed attempts to bring the Dutch into a customs union with Belgium and Luxembourg, as well as the Briand Plan.
7 Count Coudenhove Kalergi, who had been in exile during the Second World War, working at New York University, contributed to the USA's way of thinking.
8 Jean Monnet, quoted by William Walker *Nuclear Power Struggles* (Allen & Unwin, 1983) p. 13.
9 Alfred Grosser *The Western Alliance* (Macmillan, 1980) p. 164.
10 The Single European Act, Title III, Article 30, Section 6(a): 'The High Contracting Parties consider that closer co-operation on questions of European security would contribute in an essential way to the development of a European identity in external policy matters. They are ready to co-ordinate their positions more closely on the political and economic aspects of security.'
11 The Single European Act, Title III, Article 30, Section 6(c).
12 Preamble to the treaty establishing the European Coal and Steel Community (ECSC).
13 Preamble to the treaty establishing the European Atomic Energy Community (EURATOM).
14 Michael Curtis *Western European Integration* (New York, Harper and Row, 1965) p. 117.
15 The founding resolution of the Action Committee for the United States of Europe, quoted in Hans-Peter Schwarz 'Federating Europe – But How?' in P.D. Dagtoglou ed. *Basic Problems of the European Community* (Oxford, Blackwell, 1975).
16 Roy Pryce *The Politics of the European Community* (Butterworths, 1973).
17 ECSC Treaty, Chapter III, Article 26.
18 ECSC Treaty, Article 27; EEC Treaty, Article 148; EAEC Treaty, Article 118.
19 ECSC Treaty, Article 26; EEC Treaty, Article 152; EAEC Treaty, Article 112.
20 ECSC Treaty, Article 9; EEC Treaty, Article 157; EAEC Treaty, Article 126.
21 ECSC Treaty, Article 21; EEC Treaty, Article 138; EAEC Treaty, Article 108.
22 Roy Pryce *The Politics of the European Community* (Butterworths, 1973) p. 95.
23 John Newhouse *Collision in Brussels* (Toronto, George J. McLeod, 1967) p. 63.

24 Ibid.
25 Pryce, op. cit., p. 19.
26 Newhouse, op. cit., p. 132.
27 Single European Act, Title V, Article 130A.
28 Ibid.
29 Raymond Aron 'Old Nations, New Europe' in Stephen R. Grauband ed. *A New Europe?* (London, Oldbourne, 1964) p. 61.

7

The State and War

Philip Windsor

States make wars, but man makes war. The relationship is both obvious and obscure. Without the warlike proclivities of man, states could not function in the way they do – they could not make wars. Yet man forms the state in order to overcome the war of all against all, which Hobbes argued was his natural condition. And the paradox is wider in scope than it might seem at first sight.

Those who seek to explain the causes of war in terms of man's condition – whether they do so from an ethological base (relying on notions like 'territoriality' or 'aggression' as some kind of cause subsumed in the effect), or on the basis of a system which drives its participating elements into periodic bouts of violence – would be hard put to explain why the brutish animal, the progenitor of the system, should have created the state in the first place. If his irenic aspirations had not impelled him, why should he have bothered? Conversely, why devise a system which depends on violence as the ultimate sustaining form of legitimacy? There is an inherent tension between political man, mediator between conflicts of interest and value, and man the architect of a sort of order between states which relies precisely on the *ultima ratio*, the recourse to war. Moreover, the whole system of international society is posited upon this tension and works because of it.

In some ways, of course, all this is familiar. Thomas Hobbes was perhaps the first to articulate man's paradoxical nature in society. But despite his startlingly modern method (beginning with a discussion of human psychology and of relating the considerations which derive from that to those of politics), he came down to an argument from necessity: it was in people's best interests to settle for Leviathan. Now, in terms of an heuristic experiment, his work provided an immense stimulus to thinking about the criteria of both social and international behaviour; but in the end, it served to make the dilemmas explicit – in terms of the conflict between social authority at the national level and the anarchical character of international society. But that only emphasizes that war has been the best (perhaps the only?) method that human beings have found to resolve these tensions. It still leaves the question 'why war?'

Ha-ha among the trumpets

All states are founded upon the assumption that they have the *right* to make war, even if only in such terms of self-defence as are spelled out in Article 51 of the United Nations Charter; and virtually all states prepare for war. Even Switzerland, whose most celebrated military achievement is the destruction of an apple, maintains a fomidable military machine, actively intercepted the Luftwaffe when it transgressed Swiss air space during the Second World War, and actually has a *monument aux morts* to those who caught pneumonia while patrolling the frontiers at that time. In the case of Britain, the only year between 1945 and 1989 in which there were no combat casualties in the armed forces was 1968. The grip of war upon the nature of the state is so extraordinary and pervasive that one might almost argue that war is a defining characteristic of the state itself. Yet the same United Nations Charter which permits this recourse to violence also declares that 'Since war begins in the minds of men, it is in the minds of men that it must be ended.' Here is an international document which not only recognizes but explicitly emphasizes the tensions between man, the state and war.

In using these three categories for the title of his classic work, Kenneth Waltz appeared to acknowledge the tensions. In fact, he left matters at dividing them into separate levels of explanation. What this method of procedure does not take into account is the way in which one state might go to war against the aggression of 'man' in another state. But this is how many modern wars have been seen by their participants, at least since the First World War, which brought the relationship into the open. (The inscription on the monument at Hyde Park Corner to the members of the Machine Gun Corps who fell in that war reads: 'For Saul hath slain them in their thousands but David in their tens of thousands.') War in this sense provides the ultimate link between man and the state, even though this is seldom acknowledged and though it is perhaps only the Third Reich which articulated it and glorified it. One might therefore propose a preliminary answer to the question 'why war?': that it reconciles man and the state by conferring upon each a supreme legitimacy in its relation to the other.

Of course, the way this question is posed is essential. Up to now it has been posed purely in terms that suggest that the state and civil society are identical

– and this was indeed the conclusion of Hobbes's argument. Hegel, however, distinguished sharply between state and society and in doing so helped to illuminate the nature of war. But for the present, I would wish to persist with the question of why the irenic creature who founds the state in order to end the war of all against all should continue to agree that war is a legitimate, necessary and defining function of the state in its relations with other, equally legitimate states.

The notion of agreement is vital here. Wars have their ceremonies, their rules of engagement, their own corpus of international law. Indeed, a glance at the history of the Nuremberg and Tokyo trials will make it abundantly clear that 'civilization' was far more horrified by violations of the rules of war than by the systematic extermination of people in conditions to which war lent no appearance of justification or rationality. It was as if modern man were determined above all to preserve the propriety of going to war.

Perhaps this is because war is doubly an act of liberation. In the first and obvious sense, it liberates man from the constraints of civil society, in which violence and killing are forbidden. Once the rules of engagement apply, man can kill his fellow in a new *order* superseding the old. *'L'ordre regne a Varsovie'*: it can not be a purely linguistic accident that the word for military command and that for social decorum are identical in so many European languages. One might even hazard (though their language is ambiguous here) that the defendants at the war-crimes trials were not only copping-out but were unwittingly pointing to a deeper confusion when they argued that they were merely obeying 'orders'. So far, and in such terms, war is perfectly compatible with the purposes of the state and conducive to its maintenance; but every military commander from Claudius to Clausewitz has recognized the implicit threat – when man is given 'license' (another double meaning?) to kill, he becomes godlike in his dealings, unrestrained by considerations of humanity.

Military discipline and political control are vital if the released violence of godlike man is to serve the ends of that civil society which his new capacities have superseded. And without political control, even military discipline only reinforces the self-worship of those who claim to supersede the civil order: the posturings and paraphernalia (let alone the atrocities) of those who stage a military *coup d'état*, whether in Athens or Buenos Aires, bear ample witness. The 'order' of 'discipline' can itself be inimical to the order it is meant to serve. Yet states, geared to war as they are, nearly always find standing armies indispensable (Costa Rica is the exception that springs to mind). After the Glorious Revolution, the English Parliament forbade such forces. The effort to reconstitute society was incompatible with their existence. The same happened after the Russian Revolution. But the constraints of state-to-state relations soon brought them back – in the case of England by a constitutional device, in that of Russia by a Central Committee decision and the establishment of the Frunze Military Academy. In both cases, and in those of other states in between that were concerned with rewriting the social contract, the tensions between the preparation for external war and the survival of the state in terms of its own internal criteria were recognized; but the principle of war emerged the victor. Godlike man survived, and so did war.

But while the tensions of this first characteristic of war as an active form of liberation are readily apparent, they are insignificant compared with those of the second. 'Courage', wrote G.K. Chesterton, 'is almost a contradiction in terms: it means a strong desire to live taking the form of a readiness to die.' It is here that the godlike propensity of war comes most clearly into its own. The ability to kill is not the ultimate criterion of liberation: it is the readiness to die. Chesterton loved paradoxes, but he did not take this one to its final conclusion. That conclusion can perhaps best be expressed in the words of two very different Frenchmen. In the last lecture that he gave at the London School of Economics, Raymond Aron concluded with the words: 'Unfortunately, man is a courageous animal and will dare anything to prove his courage'; Jacques Monod, in a different vein, wrote of the 'heroic indefatigable effort of mankind to deny in despair its own contingency'.[1] Taken together, these two sentences provide an approach to the under-standing, and also to the resolution, of Chesterton's paradox. War is the ultimate illustration of human contingency. In battle, nobody knows whether he is going to stop a bullet, as the saying has it, or whether he has another minute to live. Terror and tedium are the themes of every campaign; yet when battle is joined, astonishingly few soldiers refuse it. If they did, there would be no wars and all human history would be different. But in fact the courageous animal, daring anything to prove his courage, transcends these ultimately contingent circumstances and, staring death in the face while running away from it, asserts his liberation.

At the psychological level, one might simply argue that this represents a release from the humdrum rules of prudence and circumspection in everyday life, and a fairly straightforward relationship between the confrontation of fear and the exhilaration of danger. In such terms, it is easy to accuse writers and raconteurs, from the most ancient of Greeks to the most modern propagandists, of glorifying war and overlooking its sordidness and brutality. Yet one might point out that all true writers from Homer onwards have recognized its squalid nature as well as its heroic, and also ask why the propaganda has any appeal at all. Human beings knowingly risk their lives when they go to war. If it were not for the nature of that risk, that bet, one might suspect that war would have no attraction. The psychological/ propaganda explanation is scarcely sufficient. When the writer of *Job* exclaims of the war-horse that 'among the trumpets he saith ha-ha', he is recognizing a much more fundamental human demand: the assertion of courage against contingency. In this sense, war is simply the ultimate expression of all the achievements of peace.

In terms of this argument, then, war is both a human institution of which the constituent elements are a threat to the state and to civil society even while being indispensable to their perpetuation – and at the same time the final form of drawing human activity together. In terms of the first set of criteria, and as indicated earlier, the state system functions by virtue of the very tensions inherent in war and in the distinction between the aspirations of civil society and the 'order' of war. In terms of the second, there is no real distinction to be made between the nature of war and the nature of peace. In terms of the first, the distinction between the one and the other lies in the licence to kill. In terms of the second, the engagement of courage with contingency means that the achievements of peace and the acts of war can seldom be distinguished. Apart from the fact that this dual nature of war creates difficulties for conflict researchers (unless they are really after social entropy) and polemologists in general, it sets up problems for the state operating in an international structure of states. It is here that Hegel's distinction between the state and civil society is of particular importance.

Arms for oblivion

The importance of that distinction should become apparent soon. In the interim, it is worth noting that within the Hobbesian scheme war is exceptional *because* it is legitimate. If human violence were simply part and parcel of the state of nature, more or less general and undifferentiated, war would be the norm, and as such would not raise any questions. It is the ordered, legitimate, hierarchical character of war which distinguishes it both as the most extraordinary of human activities and as the most peculiar of the considerations that humans address themselves to when they consider the nature of their own doings. Quite apart from the considerations already mentioned, manifold attempts have been made to treat war as an outcome of a particular form of social organization, e.g. Auguste Comte's treatment of the relationship between war and feudal society, and the conclusions of people as diverse as Aron, Max Weber and a score or so of American sociologists who argued that a different relationship had come about, between the character of war and that of industrial society. Despite their best efforts, the practice of war remains as elusive and as deep-rooted as ever when anyone attempts to come to terms with it. Indeed, even the astringent philosopher of war, Carl von Clausewitz himself, who confessed in letters to his much loved wife how greatly war raised his spirits but who at the same time spent his life in a dispassionate dissection of its undertakings, couches his whole argument in terms of the central mystery of the phenomenon and of the separateness of its various manifestations. As Aron has shown in his two works on Clausewitz, the monist view of war itself can only be understood through an appreciation of the different levels of what is involved in war and also through a sense of its diversity, both in time and place. Why?

The short answer might be that all wars, however grandiloquent the *monuments aux morts*, are soon forgotten. It is the exceptional character of war, the supreme social order crossing paths with the ultimate wager against the contingent, which ensures that this is so. The effects of war remain. The First World War destroyed/transformed the nature of European society. The war of 1973 did the same for Israel's relations with its Arab neigbours. The very nature of thinking about war itself, of the literature of war and even of everyday language was utterly changed by the European experience between 1914 and 1918,[2] as was the character of Lebanese society by the Israeli invasion of 1982. But in neither case was any terrible beauty born. Yeat's 'noble lie' about 1916 in Dublin might have had some meaning in the limited context of the Irish rebellion; but it was in turn given the lie by the refrain of one of the most famous songs sung by British soldiers in the First World War: 'And we'll never tell them. . .'. The experience of war, and its meaning for godlike man, *cannot* be transmitted to civil society.

When war is over, it is all over. Goodbye to All That. The First World War produces the Lost Generation and its counterpart, the Jazz Age. It also produces the poisoned romanticism of those who in Germany embark upon the Second World War to rectify the outcome of the First. And the Second World War, in the West, produces the Welfare State, even though the architects of that new cathedral had connived at some of the most barbarous slaughters in human history. This failure of historical memory is probably also inherent in war itself. The extraordinary legitimation which civil society accords to the act of war and which makes it such a highly *specific* phenomenon, distinct from war in the state of nature, also means that war, as the act of such a society, has to be kept at arm's length. It constitutes an exceptional phenomenology, related to the nature of society but also self-defining. Hegel puts his finger on it: 'In war, war itself is characterised as something which ought to pass away.'[3]

In these terms, *oblivion* is the necessary answer of civil society to the exceptional phenomenon of war. But that raises the next question: namely, the relationship between the nature of war and of civil society. If, in the Hobbesian scheme, war is exceptional by virtue of its legitimacy and therefore doomed to oblivion when the civil order reasserts itself, how can one address the relationship within the terms of Hegelian thought?

It will be obvious from what I have argued hitherto that war can be regarded not only as what Kant would call an 'unsocial sociability', but also as an act of transcendence – certainly within the form that Hegel argued the master–slave relationship. But while this was a parable for history, one might say that Hegel cheats a bit by arguing from the individual transcendence in the combat between the future master and slave to the potential for historical transcendence in humanity itself. Yet, within the latter context, war is socialized transcendence: a most peculiar negation of the negation. Now, this means either that, in terms of the development of human society and the manifestation of the spirit, that war is also exceptional, forgettable and ultimately meaningless (relegated at the end of the day to a Hobbesian dustbin) or else that its significance must be appreciated in a wider perspective.

But Hegel emphasized the importance of war in the development of the human spirit. (I am taking it for granted here that Hegel does not separate the Spirit from Man even though certain passages in the *Introduction to the Philosophy of History* might lend credence to that view.) How, then, can one characterize the importance of war when Hegel himself both insists upon it and emphasizes its exceptional phenomenology?[4]

One might suggest that it goes something like this: man becomes community (though not state) through language. The function of language is the creation of community, but the state still depends upon some understanding of a social contract. It is the becoming of the community into the state which starts war. This might sound highly abstract, but some consideration of the history of Israeli–Arab relations during the Mandate period in Palestine and after, or indeed of the barbarous wars between the *langue d'oeil* and the *langue d'oc* or between English and Welsh, might help to illustrate what is at stake. And the conclusion to be drawn from that is that war is epistemologically anterior to the state. It is the war of communities which creates states, and war as such is not only the expression of community but also a form through which the social contract comes into being – a point very well understood by the Founding Fathers of the only state which explicitly bases itself upon a social contract, namely the Declaration of Independence and the American Constitution.

Now, this suggests that within the Hegelian schema there is an inherent relationship between war and the state; and certainly some passages in his works would reinforce that impression. But in discussing this point, one consideration is crucial; namely, that adduced above. Hegel is against the Liberal identification of the state with civil society. Indeed, the whole basis on which he could argue in his last lectures that the state *could* be the vehicle for the Spirit was precisely that it was not bound to the stasis of civil society, as it had been in earlier schemata.[5]

On the other hand, he does not see the state as some form of abstract motion engaged in constant self-referring transcendence, but as a concrete entity in opposition to other states. The importance of the state for Hegel is that it provides the arena for a process of historical selection – not natural selection in the terms in which it was subsequently vulgarized but spiritual selection. If that proposition is accurate, it helps to reconcile his apparently contradictory positions. On the one hand, 'in war, war itself is characterised as something which ought to pass away'. On the other, war is part of the process of spiritual selection between the communities which are in the process of becoming states – a spiritual selection which in Hegelian terms can permit a new relationship to develop between the *Volksgeist* and the *Geist*. In this sense, war is not simply an exceptional phenomenon: it incorporates the transcendence of the master–slave combat in a new historical relationship between states and cultures; and by the same token, has an historical rationality of its own. It can provide the criterion for *Sittlichkeit* – a term feebly translated into English as morality. The argument is now at the opposite pole from Hobbes's original starting point. War becomes the progenitor for freedom.

An admixture of other means

Hegel's position was completely antithetical to that of Kant – who argued for the application of Reason to an international ethical life. The self-centred ethical community which had become the Hegelian state could admit of no such thing. It was bound to pursue its interest historically, not only by war but also by war. And its interest, if it understood what it was doing, could also become part of the manifestation of the spirit of freedom. In terms of the subsequent history of state activities, Hegel certainly appears to have the advantage over Kant, though in terms of his own criteria he would be hard put to argue that there has been any correspondence between the incidence of war and the growth of historical freedom. There is a clear-cut reason for that.

Hegel's historical experience was that of the Napoleonic age, carrying the impact of the French Revolution across the societies of Europe. His whole majestic work rested upon the proposition that through his experience he could step outside history, understand its course and indicate its potential fulfilment.[6] It is not difficult to imagine how, when confronted with Napoleon, he could conceive of war in terms of its spiritual instrumentality. But his contemporary, Clausewitz, whose whole life was determined to an enormously greater extent by Napoleon's career, came to opposite conclusions even while reconsidering the same events over an almost identical period. (Both men died in the plague of cholera of 1831.) Clausewitz was fully aware, as his writings amply demonstrate, of the revolutionary potential of war and of its social implications. But the man who has been characterized so often (and so wrongly!) as an Hegelian, was dedicated to the preservation of a political – though not social – order. In this respect, he stands in marked contrast to Hegel.

Hegel was concerned with the instrumentality of war in one way, Clausewitz in an entirely different manner. For Hegel, war could become an instrument of human transcendence in the eye of Reason. For Clausewitz, war could be the instrument of the preservation of the state order, provided that it was understood. Hegel was forcing the phenomenon of the state to come to terms with the phenomenon of war. Clausewitz was trying to persuade war to come to terms with the demands of the state. His underlying concern throughout was to preserve the European state system at a time when it was threatened by the Napoleonic experience. In such terms, if one is to embark at all upon the futile task of categorizing Clausewitz in terms of his wider philosophical inclinations, he is nearer to Kant than to Hegel: for him, the European state system did represent a kind of international order, itself an application of reason. The difference is, of course, that for Kant, the application of Reason could create a perpetual peace; for Clausewitz, it was necessary to apply reason to war to ensure that its violence did not threaten the existing political order – of which war was anyway a constituent element. That seems to me to be the fundamental meaning of his most famous aphorism: war is a continuation of politics with an admixture of other means.

But this implies not only that war can be brought under political control but also that if it is, it can be instrumental for the purposes and maintenance of the state. Can it?

Earlier, it was argued that the initial tension between states making wars and man making war had the effect of consigning war to oblivion within the terms of civil society. Its transcendental claims are so immense that, rather like falling in love, within a very short period people remember *an* experience, they don't remember *what* they experienced. Even in Britain in 1985, most people found it almost impossible to recall the emotions which swept a nation when the state went to war to reconquer an outcrop of its own civil society 3 years earlier. Now, Hegel's bold and comprehensive attempt to make war an agent of transcendent history suggested that the terms of the *Volksgeist* and of the *Geist* could ultimately be reconciled. But his argument depended on a prior assumption: that of the unchanging nature of war itself. And Clausewitz, after all, also argued on a basis of permanence. His very attempt to create a monist approach to the nature of war, even while arguing for a duality in its phenomenology, and his careful distinction between the three levels at which war is conducted, all attested to this.[7] Such assumptions were well justified in both cases. The social nature of war was already undergoing a transformation from the effects of the *levée en masse* and from Napoleon's campaigns. But apart from the fact that Napoleon was handling bigger bodies of men than ever used before, there was little change in the technological character or in the actual conduct of warfare. Some rather inefficient artillery had been developed, but the outcome of battles still depended upon the charge and upon close fighting. Napoleon, for all the celebrity of his advance on Moscow, did not march nearly so far as Alexander the Great. And armies still marched.

Clausewitz and Hegel both died 6 years after the construction of the world's first railway. But there was no particular reason for them to see either the enormously rapid growth it would have or its devastating implications.

The original track between Stockton and Darlington was 12 miles long. By the time of the American Civil War, 40 years later, there were 40 000 miles of railway in the world. But, as that war showed, it was not the railway alone which transformed the nature of armed conflict. Certainly, it was this peaceful development which now enabled thousands of men at a time to be brought to the battlefield instead of having to march there as Alexander's and Napoleon's armies had done. But, had it not been for the invention of the machine gun, the outcome of battle would still have been decided by the charge and close combat. It was the combination of the railway and the machine gun which not only made it possible to bring thousands upon thousands to the scene but also to slaughter them by the thousand when they arrived. And when Saul gave way to David in this manner, it was not merely a change of scale – it was a change in the social nature of war. The logisticians who commanded the armies of the First World War had appreciated the importance of the railway but not that of the machine gun. They still relied upon the charge to achieve victory. Man, the courageous animal, complied on all sides. But as he was unremittingly mown down and, as defeat after defeat was inflicted on his commanders, whole societies were drawn into the war.

The 1914–18 war threatened to make a nonsense of history in terms of any Hegelian instrumentality and it certainly made a nonsense of the Clausewitzian state order. Indeed, in such terms, it destroyed a majority of the states or empires which participated in it. War, the supreme activity of the state, had now become a threat to the state itself.

The reason is clear. When whole societies, instead of armies, go to battle, the limited ends of state conflict are no longer appropriate. The *levée en masse* was fed on the myth of the Revolution, but even that was a relatively limited *levée*. The continual discharge of mass after mass of civilians-in-uniforms into the field of fire meant that war had to be fed on myths of bigger and bigger proportions. In some cases, the myths are clearly well rooted and socially stabilizing ('making the world safe for democracy'), in others there was an implicit promise of social revolution ('a land fit for heroes to live in'), in others of course the promises were simply insufficient to sustain the state – and it just disappeared. But, for all the universalist aspirations of the League of Nations, what the First World War had demonstrated in virtually every case was that the *Volksgeist* had gone to war with the *Geist*. The technological and social transformations now matched; the relationship between war and the state had been broken; a war of all against all on a global scale had broken out, and it did not stop at Versailles.

Whom his great father did in ignorance kill

War, in Hegel's terms, had been the father of the state – at least in the sense that it was through war that the community became the state. This view was oddly echoed later by Charles de Gaulle when he declared that '*La France s'est faite à fil de l'épée*'. He was right historically, but in adducing it to contemporary circumstances he was anachronistic. War was now seen, as both the League of Nations Covenant and the United Nations Charter indicate, as a threat to the international order and to the existence of the state itself. The ignorant father was now killing his own offspring, as Rustum killed Sohrab.

Certainly, this dates in part from the experience of the First World War which, writing at the time, Edmund Blunden had already characterized as a new God. But it went further: The recognition of this God was now to deform godlike man. The 'licence' to kill became predominant. The readiness to die – scarcely a matter of choice even in 1914 – lost all significance when war took the form of the mass obliteration of cities. Crowding into a cellar and hoping to survive while firestorms rage overhead, or even waiting for the moment when the doodlebug goes silent, are not instances of the transcendent courage previously attributed to engagement in war; they are the triumph of pure contingency. Equally, godlike man, authorized to kill his fellow combatant in something at least approaching a fair fight becomes both diabolic and impersonal when he can incinerate thousands from a position miles up in the air or, ultimately, millions by pressing a button from 8000 miles away.

In standard debates between unilateralists and champions of nuclear deterrence, between governments and peaceniks, questions of this order are usually treated in a purely phenomenological and probabalistic sense; that is, in terms of whether the posture of nuclear deterrance makes nuclear war more or less likely. But the fundamental question which is at stake (certainly in terms of how one thinks of what it is to be human, whether one calls that the *Geist* or not) is what it is that states now engage their citizens to do. Preparing for war now includes preparing to commit genocide, rather fast. War could once have been said to be the external guarantor of the internal cohesion of the state – even despite of Jenkins' Ear. But in the present circumstances, even the very nature of preparation for war promotes the disintegration of civil society and of the authority of the state. Without the in-built preparation for nuclear war, it is doubtful whether the Greens would have taken off, Greenham Common women have found a common cause, or a Secretary of State for Defence have found it necessary to dress up in a flak jacket to stage a dawn raid at RAF Molesworth. (Winston Churchill, as Home Secretary, attended the siege of Sydney Street in a frock coat and striped pants. Michael Heseltine emphasized the decline in the dignity of the state when he clambered into camouflage. The Diary of Adrian Molesworth?) Not only war itself, but now even the nature of preparations for war threaten the legitimacy of the state. The state as the vehicle for the manifestation of the *Geist* has lost any purpose it might once have had – though this is of course not to say the same thing as that the *Geist* is dead.

But, in terms of what was argued earlier, there can be no manifestation of the *Geist* without a concrete historical form, and that which was its form has now given way to the preparation for the self-destruction of the spirit. Why should this be so?

There are three levels at which this question might be answered. The first relates to the changing nature of war; the second relates to the changing symbiosis between war and the state; and the third relates to an emerging differentiation between states and the nature of man in those states.

In terms of the changing nature of war, its instrumentality has been largely vitiated by its instruments. It is not simply, as already indicated, that war can now become a matter of remote-controlled mass slaughter. It is also that human beings are now trained, as a matter of course, to inflict not just pain, not just wounds which might or might not prove lethal upon their fellows, but in fact the most horrible atrocities. The USA won the campaign of the Tet offensive in 1968; but it was the photographs of that campaign, especially of the use of napalm, which began to convince the American public that American troops should be withdrawn. Out of an unexpected military defeat, General Giap gained an equally unexpected political victory. Yet this was not because of anything that the Viet Cong or the North Vietnamese regular forces achieved, it was because of what the Americans did. The catch-phrase 'we had to destroy it in order to save it' is eloquently expressive of the changing nature of war and of the fact that it is now almost impossible to think of war as instrumental to the purposes of the state.

This contention, however, is only incidental to a wider consideration. Clausewitz wrote that the inherent logic of war should lead all wars to become absolute. In reality, though, the absolutist logic of war was tempered by the everyday forces of friction. For him, absolute war was an Idea determinant of war's nature, but not an accurate historical or phenomenological description. The twentieth century has obviously brought absolute war into the realm of reality, and it did so through a process of invention. 'Total war' was not a phenomenon considered by Clausewitz but an enterprise decreed by Hitler. The response of the Western democracies, Britain and America in that historical order, was first to wage total war from the air and then to transform it into the potential of absolute war through the development of nuclear weapons. Britain began the process through fear that the totalitarian monster Hitler might get nuclear weapons first; America completed it through fear that the totalitarian monster Stalin might otherwise produce thermonuclear weapons on his own.

Yet, having invented absolute war in response to total war, the Western democracies found that this very condition had made it increasingly difficult for them to wage any war which was effectively instrumental for the state without thereby incurring the risks of absolute war itself. (Hence, the proliferation of confused and almost desperate literature about 'limited war)'. This is not, of course, to suggest that various powers have not attempted to engage in limited wars – many do so all the time as already indicated – but it is to suggest that even the existence of the discourse of limited war makes it clear that the purposes of the state can scarcely be served by war today.

In part, one might explain the difficulty by the straightforward reflection that states which have become muscle-bound by the process of inventing absolute war find it tricky to wage 'normal' war, while fighting, as they see it, with one arm tied behind their backs, or else without incurring the risk of that which they have themselves brought about. There is, however, a further difficulty. It is that states fighting 'limited war' can find themselves opposed to others, or to other movements, which are fighting total wars. Such, again, was the case of the USA in Vietnam. In a context of that nature, it is increasingly difficult to claim that fighting war serves the interests of the state – as was clearly recognized by Henry Kissinger when he said of the war in Vietnam that 'the US would not have recognised victory if it was staring it in the face because we didn't know what we were fighting for'. The implicit confession here is that American state interests were conceived of in a global context – as an all-out struggle between two, mutually hostile, social and ideological systems which implied total war just as the case had been in the First World War – but that the nature of the war had to be kept under control because of the fearful considerations attendant on absolute war. Such a condition not only doomed the USA to fighting a limited war but, by the same token, left its Vietnamese opponents free to fight a total war with all the means at their command. In the circumstances, it is not surprising that those engaged in total war beat those engaged in limited war.

To some extent, and perhaps in a rather circuitous manner, states have recognized the new 'limitations' imposed on war. Convention now has it that it is inadmissible to acquire territory by force. Lithuanians or Palestinians might be interested to hear of this, but the rule has held to a surprising extent. The reason is conjectural, but it might have something to do with the earlier distinction drawn between community and state: a community, which once became a state through war, did so by securing territory. Territory provided the defining conjunction between war and the state in the process by which the community was itself transformed. The extraordinary hold which two rather uninteresting islands still have over the Argentinian imagination says something about the power of that conjunction. Yet British diplomacy was successful in the rather unsympathetic environment of the United Nations in getting the General Assembly to condemn the Argentinian action of April 1982. An instance such as this might serve to illustrate the extent to which states now fear the intrusion of war into what was once its natural domain; wars fought over such all-important issues as the right to territory can become total, and the total can breed the absolute. Indeed, a state can occasionally play diplomatic games with such dangers. It was the nuclear alert of the American forces in 1973 which, as one might say, precipitated an end to the war between Egypt and Israel. A war in this instance fought for the recovery of territory but, even as such, one that was threatening to get out of control.

The question of territory is but one example of the manner in which the war has now brought the *Volksgeist* into conflict with the *Geist*. The emergence of total war is the primary principle through which this occurred and is in that respect the first of the three levels indicated above – that is, the changing nature of war. But why total war? The answer to that relates to the second level; namely, the changing symbiosis between war and state.

I have suggested that the transformation of war between the Napoleonic period and the nuclear era was not merely technological in character but also social. Earlier, the argument was put forward in terms of the kinds of causes for which civilians in uniform would be prepared to fight and to die. But there was an implication, not yet spelled out. It is that war became total *because* the state had become the whole of civil society. I was arguing at the beginning that a state can make war against the aggression of 'man' in another state, but this ignored the consideration that man has become increasingly absorbed into the state. (The paradox here is that as the state becomes more comprehensive, so it also becomes more of a sectoral interest in its dealing with civil society: witness the Polish state and its attempts to grapple with the phenomenon of Solidarity, and also the British Government's attempts to cope with the problems of civil rights in contexts as diverse as that of the GCHQ or the miners' strike.[8]) But Nietzsche had already elucidated this paradox in 1876. He pointed out[9] that the emergence of the Welfare State would also produce totalitarian, as well as total, wars. The inscription at Hyde Park Corner would certainly appear to provide evidence for his view – and there is little need to go further and dwell upon the details of the Dresden raid. The conclusion appears inescapable that the comprehensive state has engaged increasingly in total war, whether poisoned by ideological effects or not. Yet, the closer war approaches the degree of totality, the less instrumental it becomes for the comprehensive state. The outcomes of the First World War, the fate of the Third Reich in the Second World War, even the severe threat to the internal cohesion of Israeli society after the onslaught on Beirut in June 1982, all seem to suggest that, both in the international and the internal context, a civil society must now either feel encumbered with the guilt of the state which wages all-out war, or else reject its own criteria and glorify the war for the sake of the state. (In case of possible misinterpretation, I would wish to make it clear here that I am not in any sense drawing a parallel between Israel and the Third Reich, but am trying to emphasize that, across the board, war has changed the relationship between society and the state.) President Reagan rather awkwardly recognized the same thing when he went to Bitburg: it was impossible to distinguish between the act of recognition as between two societies and the condoning of the horrors of total war as practised by a state with which the USA itself had been at war at the time.

In the context of modern war, Leviathan has been defeated, as has the *Geist*. The case of modern Germany illustrates this most clearly. The society flourishes and is in many ways remarkably successful. It has also yet to come to terms with the activities of the previous state – and there is more than a hint that if it were to try to do so the society itself would be at risk. The case, however, is not unique: in the Soviet Union there was an almost near reversal. Endless celebrations of the Great Patriotic War were used to ensure that the citizens of the USSR did not re-examine the atrocities of Stalinism; and in this way the state could reign unimpeded by the demands of civil society. That might appear at first sight to be Leviathan's quirky triumph, not his defeat. But the USSR clearly demonstrates that the state can function neither efficiently nor justly without the acquiescence of society, and that, in terms of the criteria set forth in Hobbes's famous Chapter Thirteen, Leviathan has manifestly failed. One might also adduce the case of Japan and of the conduct of the Western democracies, both during and after the Second World War; but the point has been made. It is now very difficult indeed to conceive of war as being conducive to the maintenance of the state, as it was held to be within traditional forms of thought about the relationship between the two. The symbiosis has changed, and the relationship has become at best arbitrary (e.g. the Falklands), at worst fateful (e.g. Israel at the same time).

All this, however, might appear to be narrowly focused on the industrialized world – and it is true, of course, that the comprehensive state appears in industrialized societies. In this sense, it might be the case that Raymond Aron and others were right to argue, against Auguste Comte, that war has become a phenomenon of the industrialized society. But such propositions take little account of the wars in the Third World, nor of the third level of argument indicated earlier in this section: that of the emerging differentiation between states and the nature of man in those states.

The Third World has been rich in wars. Unlike the wars between the industrialized Leviathans, these have largely been wars *for* the possession of the state. In that respect, they might be said to be wars of an old-fashioned kind; namely, the conflict of communities in the process of becoming states. As such, they reflect something of the traditional nature of man making war. Yet they take place within the modern global context of the universalized state system, and that of the global spread of modern instruments of war. Traditional, even primitive, engagements now make use of the most up-to-date apparatus for killing on a large scale. The result has been two-fold. In the context of the globalized state system, boundaries remain fixed, as can be seen in the workings of the Organization of African Unity (OAU), and the territorial relationship between man, the state and war no longer provides a means of resolving disputes. At the same time, within these fixed boundaries the conflicts of communities which have not yet become states in anything but name (the cant term for the recognition of this fact is 'nation-building'), fought out as they are with modern means of mass destruction, result in a singular ruthlessness often verging on genocide. The full panoply of total war is seldom available in such circumstances, but the underlying assumptions of modern warfare, allied to the equipment which *is* available, do much to compensate. Indeed, in Cambodia, the genocidal war of 1975–6 was seen as the means of a particular form of modernization.[10]

War for the possession of the state has therefore come to be a different phenomenon in the modern context from what it was, say, at the time of the English Civil War. The fox-hunters chasing between the lines at the battle of Edgehill would not have been able to recognize how a war could become totalitarian even before the nature of the state itself had been ratified. Milovan Djilas was able to recognize this, though.[11] In *Wartime*, the volume of his memoirs dealing with the Second World War – in which one in eight of the entire population of Yugoslavia was killed – he recognizes the similarities between the courage and the ferocity of the Germans and of the Partisan forces, and remarks: 'We were all driven by the same dark force.'

Even for the Third World, therefore, and most particularly for the Third World, the modernization of war has taken place without reference to the historical transformations of society. If war has indeed become a vehicle for the modernization of society, this does not mean that it is thereby historically instrumental. It merely means that the cohesion of a society in the process of becoming a state is now more at risk from war than ever before – unless, of course, a dominant group really does embark on genocide. That might do the trick in terms of cohesion, but would obviously not do much in terms of society.

The conclusion is that at all three levels – that of the changing nature of war, that of the changing symbiosis between war and the state and that of the emerging differentiation between states – war has lost both its social and its historical instrumentality; and, in Hegelian terms, has become a form of preparation for the self-destruction of the spirit.

The parent of all things

The conclusions reached hitherto do not, of course, imply that war will cease. Intellectual discourse is not an 'unacknowledged legislator of the world'; and the interdependence between war and the state will certainly continue, even though it is becoming painfully apparent that war can no longer serve state purposes. The appeal of war will continue too: the existential bet, and 'all the panoply of glorious war'. Considerations of that nature will not be resolved by conflict researchers.

Indeed, Heraclitus was no doubt right. Strife *is* the parent of all things. But at the political level, that of the activity of the state, it is becoming increasingly important to recognize that there is no relationship any longer between Heraclitus and Clausewitz. For Heraclitus, strife was a metaphysical ancestor of thought. For Clausewitz, the use of war was that, if well understood, it could preserve the state system. The behaviour of states has been such as almost to meld the considerations of the two: to treat war as a form of Heraclitan strife, a universal *fons et origo*, in the name of a Clausewitzian system. While it was possible to keep war under control – morally in terms of the Just War tradition, politically in Clausewitzian terms – this was a reasonable act of confusion. But the reason that there has been no mention of Just War hitherto is that in the circumstances of today it is virtually impossible to continue fighting for very long or in any extensive theatre without violating the canons of the Just War.

Strife can perhaps take other forms – just as the rioting mobs that helped to determine much of Western political history in the nineteenth century gave way to the strikes and picket lines of the twentieth century. But even if a transformation of armed conflict ever comes, that will be a very slow evolution. In the meantime, the important thing is to recognize that while war continues, it will increasingly become the enemy of the state rather than its servant, and a threat to civil society rather than its protector – and that even the great military virtues of courage, discipline and restraint will do little to change its changing nature.

Notes

1 Aron's lecture was published as 'War and Industrial Society: A Reappraisal' *Millennium, Journal of International Studies* 7, 3 (1978). Monod is quoted by Leszek Kolakowski *Religion* (Oxford University, 1982).

2 An interesting exploration of this change in language and assumptions is Paul Fussell's *The Great War and Modern Memory* (Oxford University, 1978), but even that is only a footnote to the work of Walter Benjamin and to Erich Heller's *The Disinherited Mind* (Cambridge, Bowes and Bowes, 1952).

3 T.M. Knox (ed.) Hegel's *Philosophy of Right* (Oxford, Clarendon, 1952) p. 215. Hegel's comments on war are contained in pp. 324–8, 334–9 and 351.

4 I wish to acknowledge my debt to Dr Zbigniew Pelczynski, and in particular to a paper he gave to a seminar at the LSE in the spring of 1985; see Z.A. Pelczynski ed *The State and Civil Society* (Cambridge University, 1984).

5 See Klaus Hartmann 'Towards a New Systematic Reading of Hegel's Philosophy of Right' in Z.A. Pelczynski ed *The State and Civil Society* (Cambridge University, 1984) pp. 129–35.

6 This is, of course, drawn from Alexandre Kojeve *Introduction to the Reading of Hegel* (New York, Basic Books, 1969).

7 See Raymond Aron *Clausewitz, Philosopher of War* (Routledge and Kegan Paul, 1983).

8 It was Professor J.A.G. Griffith of the LSE who, to my knowledge, first pointed this out.

9 In 'Human, All-too-Human' in Oscar Levy ed *The Complete Works of Friedrich Nietzsche* (Edinburgh, Foulis, 1909–13) Vol. 6, p. 349.
10 Cf. Ben Kiernan *How Pol Pot Came to Power* (Verso, 1985).
11 M. Djilas *Wartime* (New York, Harcourt Brace Jovanovich, 1977) pp. 440–50.

8

On the Withering Away of the State

Cornelia Navari

Predictions of state withering have been a recurrent feature of modern political analysis and its focus on the social condition since the nineteenth-century. Liberal reformers expected industrialization and the requisites of 'modern' society to reduce the role of the state, internationally as well as domestically. Concern with social reform, the emergence of the 'social question' and the beginnings of sociology were also reducing the state conceptually to a social by-product of a more relevant social process, dependent on society's emerging forms. In their notions of the evolution of class, marxists went so far as to foretell its positive disappearance. By 1910, legal pluralists, together with liberal economists began to positively enjoin its dissolution. After the Second World War, the process speeded up: in approximately 10-year cycles, theorists of international interest groups, multinational corporations and global warming, each in turn heralded some bad news for the state, either evaluative or predictive, each as a result of some new social evolution, each to a flurry of protest. Indeed, much of the development of international relations theory has emerged from quarrels between the state-withering and the state-maintaining schools.

The advocates of withering have covered the range of the analytical spectrum: systems theorists, realists and political economists, as well as pluralists, socialists and marxists, have each joined the current at some time to announce that the state is about to be surpassed, is becoming increasingly irrelevant, is losing grip, is losing its ability to control, or its imaginative evocation.

The bases for such claims have accordingly varied, with as many quarrels among the withering theorists as between them and the advocates of non-withering. Two generations of pluralists have rejected the marxian analysis of class struggle and substituted a sort of generalized utility thesis, in which the variety of groups composing society would no longer require state mediation to secure their interests.[1] In the early 1960s, the realist, John Hertz, moved from general social or group requisites to strategic utility: the discovery of the penetrability of the state's 'hard shell', through nuclear weapons and the inability of the state to provide for security.[2] Later that decade, strategy was declared irrelevant and interdependence was elaborated, a complex of new issue areas, often called 'low politics', which were deemed increasingly central to modern political life and to enjoin redefinitions of sovereignty.[3] Today, economic utility has re-emerged, together with a new biological determinism. (Political economists point out that some 30 per cent of contemporary world trade is intra-firm, not inter-state, trade.[4])

Whatever the variety of claims, however, and whatever their theoretical starting points, most theorists of withering share striking common features. If we were to generalize the range of arguments, we would see, as a fundamental postulate, that there are tasks which states are meant to perform and which are central to them. These may be security, economic management or the control of trade, but each is none the less somehow integral to the state, so much so that loss of capacity to perform it qualifies a state's stateness. Secondly, there is the claim that such tasks either can no longer be done by the state, cannot be done by it alone, or no longer require to be done, with the logical corollary. In each case, the state withers because it is inappropriate to some relevant or more relevant social requirement, because it is not useful, and because things that society requires to be done either cannot be done by a state, or the state is not the best organ to do them. It is thus 'destined' to decline. Moreover, many evaluations of whether or not the state is indeed withering base their analyses on a range of functions it must perform (and its performance of them) to evaluate its (continued) viability.[5]

This would appear commonsensical. It seems sensible to hold that when a state cannot do a central social task, this somehow reflects not just on this or that state but on the state itself, and many people think they ought to evaluate the state on such grounds. Many of these arguments represent, however, less common sense than a particular theoretical view of the state: the social function theory of the state.

Functionalism was a natural intellectual ally of rationalism, where it took the form of utilitarianism. As a formal theory, however, its roots lie, in part, with systems science and, in part, with evolutionary biology. Translated into political theory, its most elaborated versions hold that the state or 'governing function' is part of a complex whole which it serves – the state exists because it is useful to society – and that its form and scope perform some socially useful purpose. Were it, therefore, to cease to perform the uses which gave it scope and form, were new functions required in relation to which its present shape is rendered inappropriate, some revision in both form and function would inevitably follow. The long history of prognostications concerning state withering belong generally to the functionalist school, and it is functionalists who have been the most consistent advocates of withering.

Leaving the problem of evaluation by function aside for a moment, there are problems with this conception of the state, frequently adumbrated.[6] An obvious one is the view of the state as a machine or instrument. This metaphor immediately presents itself with the problem of the designer of the machine and with the assignment of its 'purposes'. We may understand a vehicle with a purpose, such as an automobile, and designers of automobiles, but who designs the state and determines its purposes?

More immediately, there is the process of withering itself. The precise mechanics of withering are seldom laid out by the proponents of such theories, and their weakest point is the link between a perceived loss of function and its translation into a changed form for the state. Are we to suppose, for example, that civil servants, aware of their uselessness, resign their jobs *en masse* to take on more socially useful functions? (The specialists on bureaucratic politics inform us that this is exactly what bureaucrats do not do.) Are we to suppose that the state, simply mirrow-wise, conforms to new, widespread and more limited notions of itself? In fact, the state has steadily absorbed more of the social product, precisely during the period of the (many) prognostications of its withering.

The notable exception is, of course, Lenin, who did try to outline how state withering might occur, and who, in a dearth of neglect for this rather vital question, is to be congratulated.[7] With Lenin, however, there is reason to doubt that the state withers at all. What is the administration of things, after all, and how does it differ from a state?

When, moreover, the state does not wither, this school explains the retention of the state by the discovery of 'new' purposes, like the preservation of now-altered forms of capitalism, or residual defence purposes.[8] This is a specious form of argument, for some purposes can always be found for a state, by someone. It also undercuts the argument, for it must surely be the case that if the state does reflect social needs, there must be some fairly widespread agreement on what those needs are – they can surely not be that hidden or contentious – and continuous (and wilful) redefinition of them must cast doubt on the fundament of the analysis.

Is it not possible to do better than this? Can we not try for an under-standing of the state within which to place such developments as international interest group formation, multinational corporations, revised defence conceptions and ecological disaster, with a view to forming some reasonable expectations of the implications of such developments for the scope and capacity of states, which is not at the same time circular or tautological? The formal requisites for such an understanding are two-fold:

first, we must define what is to stand for withering which is reasonably objective and palpably determinable; we also need a theory of state growth and decline which cuts through the circular thinking of the social aggregation theorists, which establishes causes that are distinct from consequences, and which will alert us to identifiable circumstances conducive to withering (and within which it might possibly occur) and circumstances in which withering is unlikely.

Withering and its dynamic

Withering was first envisaged by the early rationalists and taken up by the liberal or pluralist school of political analysis. Both held that man had natural and self-sustaining 'rules' of social organization and that the state was a reflector of those rules. In these schools, much of the *ancien régime* was held to be 'useless' or inappropriate to natural laws and could be done away with, without harming social cohesion. Indeed, to reform the old order in ways more conformable to man's nature was held to place social organization (and the state) on a sounder footing. To each, withering had, thus, a fairly distinct meaning: it involved limiting the state to tasks essential to a state and for which it was in theory 'instituted', and allowing man's natural instincts to manage the rest of public affairs. Of course, there was always debate among the liberal theorists as to the proper realm of the state and its extent. But there was always held to be a sort of mythical line between what was public, what within the public was the state, and what the domain of the private. (Some liberals had a notion of natural organizations like the family or the church which would control man's behaviour, and hence also of corporate man, alongside man the citizen; these corporations were public but not state.)

Given the origins of this thought, we may at least arrive at a tentative definition of withering. It lies in the realm of the 'silence of the laws', or the restrictions on public and, more particularly, government policy. By these ideas, the state 'withers' when it hands functions over to the market, or non-state bodies, when government expenditure and taxation lessens, and when it restricts itself to certain domains.

Let us take on the dynamic of withering by referring back to the assumptions of functionalism. First, functionalism assumes that the state is solely an outcome of social forces; it assumes, that is, that there is no logic, purpose or interest which inheres in being a state itself. Secondly, functionalism assumes that all events are in some sense purposive, that they produce an outcome in keeping with the original impulse, in its direction and in an 'intentional' or purposive relation to it. It assumes, in other words, that there are no unintended consequences which dictate state behaviour. The first we may call the denial of any logic to being a state; the second we may call the denial of any grammar of power which is not attuned to a social purpose. It is to these that we must now turn. I will argue that there is certainly a logic in being a state, and interests which are state interests, as opposed to social interests. I will also argue that there is a grammar of power, quite apart from the logic of being a state, which dictates state and social behaviour. In other words, I will argue that there are unintended consequences of action which powerfully affect states and their prospects for 'withering'.

The logic of a state

We may apprehend the possibility that the state has a logic in the performance of governmental tasks. We may, that is, agree with the functionalists that the state is a task doer, and with the rationalists that it constantly chooses among ends and means. Government is the active agency of the state; it has speech and purpose, represented by its policies; and its choices are decisions or policy directions. The question is what or who do its choices 'represent'?

This question has always been at the heart of democratic theory, one of whose main concerns was how to make the state 'represent' more than merely itself. It was raised most pertinently by Rousseau in his distinction between the General Will, the Will of All and the Particular Will – commonly understood as the good of all, the good of the majority and the good of the individual. But it took on a particularly pertinent and indeed poignant aspect with the modern Welfare State when the question became how to advise government on the welfare function – the best mix of policies that would achieve a general social good. The question was not merely whether the social good or general will could ever be more than a majority among a sum of particular wills (which Rousseau thought it ought to be), it was whether even 'majorities' rule, a question raised in its most logical form by Kenneth Arrow in 1951 in the famous 'General Possibility Theorem', now simply called the Arrow theorem.[9]

Formulating the idea of the state in a classically functionalist manner, the social theorist, Abram Bergson, reported Arrow's finding in a somewhat doleful manner:

> The official is envisaged . . . as more or less neutral ethically. His one aim in life is to implement the values of other citizens by some rule of collective decision-making. Arrow's theorem apparently contributed to this sort of welfare economics the negative finding that *no consistent social ordering could be found* in the counseling of the official in question.[10]

Arrow's conclusion was that a choice could represent nothing more than the preferences of the chooser; and, accordingly, government policy nothing more than the preferences of government.

A state's interests are expressed by its preferences. Interests are expressed by choices: that is what an interest is, a denomination of choice. Choices are expressed by policies; the statement that France's interests are served by its policies is not a tautological statement, it is a necessary statement. It is also a meaningful statement; for once we see that a state's choices represent and can only represent its own preferences, that so-called social choice is actually public choice and in reality governmental choice, we see that they must accord with the governors' interests, since they can represent nothing else.[11]

If the state expresses not social purposes but the preferences of the state, if further it is seen that governments are handing powers to the people, to representative groups, to social organizations or to the market, the corollary must thus be that this activity is its preference, that it is willing itself to wither. For, if withering of the public power is a public act, if it, like all acts, is a choice of the actor, then withering must be an act of the state, of the public power itself.

That a state should prefer to wither, that it should prefer to divest itself of responsibilities and return those responsibilities to management either by the market or by relatively autonomous social organizations, or even to outsiders and non-nationals, may seem a contradiction to the logic of being a state. It may seem absurd to suppose that a state can prefer a diminution of its own powers as part of its own logic. Yet it is neither logically absurd, nor historically unknown. It is historically the case that the 13 colonies divested themselves of potential prerogatives and as a logical corollary of their well-being as states (the fear that they would hang separately if they did not hang together.) Germany and Italy after the war chose limitations of their own sovereignty, as part of the logic of state enhancement (the powers they preferred could not be got but by such diminutions).

In what circumstances does it make sense for a state to wither? Logically, a state may prefer less of itself when its aims lie beyond politics in the preservation of a religious or natural order. In these circumstances, all that will be needed by a state will be a sufficiency to protect that order by depredation from outside, from other states. It will also prefer less of itself when the logic of being more would disturb a present equilibrium necessary for its existence (or its existence altogether). It would also be logical for governors to choose less power when having less would ease their governing tasks or provide them with more resources than they would otherwise have.

A.W. Hirschmann provided one logic of state withering in his 1945 argument on the costs and benefits of economic nationalism, in which he calculated the costs of cutting off from the outside world and the price involved in pursuing economic autarchy, providing, in effect, one account of circumstances where it made sense for a state to choose less of itself.[12] H.G. Johnson widened this account to include the psychological satisfaction of nationalism (which states could draw on, in effect, to balance some of the economic costs) in another account of economic nationalism, and S. Kuznets related the proclivity to openness, and less state to size, in a parallel exercise.[13] But the most subtle and nuanced theory to date, which provides a logic of state withering, may be found in Anthony de Jasay's *The State*.[14]

De Jasay notes that states do a variety of things: some merely protect a reputed natural order, while others represent, take sides or redistribute. He then provides a logical continuum of five ideal-type states from the natural-order market state, through the democratic state (the state which represents), to the adversarial state and the redistributive state, ending finally at the state-market state (from 'less' to 'more' state). Using this typology, he illustrates conditions where it is rational for the democratic state, the state which merely represents, to begin to choose sides – to become the adversarial state – when merely representing impedes its ability to construct policy or to survive. Equally, in choosing sides, the adversarial state may find it profitable to begin to redistribute, as a logical requirement of its adversarial function: it may find its adversarial function, its capability to reward one side over another, enhanced if it begins to shift resources around, if it becomes redistributive. It is also logical for a redistributive state to develop totalitarian forms, if the means of its redistribution run out. Equally, however, it is quite possible for the logic to run the other way. Thus, the 'redistributive drudge' may find its tasks eased to return certain social functions to society when its resources run out, and to lessen the burden of redistribution; for the adversarial state to become tired of choosing sides and to settle for the merely representative or even the market state; and for the democratic state, tired of trying to balance a host of aims, to aim for the natural-order state.

The denominator of withering – whether a state will prefer less of itself or more of itself – is a function of its capabilities at the moment of choice, its requisites for the job at hand. That is, if the adversarial state does not have the requisites to continue in its adversarial function, if it finds that mere choosing of sides is not sufficient to win consent – and may indeed be losing it – it may attempt to widen its appeal by recourse to redistribution. Redistribution will bring it more capacity, more goods with which to win friends, and certainly new loyalties. For, whereas previously both sides were sliding into discontent, one will now be more emphatically on its side, and it will also have earned consent to repress the other. On the other hand, the redistributive state, faced with an exhaustion of resources for redistribution, may declare the redistributive game at an end and institute the merely representative or the natural-order state, depending on where it may find support.

States maintain themselves by different mixes of consent and repression, from the consent of the many (and the repression of the few) to the consent of the few and the repression of the many. This is a common observation. De

Jasay notes, however, that any governing mix is along a scale which may be conceived more precisely: from the lightly rewarded many and the heavily repressed few to the heavily rewarded few and the lightly repressed many. Where a state does not have sufficient resources to lightly reward the many, its logical alternative is to reward fewer, but more generously. (Logically, it can never make sense to heavily reward the many.) In each case, the 'rewarded' will act as its lieutenants. The state will expand or contract accordingly.

The particular mix between the lightly rewarded many and the heavily rewarded few may be said to represent each state's centre of gravity, which can be shifted, depending on where any state starts, its aspirations and the toleration of the population for government, to release resources. To shift in accordance with the maximization of its resources would constitute a logic for a state.

Given the variety of social mixes and the different bases of state legitimation, we cannot assume developments uniformly disturb all states, or provide them with the same opportunities or incentives. Multinationals may be a salient issue for the state with a deep intervention in its economy, and which heavily depends on redistribution, but they may present a neutral phenomena for the King of Morocco, a traditional ruler, or if they do disturb, it will be for very different reasons. Capital flight, on the other hand, heavily rewards the few at little cost to the state not concerned with redistribution, which is no doubt why some states tolerate it: it has been opportunistically incorporated into their reward structures. For the redistributive, however, it must be an anathema, as it removes from the state a potential redistributory asset.

Nor should we assume that less states are weaker states, or even less statish. It is not obvious that Greece with one public/private balance is less a state than Sweden, or that the USA which eschews sometimes even the adversarial, is less strong than the Soviet Union. The question is the balance of resources each provides the state at any moment, against the balance that might be provided by other mixes.

Thus, so far as gauging the likelihood of any development, such as a global market, for state withering, the first and essential question to ask is how such a development fits into any single state's particular governing logic – its centre of gravity, its governing mix and its potential resources – and how it affects the resource base required by that logic.

The grammar of power

When a state chooses, however, it does so within an environment of givens which powerfully affect its choices. These are opportunities and limitations not of its making but which emerge from historical developments, prevalent ideas about state and society and the aspirations of citizens. Opportunities and limitations not of its, or indeed anyone's, intentional making we may call the grammar of power.

There are numerous postulates of such a grammar; for our purposes, however, let us begin with Bertrand de Jouvenal, a justly famous grammarian of power.[15] De Jouvenal adduced three main sources to the unintentional growth in the absolutist power of the modern state: revolution, atomization and subjectivism. Each was, in turn, a sub-category of a more general phenomenon which we may call 'rupture'. Revolution was a rupture with the past, atomization that of 'every private tie between man and man', and subjectivism was the resultant of a break with natural law.

Rupture with the past brings with it, he notes, the 'apparent disappearance of every constraint'. In fact, however, it produces only the disappearance of those which do not emanate from the state. The breakdown of tradition creates 'opinions of equal validity' (or subjectivism) and makes the state the judge among subjective preferences. Atomization creates the demand for new rules in a situation of social change. When the state is the only source of constraint, the salience of the state becomes, accordingly, enhanced. This is the main reason why the break with all traditional constaint, so often seen as disruptive to state power, actually enhances it: it turns the state into the only source of constraint. It can also choose which constraints to impose. (And where the state can choose, it, like any other chooser, is free to suit its own preferences.) Where there are opinions of equal validity, the state will be called upon to select among them. (And where a state can choose . . . .) Finally, the demand for new rules in a situation of social change increases both a state's substantive legislative rights and its political salience. (The dissolution of a natural law order, its substitution by human and positive law giving, and the development of subjective and transitory rights – rights which maintain validity partly because they are seen as changeable – have also been emphasized by Gianfranco Poggi: he notes they give the state the ability to tailor the legal order to any conception of its needs, virtually unimpeded.[16])

De Jouvenal also notes that 'when power runs with the current, it will appear strong, where it runs counter it will be found to be infinitely weak'. And the less flexible the usage, and the more tied to dogma or doctrine, the 'less latitude has command'.

The practice of asking the state to intervene, to supply policies for the poor, or against trade unions or the capitalist class (de Jasay calls this 'taking sides'), also enhances it. In the process, the state becomes very informed as to the particular characteristics of each side. Also, in asking the state to take sides, we are asking the state to choose, and where an agency is free to choose, it is free to seek its preferences. Standard setting by central authorities, arbitration and surveillance also serve the state and enhance it. When we ask the state to set standards, we allow it a tailoring freedom. Arbitration and surveillance of trends give it information; in consequence, it becomes more knowledgeable and its knowledge is like a reserve which it can store against a rainy day. (Such knowledge can, for example, lay the foundation for choosing sides.)

It is a pervasive assumption among functionalists that arrangements that create losers are somehow bad for the state because there is now a disaffected group which can protest or rebel. This is a dangerous assumption. The creation of adversary relations poses a potential for increasing state power, so long as it also creates winners. The winners become dependent on the state for the protection of their gains, while the losers become dependent on it to change the arrangement. Continuously adjusting the balance, moreover, and the prospect of balance change, provide the state with an almost inexhaustible source of relevance.

When governments seek to change the balance between consent and repression, their powers are also enhanced, a surprising effect to some. In the case of the lifting of repression they become, paradoxically, the liberators of the oppressed, suddenly gaining legitimacy. In the case of consent, they also become the donors of desirable gifts – a willingness to bargain and the potential fruits of any such bargains. (It is for this reason that states discover powers at the moment they are prepared to give them away.) In the case of repression, its avoidance. (Rationalization involves both coercion and bargaining, and hence always bestows power on the rationalizer. Where government is the rationalizer, it is also given powers to determine the criteria of rationalization. And where the state can choose . . . .) Each is, however, only a temporary power and will dissipate at the end of each redistribution cycle.

Modern intradmundane ideology which proposes altering social conditions, and its concomitant, social engineering, also enhance authority. The notion that good can be achieved by policy makes the state first responsibile for a social task, then it gives it the instruments to carry out that task. In the process, the state takes on a lot of administrators, gains rights to carry out its duties, and also inevitably becomes the arbiter of its own definitions of its duties. (The degree to which any task is deemed by some social movement or other to require the intradmundane action of a secular authority always serves the state; any such instance widens authority's scope and its realm of choice.) Accordingly, demands for redistribution are no sign that a state has lost capacity; they are the crucial foundations for increasing it, whatever superficial confusion or criticism of government, and state, attend such demands. (It is also the case that the more issues are politicized, the more salient the state becomes.) Above all, there is the functional idea of the state. The idea that the state can do good is one of the most powerful feeders of state power. By extension, we might observe, withering is best served not by locating dysfunctions, or political disputation and dissatisfaction, or even rivalry by another state (which may increase loyalty) but in disillusionment with the state, and rival authority of a non-state sort.

The state's logic exists within such conditions, and the analyst interested in gauging the likelihood of specific developments for withering must take account of both.

Globalization and the multinational company

By the end of the nineteenth century, modern social thought had produced the demand that the state should be all things to all people; that it should be mother, father, economic guardian, guardian of culture, equality regulator, etc. Few states chose this entire range, fascist Germany and the Soviet Union under Stalin being the major exceptions. The Western liberal state, by the post-war period, had settled for the managed open economy and the mildly redistributive, to be financed by tax revenues accrued by economic growth. The growth formula was in general capitalist; that is, leaving choice to the citizen. It was also the political formula: citizen choice, together with growth, a comparatively prosperous basis for growth and the mildly redistributive, won it consent.

Within this mix, the independent company was an important resource, an agency and promoter of growth, a gatherer of both élite and popular consent, a source of tax revenue and a critical capital source.[17] It was also, of course, the trader, supplier and translator of growth opportunities abroad to the local rentier. Independent companies were not merely compatible with the liberal state's liberal ideology, they were vital instruments in its governing mix.

The combination of open liberal orders, relatively open financial exchange and autonomous companies produced, of course, unintended consequences. Few predicted the massive growth of the multinational company, the resultant growth of the international financial market or the extent of interdependence, in either of its two senses: the translation of disturbing impulses or mutual dependency. (The growth of international competitiveness was chosen by some; unforeseen by others.) It also produced the capabilities of 'transfer price' manipulation, and the distribution of profits away from heavy taxers.[18]

However, these developments also produced demands that multinationals be more heavily controlled; they provided opportunities for adversarial politics on the part of states, who placed themselves on the sides of peoples against wicked multinationals (or, alternatively, on the side of modernization against slothful people), and a spate of useful advice on how to handle the threat of multinationals.[19] In consequence, the state acquired, in some instances, a potential increase in bargaining power (when the state becomes adversarial, it is automatically in a bargaining position); it also became more knowledgeable.[20]

How these opportunities have been used varies from state to state. One telling example is, however, India, which early on in the game set guidelines for foreign investment.[21] These have allowed it to protect indigenous capitalists, and set the framework for a variety of minority ownership schemes and joint public–private and private–private ventures. The virtue of such arrangements, viewed in terms of the logic of a state, is not whether they aid development, but that they allow the state to offer rewards to regional and federal trustees, winning their consent in the process. (India is a state whose unity and hence centre of gravity rests on heavily rewarding a federal and regional few, who bring followers with them.)

The fact that a multinational becomes contested is not, overall, a bad thing for a state, depending on the grounds and the form of relief sought. If it is contested on the grounds that state planning is disrupted, this denotes a victory for state planning: the state will have won consent to control multinationals in the name of the plan. If it is contested on the grounds that people are suffering, it wins the right to redistribute, if it chooses, or to place harder conditions on the company, and on the terms of its own choosing. The state is thereby given licence to enquire what purposes multinationals ought to serve, and of course to choose them, while its role as the protector of the people and the economy is enhanced.[22] If this process is generalized into an international process, i.e. if a number of states simultaneously are under attack by citizen protest, this is even better for states, because it places them in a market control situation and allows them even more leverage *vis-à-vis* companies to set terms for the legal rights of entry and to claim benefits.[23] Needless to say, these may also be highly selective, allowing the state considerable refinement in selecting what goals precisely it wants multinationals to serve, and in what sectors of the economy.[24]

Ensuing disturbances generally raised pressures for compensation, but few really enhanced redistribution in Western States. (Mrs Thatcher deployed the multinational to clock down from the redistributive to the adversarial. She used the international company to undercut the power of the trade unions while winning consent from a new set of workers who were free to draft their own contracts.)

In general, the value of openness, and the likelihood of a welcome to at least some sort of multinational, on the part of a state, depends on the proportion of recipients of the benefits of openness, at different degrees of national autarchy. This proportion, seldom looked at by the proponents and opponents of multinationals, is a key initial variable.[25] Its nature and relative degree of sophistication are also important. In Singapore, where a large native mercantile interest existed at independence, the multinational was a positive boon. An ideology of export orientation, together with the practice of joint ventures and production for export (which was, moreover, externally financed) ensured participation and reward to locals and secured the loyalties of a large open élite (from heavy to light rewards). In such states, the multinational provided investment, participation, training and intermediation at practically nil social cost, so long, however, as the state agencies retained key patronage roles. In West Africa, there was also a trading tradition – however, with some important differences. The 'native' traders were largely domestically oriented and small-scale at independence, while the large mercantile structures were expatriate in origin. There was, none the less, growth potential (and, hence, constant fodder) in the domestic trader. To gain both domestic support and key domestic allies, these states adopted redistributive policies, involving moreover redistribution from the expatriate, international and sometimes multinational (generally primary) producer and marketer, in part to the urban poor and, more importantly, to the native proto-industrial producer or marketer. A variety of economic nationalisms and collective ideologies justified control and taxation, including large extractions in some cases. Controls, however, were moderated to ensure continued operating attractiveness, to produce both a continuing taxable resource and 'intermediation', access to the international market and guaranteed sales, and sufficient openness for the larger domestic economic interests. By this means, governments held on to their resources, heavily rewarded some key trustees, while winning admittedly variable degrees of popular consent, partly through an adversarial role *vis-à-vis* 'foreign influences'. (The consent/repression balance in new states alters with confusing rapidity.) In Tanzania, on the other hand, one of the poorer states, and with a large majority of peasant producers, the government had fewer resources to carry out even mild redistribution and fewer potential receivers of the benefits of openness. Moreover, and partly in consequence, no independent company policy could really offer an appropriate pay-off, to enable government either to heavily reward the few or to lightly reward a consent-rendering many. The logical alternative was to close the economy and extract from the base as a whole, employing a socialist ideology combined with a rural reform programme.[26]

The overrall economic rewards produced by multinational companies to poorer states are not irrelevant to governing logic, as the above analysis might suggest, but they should be seen in political terms. For example, where a multinational is draining resources *which would have been there otherwise*, government is in effect running out of potential rewards and must rely on rewarding fewer, which turns of course on further controlling the market, and more state. Far from inducing withering, the multinational is inducing a shift to the redistributive but with, additionally, a narrowing basis of redistribution – the clientelist state. This may serve to explain at least some instances of the clientelism, élitism, poverty, multinational company mix. Such states are not, of course, strong, but there is assuredly more state. (One must also say, to those who believe this is an intolerable situation, that the solution is not more state still, but policies directed steadily and over time to increasing per capita income, a policy which is not only better for the common man, but also good for the state, because it increases both its choices and its resources.) However, it is not multinationals which are the determinants of such choices, but the overall governing mix.

On the other hand, multinationals do not automatically enhance or push towards the free market state. On the contrary, as H. Johnson has noted, they have little interest in spreading knowledge, investing more than they have to or enhancing economic growth.[27] Their natural form is monopolistic or oligopolist and 'higher tariffs worry them very little, and may offer them more secure markets and safer prospects for planning';[28] and they have little automatic economic 'spillover'. (This is one of the economic complaints against them, that they may operate within an enclave.) Hence, they have little difficulty operating in the closed economic order. Moreover, because they are well placed to enhance the rewards of the élite, they may be a boon to the heavy-rewards-to-the-fewer state. (Hence, also, their compatibility with socialist economies; the Soviet Union used them to reward more heavily the slightly more among its trustees.[29])

The rigours of interdependence and international competitiveness have produced the growth of the state company. The two formulae noted by Vernon are the use of state-owned companies to favour an indigenous producer, and the national champion in a key industry who sells to state agencies and other state-managed companies. Goldberg has noted a 'mixed pattern' in which the national market is served partly by integrated multinationals and partly by national champions, often engaged in joint ventures with other national champions. He observes that 'a mixed industrial structure increases the bargaining power of governments and decreases the need of government support'.[30] From the point of view of state logic, this is a good bargain. Let us also note, moreover, that within this mix, governments choose to meet some of these problems by the employment of the multinational. To be adversarial on the side of international competition, using a variety of companies to carry modernizing impulses, allows government to choose what industries to encourage and what new techniques to introduce. It also allows for the disciplining of trade unions and produces a 'social opposition' to retrograde practices and retrograde industries.

Not the least effect of globalization, however, is the cross-cutting nature of the ties it produces. In any complex economy at any one time, some enterprises will assuredly benefit from isolation but others will suffer. This mix, in turn, allows the state authorities a high degree of selectivity in the mode of protection, its timing, the sector to which it will be applied and its duration. It allows, in other words, the state to *choose*.[31]

In discussing the implications of globalization and the multinational company for state autonomy, some political economists have employed the concept of a 'sovereignty cost'.[32] This is a misapplication of economic logic to political reality. States do not necessarily pay any cost in reducing or limiting the exercise of their legal rights and may gain considerably, both in loyalty and in the ease of the governing task. If political economists insist on this concept, they must identify such costs and from whence the loss ensues. If, moreover, it is a sovereignty cost, then it must be shown to be derived from some feature integral to the scope of government or to the unity of the sovereign power (the degree to which power is shared, divided, impinged upon, etc). If the latter consideration does not deliver the analytical purchase desired by the analyst, then he or she is not talking about sovereignty at all, but about choice, which may or may not be related to the formal attributes of sovereignty.

It may be, of course, that dealing with multinationals forecloses choice and introduces an inflexibility into policy making which would not have been there otherwise, but such a case is seldom clearly argued. The original and contrary argument was that multinationals enhance government choices, and such an argument, while superficially persuasive, may also be vulnerable to refutation. To demonstrate, however, that multinationals do not deliver the freedom (or any other good) promised by non-official sources of investment, is not to demonstrate a sovereignty cost; it is only to demonstrate that the claims made for this form of investment were overstated.

International legal regimes

Much recent effort has gone into showing the consistency of regimes with state preferences. In particular, Steven Krasner has adduced a close relationship between regime continuation and state external needs, and Gilpin has related the features of regimes and their stability to the foreign policy interests of the hegemon.[33] Keohane, writing in response to the hegemonic theorists, has, moreover, demonstrated a set of likely responses to the disappearance of the hegemon using a sort of rational choice logic combined with a mild functionalism or social logic (but which is in fact practical inference).[34] The question here, however, is the way regimes relate to different states' overall governing tasks, not merely their foreign policies.

When we ask this question, we should note first of all that regimes may be differentiated by the very different gifts they bestow. Some provide aid and trade packages to reward and redistribute. Some maintain the capacity to be a state (by the actual financing of a state apparatus). Some enhance predictability, while others enlarge political scope (the legalization of new matter; see Chapter 5) and enhance the legal capacity of states by, for example, making enforcement a matter of international obligation. There is no simple generalizable fact about regimes, such that we may deduce similar consequences from them, at least from the point of view of state logic and state withering.[35]

Aid and trade packages were particularly valuable to new states in their newness, allowing them sources of reward and considerable choice in the distribution of that reward; that is, either to heavily reward the few or more lightly reward the many. Even given the restrictions imposed, these states were well served by such aid and trade regimes, in their logic as new states. They provided valuable resources in winning new loyalties and could be used to differentially reward loyalists and to punish. Equally, we may suppose that, if the new cooperative spirit between multinational companies and Third World governments leads to a wide variety of private financing, these benefits will accordingly lose value, particularly given the increasing restrictions being placed upon them by the World Bank and the International Monetary Fund (IMF). (The fact that states stop quarrelling about IMF terms, or stop quarrelling so bitterly, is not an indication of less salience, but rather that their requirements are being met in other ways.)

To achieve the benefits, states had to agree certain conditions, such as open trading regimes. But such regimes did not necessarily demand that there be, accordingly, less state. In the early stages of state liberation, a favoured ideology of development allowed a wide scope to planning, and indeed state interference, with the consequence that such regimes provided goods to a wide range of states, supporting, in fact, a whole variety of state–society bargains or repression–consent mixtures, at virtually the receiving state's own choosing – a crucial benefit, which may explain why so little fuss was made about conditionality upon independence. Open liberal orders and markets were precisely not a cost that had to be paid to receive such aid. The cost, if there was one, was the continuation of foreign-based enterprises or ex-colonial economic activity. But such continuation was seldom a real cost to a new state, since there was often little resource to take them over or little talent at home to run them, with the result that resources of employment, tax and social capacity would have been lost. Moreover, few new states had any real appetite for extensive social experiments, because few could have managed the repression capacity required by them. Developing countries had a good bargain in that they were in effect paid to allow what many would have been forced, by their own state logic, to concede anyway.

In marginal cases, however, the case is not so clear. One may speculate that the Ivory Coast or Senegal, without such external sources of aid, might have been pushed into economic closure or forms of state socialism to achieve a redistribution effect. In these circumstances, aid did promote 'open orders' and, consequently, 'less state', since they allowed for externally financed rewards, minimizing pressures for internal redistribution to do the job.

In this respect, we may comprehend the wish of states to have more latitude in the use of aid funds, in the form of untied aid, for example, or claims of economic sovereignty. All of these widen the choice of whom to benefit. The claims that such allowances would produce irresponsible behaviour, allow for widening graft or produce uneconomic development projects, may all be very true, but also irrelevant. From the point of view of the logic of a state, such widenings are beneficial; for, the wider a state's choices, the more it may serve its own interests.

The 'large' regimes, the General Agreement on Tariffs and Trade (GATT) and the IMF, are differentially related to a variety of domestic social mixes and governing tasks, with governments who exploit their provisions in a variety of ways to suit their tasks. One example must suffice. The US Federal Government, with little direct command over the economy and little popular appetite for governmental control, has a governing mix which turns on heavily repressing the more than a few and lightly rewarding less than the very many. In de Jasay's typology, it is the representative, the only mildly adversarial, and the only occasionally redistributive. That mix obviates deep or uniform intervention in the economy. The IMF structure, combined with the dollar–gold link, allowed the costs of economic adjustment to be exported, preserving American standards of living long after the condition of the economy dictated their lowering.[36] It was also part of this particular state logic, that when the external discipline of maintaining the IMF regime began to demand internal economic reform, for such was the issue when other states began to refuse to receive US-exported (and gradually increasing) costs, the USA cut the link; and in 1971, turned to enhance internal redistribution of a mild sort, to benefit exporters by the imposition of temporary tariffs, at little cost, so it emerged. (It should be recalled that changing statuses provides opportunities to win new friends, for such moments signal the redrafting of the social contract. The subsequent fate of the IMF regime is, also, a warning against supposing that such regimes have fixed statuses.)

Such regimes do have unintended consequences. One important such consequence is the creation of international secretariats and their transformation into new political actors with their own logic. These secretariats remain closely connected to the rationales of the states that founded them, but are never completely identified with them, since their regimes have demands and a logic of their own. Negotiating such regimes also involves states in a certain game logic which, in turn, effects social bargains and pushes them to less state. Were states to engage in long-term fixed legal relationships with states which control the entire social product, the balance in such regimes would prefer the larger, more extensive states. It is only by either privatizing or internationalizing that some equalization between partners can be achieved, since this removes some state capacity. For example, in the progress toward European union, states are always pushed into handing prerogatives either to the bureaucracy or to the market, and this is because the alternative would involve handing them to another state.

It is important to note, however, that no state abrogates powers to such regimes, not even to the extensive legal regime of the European Community. Since the state is logically a corporate person of will who wills its own preferences, it always retains the notional choice to withdraw, and if that choice is, from moment to moment, 'unreal' or unlikely, it is only contextually so. Should the context change, by for example another widened political framework with new goals (as has been suggested might occur with the institution of a 'common European home') which coincided with another definition of state, a 'national state' or a redistributive state or the pure market economy state, whose aims might be achieved through special bilateral relations or a looser and wider order, a state might very well decide that the inconveniences of membership outweigh the benefits, and no-one should be surprised to find that, given a new context with new choices, such a state or states would encounter few obstacles, and particularly few socially determined obstacles, in making new arrangements.

Common fate

The ecological future is, we are led to understand, a dangerous condition. It is also, however, frequently portrayed as a compellingly coherent condition. In such portrayals, there appears an unavoidable unity between different issue areas, as the multiple and interrelated sources of change in the environment are identified, producing one package of interrelated issues. A deepening crisis, combined with popular pressure on the part of peoples linked by a common fate, will drag the state unavoidably into a range of negotiations with other states to solve ecological problems, negotiations in which all social arrangements must be put on the table. In these negotiations, moreover, low politics will inevitably dominate; their outcome will be deeply affected, if not determined, by scientific and technological criteria; and the community of states will require a new complex level of rational inter-national organizations to monitor and regulate pollutant emissions, check standards and punish offenders. Hence will be laid the foundations of a new world society, out of the requisites of planetary protection.[37] Compelling though this vision may be, however, any comprehension of the logic of a state should lead us to question it in every part.

First, not all states will claim 'green' purposes: this is self-evident, because the political inclination to be green must be differentially related, not only to the level of industrialization, but also to the differential effects for governments more or less reliant on producing or purchasing raw materials. There is also the degree to which any government is seeking to buy consent by policies reliant on industrial development, the type of development and the differential access to the expensive technology on which post-modern industrial production depends. Rather than unity, we had better suppose a number of different axes of dissent.

Moreover, while many will wish to negotiate, because some potential and important long-term benefits may be gained by foregoing short-term advantage, each has a number of negotiating choices and potential points of policy compromise, along each axis, which multiply by the variety of their situations. That is, the condition of all states as a group and the multiple considerations present in green issues may be expected to produce multiple negotiations along a variety of choice axes. Governments may move on all these issues, but in no predictable, uniform or consensus manner, and with no single table or agenda.

In addition, it should be recalled, 'green' involves a slow down in the use of resources and raises the prospect of freezes at different levels of development. Moreover, some of the most crucial green decisions will affect, and must be affected by the governments of, poor populations. (Brazilian rain forests are, after all, in Brazil.) Accordingly, we must question the logical postulate of common fate, as well as that of some consequent uniform popular pressure. Populations may rather be expected to divide on the benefits of being green and in different respects. Indeed, because there are differential gains and losses in the green game, we should expect complex accounts of who really benefits and by what routes, either in becoming or in resisting greenness, and a good deal of mutual suspicion of motives, both domestic and international, at both popular and élite levels. In the circumstances, it would scarcely be 'illogical' for governments to resist, and not only because of sensitive resource questions. Certainly, we should expect that if they do, they will not be wanting support, popular as well as élite, and may play such support against their negotiating partners (or back into the domestic political arena, and in respect of quite different issues) as the logic of their situations dictate.

Even for those who adopt green (and we can expect that in the variety of Western democratic party systems which depend on co-optation of issues, green will be adopted), the road will scarcely be an easy one. There is not only the phenomenon of claiming to be green as opposed to being it, but we may expect even 'sincere' green negotiators to wish to concentrate on different issues with different degrees of commitment, depending on strategic assessments, sensitive resources questions, the strength of the political constituency being wooed and, above all, the relation of green issues to other issue areas and putative constituencies.

The latter consideration is a particularly delicate one. Green issues are translated into Western political arenas essentially through party politics and the party process of co-operation, and thus affect intimate inner-party balances as well as inter-party rivalry. Both are, then, highly sensitive to context and to intricate calculations of advantage. A recent account by Claus Offe concerning the modality of a potential translation of green issues into central issues of Western German party politics is illustrative: he proposes a declining traditional social democratic constituency of party workers and trade unions, and a shift to incorporate a new rising constituency of the middle class and ecologically sensitive, which in turn alters the boundary of political concerns.[38] This account, which depends upon a gradual decline in the salience of traditional trade union concerns, was written before the incorporation of East Germany into the Federal Republic. The latter not only raises questions concerning the incorporation of the East German labour force and the terms of that incorporation, it may also be expected to change the parameters of the green debate. It cannot be expected, after all, that the same standards of industrial cleanliness that West Germany might have supported before East Germany joined it can now be entertained, and a backward region within a country raises, and in a more pertinent way (since East Germans are now voters), the same questions concerning the *qui bono*, as between states at different levels of development.

The idea that green issues constitute a single undifferentiated low politics issue area about to claim the high ground of political debate is also very misleading. Where green issues touch on energy questions, consumption and production, this is not low politics but high politics, involving the entire economic and social life of the nation and constituting a central strategic issue for the state. Moreover, it is child's play to distinguish the relative sensitivity and salience, from the point of view of the logic of a state, as between reducing energy consumption by so many percentiles and conserving herring shoals. These issues are not only divisible, they have been divided. It is no accident, as Morgenthau would say, that the first subject of green politics to enter the high ground of negotiations between states has been fuel and energy consumption. Moreover, the issue is being negotiated in isolation from other green questions, and because of its salience. The idea that green politics must bring to the negotiating table a host of social matters which, because of their inherent technical or 'organic' linkages, must be treated together, should therefore be rejected.

The dynamics of green politics do empower technocrats and scientists. They also highlight the importance of reliable scientific and technical information, and make neutral and unbiased information valuable, empowering those who speak from apparently neutral and unbiased positions. (Though, while entertaining the scientizing of politics, we should also consider the politicizing of science.) They also, however, empower the state. And if some mythical functional opposition is to be proposed between these two, the state's empowerment must surely be the more substantial.

First, we must presume green politics are directed towards new policies and legislative programmes. Accordingly, they widen the scope of the state and its legislative prerogatives, across previously virgin territory. They are also about standards and the allocation of costs and burdens. In our subjective age, the state is the only authoritative allocator of value, and government the only authoritative standard setter. Who else will monitor, intervene, redistribute, cajole, convince and enforce, besides setting standards? If, moreover, green issues require deeper penetration into the social base, that will only serve to take government penetration deeper. To suppose that green politics decrease either the salience or the scope of the state is very mistaken; on the contrary, they increase both, dramatically. Moreover, the range of potential standards is quite large and variable, depending on the precise criteria of safety or cleanliness to be adopted, giving each state considerable scope to choose the standards that suit it, to be determined by what it deems necessary to any present political requirement. And if we understand that autonomy consists in widened choice, then they enhance its autonomy as well.

That a world society waits on the other side of green is also to be rejected as a tenable postulate. Green issues raise every question of picking sides and redistribution between states to be sure, as every agency on the sacrificing end of a green claim has made clear. But international redistribution requires no less state than any other form of redistribution. Were green to take off internationally, it would require at the very least the adversarial and more likely the redistributive. It would require more state, not less.

Notes

1 Compare Sidney Bailey *The Framework of International Society* (Longman, 1935) with James Rosenau 'International Studies in a Transnational World' *Millennium, Journal of International Studies* 5, 1 (1976) pp. 1–20.
2 John Hertz *International Politics in the Atomic Age* (New York, Columbia University, 1959).
3 Notably, Robert Keohane and Joseph Nye eds *Transnational Relations and World Politics* (Cambridge, Mass., Harvard University, 1972).
4 Anne de Julius *Global Companies and Public Policy* (Pinter for the RIIA, 1990); for a clear account of the changing fashion with regard to the state among political economists, see J.J. Biersteker 'The Limits of State Power' in P.G. Brown and H. Shue eds *Boundaries* (Tolowa, N.J., Rowman and Littlefield, 1981) pp. 147–76.
5 See, e.g. S.D. Krasner *Structural Conflict: The Third World Against Global Liberalism* (Berkeley, University of California, 1985), and R. Gilpin *The Political Economy of International Relations* (Princeton University, 1987), each of whom finds the state has continued uses.
5 The latest examinaton of functionalist analysis, with warts, is Jon Elster *Explaining Technical Change* (Cambridge University, 1983).
7 *State and Revolution* (Martin Lawrence, 1933); see David Lane *Leninism* (Cambridge University, 1981) for a recent exegesis.
8 A catalogue of accounts of the various forms of capitalism the state preserves, and the many ways it does so, is provided by R.A. Corman ed. *Biographical Dictionary of Neo-Marxism* (Westport, Conn., Greenwood, 1985); Hertz's rethink is in 'The Territorial State Revisited' *Polity* 1, 1 (1968) pp. 12–34.
9 Kenneth Arrow *Social Choice and Individual Values* (New York, John Wiley, 1951).
10 Abram Bergson 'On the Concept of Social Welfare' *Quarterly Journal of Economics* 65 (1954) p. 242 [emphasis added].

11 Responding to the claim that selling the Soviet Union wheat deprived it of its gold reserves, and hence weakened the Soviet state, Professor Peter Wiles of the London School of Economics observed, 'But if the Soviet Union prefers wheat to gold, then wheat must be more important to it than gold.'

12 A.W. Hirschmann *National Power and the Structure of Foreign Trade* (University of California, 1945) pp. 13–34.

13 H.G. Johnson *Economic Nationalism in Old and New States* (Chicago University, 1967), and S. Kuznets *Modern Economic Growth: Rate, Structure and Spread* (New Haven, Conn., Yale University, 1966).

14 Anthony de Jasay *The State* (Oxford, Blackwell, 1985); it provides a logic of state growth as well.

15 Bertrand de Jouvenal *Power, the Natural History of its Growth* (Hutchinson, 1948). The general neglect of de Jouvenal by contemporary political scientists may reflect a distaste for the unintentional as it affects political control, but we must not be swayed by such ideological concerns, particularly if our subject is withering, and its prospects. He was also looking at developments for the modern state, which makes him more suitable for our purposes than that other perhaps better known grammarian, the courtier of Florence.

16 Gianfranco Poggi *The Development of the Modern State* (Stanford University, 1978) pp. 101–7.

17 The necessity for capital, given growth policies, is emphasized throughout the literature: see J.N. Behrman *National Interests and the Multinational Enterprises* (Englewood Cliffs, N.J., Prentice-Hall, 1970) pp. 13–31; access to knowledge and technology has been rated even higher by A.E. Safarian *Foreign Ownership of Canadian Industry* (Toronto, McGraw-Hill, 1966) p. 188.

18 These problems are discussed by a large literature; for a succinct account, see Neil Hood and Stephen Young *The Economics of the Multinational Enterprise* (Longman, 1979).

19 Prominent advice givers in the literature include Paul Streeten 'The Theory of Development Policy' in J.H. Dunning ed. *Economic Analysis and the Multinational Enterprise* (New York, Praeger, 1973) pp. 252–79; see also J.H. Behrman 'The Multinational Company and the Nation-States: Another View' in G. Paquet ed. *The Multinational Firm and the Nation State* (Canada, Collier-Macmillan, 1972) and 'Multinational Companies and Sovereignty' in Courtnay Brown ed. *World Business* (New York, Macmillan, 1970).

20 Steppan's prognostication that 'the growth of multinationals may well help generate in some countries normative and administrative pressures to create mechanisms to control multinationals . . . [and] the rise of countervailing bureaucracies in which the state will play a key role' is logically well-founded; A. Steppan *The State and Society: Peru in Contemporary Perspective* (Princeton University, 1978) p. 235. T.H. Moran 'Multinational Companies and Dependency' *International Organisation* 32, 1 (1978) pp. 82–4, has outlined a state learning curve. On lessons learnt, see Osvaldo Sunkel 'Big Business and Dependencia' *Foreign Affairs* 50, 3 (1972) pp. 517–31.

21 For details, see Bharat Ram 'India Sets the Guidelines for Foreign Investment' *Columbia Journal of World Business* 5 (1970).

22 Note the conclusion of the Gray report (Canada, Information, *Foreign Direct*

Investment in Canada), that 'governmental machinery should be established with wide powers to regulate foreign investment'. The Canadian Government simultaneously announced the Foreign Take-Overs Review Bill, giving itself powers to regulate take-overs as they affected its 'key' sectors, railways, financial institutions and institutions subject to federal jurisdiction; W.R. Hahlo, J. Graham Smith and W. Wright *Nationalism and the Multinational Enterprise* (Leiden, Sitzhoff, 1973) p. 52. In his case study of the Peruvian military junta's nationalization of IPC, A.J. Pinelo observes that 'a gigantic paycheck of national political good will awaited the "vindicator" of the property': *The Multinational Corporation as a Force in Latin American Politics* (New York, Praeger, 1973) p. 150.

23 It was this development, combined with the entry of even more multinationals into the 'market for space' which led Fred Bergson to announce that 'sovereignty is no longer at bay': 'Coming Investment Wars' *Foreign Affairs* **53**, 1 (1975) p. 138.

24 Note the very different goals the various ASEAN states have set: Corazon Siddayau *ASEAN and the Multinational Companies* (Singapore, Institute of South East Asian Studies, 1978).

25 Hirschmann is essentially using such a variable (op. cit., note 12). Other exceptions are Joel Midgal *Strong Societies and Weak States* (Princeton University, 1988) pp. 93–5, 125 and 192–9, with reference to Sierra Leone and Egypt and Biersteker, who notes that 'only those nations with the least integration and hence the least internal opposition to disengagement can initiate a national strategy of self-reliance' (op. cit., note 4, p. 169).

26 T.J. Biersteker 'Self-reliance in Theory and Practice in Tanzanian Trade Relations' *International Organization* **34**, 2 (1980) pp. 229–64, also analyses the difficulties the Tanzanian Government has faced.

27 H. Johnson 'The Multinational Company as an Agency of Economic Development' in B. Ward, J.P. Runnals and Lenore d'Anjou *The Widening Gap* (New York, Columbia University, 1971) pp. 24–52.

28 Anthony Sampson *The Sovereign State: The Secret History of ITT* (Hodder and Stoughton, 1973) p. 271, notes, in consequence, that 'their role as barrier-breakers is much less sure than it was a decade ago'.

29 Reza T. Bassiry *Power vs. Profit* (New York, Arno, 1980) pp. 152–68, has a good discussion of joint ventures, the usual legal form for multinationals in socialist economies, and their compatibility with 'the Plan'; see P. Gutman and F. Arkwright 'Multinationalization and the Countries of Eastern Europe' in G. Modelski ed. *Transnational Companies and World Order* (New York, W.H. Freeman, 1979) pp. 209–11, on their use by the Soviet Union.

30 R. Vernon *Big Business and the State* (Cambridge, Mass., Harvard University, 1974) and W.H. Goldberg *Governments and Multinationals* (Cambridge, Mass., Oelgeschlager, 1983) pp. 316–17.

31 For what governments chose during the recession of the 1970s, see S. Strange 'The Management of Surplus Capacity: Or How Does Theory Stand up to Protectionism, 1970's Style' *International Organization* **33**, 3 (1979) p. 332.

32 Note Neil Hood and Stephen Young, op. cit., note 18, p. 195.

33 Steven Krasner 'State Power and the Structure of the International System' *World*

Politics **28**, 3 (1976) pp. 317–47; R. Gilpin *U.S. Power and the Multinational Corporation* (New York, Basic Books, 1975). See also Steven Krasner ed. *International Regimes* Ithaca, N.Y., Cornell University, 1983) for a variety of states-and-regimes analysis.

34 R. Keohane *After Hegemony* (Princeton University, 1984). Jon Elster, op. cit., note 6, laid out the requisites for a proper functional explanation, which he distinguishes from intentionality, and one of whose key features is non-consciousness concerning outcomes. Keohane's argument for a likely continuation of regimes, and their elaboration, is based on a conscious understanding by states of theirs and society's needs, i.e. on a type of intentional behaviour. This particular species of intentionalism, often confused with functionalism, is called practical inference.

35 Regime analysts tend not to differentiate among regimes, even those who see regimes as politically useful to states. They adduce a general regime tendency, such that all rise or fall together; see, e.g. Oran Young 'Regime Dynamics: The Rise and Fall of International Regimes' in Steven Krasner ed. *International Regimes* (Ithaca, N.Y., Cornell University, 1983) pp. 93–113.

36 Peter Katzenstein has distinguished states who export the costs of adjustment, states which pre-empt them and states who must simply live with them; he believes the US no longer has the power to export nor the policy instruments or internal domestic command to pre-empt: *Small States in World Markets* (Ithaca, N.Y., Cornell University, 1985) pp. 1–31.

37 For example, Richard Falk *This Endangered Planet* (New York, Random House, 1971) and Jan Schneider *World Public Order of the Environment* (Toronto University Press, 1979).

38 Claus Offe 'Challenging the Boundaries of Institutional Politics: Social Movements Since the 1960's' in Charles Maier ed. *The Changing Boundaries of the Political* (Cambridge University, 1987) pp. 100–1.

9

Hegel, Civil Society and the State

John Charvet

The contemporary rediscovery of the autonomy of the state carries with it implicitly or explicitly a distinction between state and society – between the specialized political institutions of a collection of people on the one hand and the economic and social institutions of that same collection on the other hand. The state's autonomy is, in part, its autonomy *vis-à-vis* other states. But such power of independent action in the international sphere is a dimension of the autonomy that is the concern of this chapter – the domestic autonomy of the state in relation to its own society. Because state and society would appear to be bound together as the institutions of the same collection of people, the domestic autonomy of the state cannot be that of an external power in relation to its society, for that would involve denying any unity to the two elements. The problem, then, that the distinction between state and society creates, is how to differentiate them so as to allow for their relative independence of action and at the same time how to comprehend them as an essential unity. Because such an understanding is precisely what Hegel offers in his conception of ethical life, it would seem helpful to pay close attention to what Hegel has to say on the matter.

From one point of view, civil society in Hegel's thought is an aspect or dimension of the state. From another point of view, civil society and state are different but interdependent sets of institutions. The former standpoint involves an understanding of the state in a wide sense to mean an independent ethical community governing itself through specialized political institutions. The latter standpoint limits the meaning of the term state to the specialized political institutions. The differentiation of civil society from state in the narrow sense arises from Hegel's incorporation into his political philosophy of liberal principles enjoining respect for individual rights to life, liberty, property and contract. The economic and social life of the community has to be organized through the exercise by individuals of such rights. A boundary, then, arises between socio-economic and political matters in the same manner as in classical liberal theory. Yet the result in Hegel's philosophy is very different because of his underlying holism which turns the liberal principles into subordinate forms necessary for the ethical community to achieve full self-determination.

The ethical community

An ethical community is in its ethical aspect a system of rights and duties, and in its communal aspect it is such a system understood as expressing the good of a whole. The ethical order is thus not an abstract set of rules valid for individuals as such, but what Hegel calls a *Sittlichkeit*, the way of life of a people. The system of rights and duties specifies a person's place in and contribution to the whole, so that in adhering to it the individual thinks of himself and his good not as an abstract individual, but as a member of a whole.

Hegel calls such an ethical community an 'ethical substance' of which the individual members are accidents. By substance, he means an independent or self-subsistent entity, but it is at the same time a mental substance or mind, so that it exists as a subjective consciousness.[1] It does so in the consciousness of its members as members of the whole, in so far as they identify themselves and their good with the good of the whole. What is the relation to the objective ethical order of the communal mind? It is the form through which in domestic affairs this mind realizes is good. But as a particular individual entity in relation to other such ethical substances, it may find its existence threatened by their actions, and then the rights of individual members and lesser associations as specified in the ethical order may have to be sacrificed in the struggle for existence of the whole.

The communal mind is not, of course, something external to the individual member. It is identical with his consciousness as a member of the whole. But any particular individual in thinking of himself as a member of the whole is thinking of himself as member of an entity that transcends his particular existence. As a particular individual he is, thus, an 'accident' of the ethical substance which is the whole.[2] Yet in so far as he wills the good of the whole in doing his duty by the ethical order, the communal mind is present in his will. It is identical with his will. He thus raises himself out of his particular limited nature and fulfils his potentiality as ethical being.[3]

However, for the individual to achieve his liberation in this manner, he must know that the ethical order is just the communal mind's self-formation and that the communal mind is his mind as member. In the simplest, most immediate forms of ethical community this knowledge is not present. The individual can know these truths only if he can distance himself from the community by calling in question its norms, make valid claims for himself on his own account, and thereby come to see that these claims must be grounded not in his separate individual nature, but his nature as an ethical or communal being. In other words, the individual must come to believe that value inheres in himself as an individual in order to arrive at the realization that it inheres in him fully only as an ethical, i.e. communal, being, only in so far as his will is a communal will. He cannot immediately grasp this truth, since he can learn to act morally only through learning how to behave in accordance with a way of life that appears to him to contain absolutely valid requirements independently of his will. He unreflectively identifies his own good with the good of the ethical order and that good with the good of his community. But the ethical order seems to him to be something given, established by the Gods, and not the product of his own nature.[4]

The rise of individualism

Hegel believed that the naîve, unreflective form of ethical community was perfectly realized in the Greek city-states and that this ethical order was in fact destroyed by the rise of individualist ideas, which over many centuries developed into modern liberal conceptions of the nature of the individual and his relation to the state.[5] Individualism for Hegel has two fundamental aspects. First, it is the idea of what Hegel calls independent or abstract personality. This is the view that value inheres in the individual as a separate unit, or in other words that the individual person is essentially a free being and as such has rights. These are the natural rights to life, liberty, property and contract. Secondly, it is the idea of subjective freedom. By this, Hegel means the view that the individual is not in fact *adequately* free merely as a person with rights, because he may not have taken responsibility for his will and adequately formed his natural impulses and desires in accordance with what he recognizes to be good. According to this view, the individual is free only in so far as he is *self*-determining. He has, accordingly, a right to form himself by normative requirements which he can recognize to be valid. This right transforms all aspects of ethical life: in marriage it introduces the principle of the free choice of partners; in civil society it takes shape as the right to find one's satisfaction and welfare in one's work; and in the state it is the basis of the ordinary man's participation in politics, giving him the right to form himself in accordance with his recognition of the common good as his good.[6]

That it is possible for a distance to emerge between an individual and the *Sittlichkeit* of his people is because a people or nation is itself only a vehicle of cosmic mind, and individuals are always more than mere embodiments of a national mind. Since the object of cosmic mind is self-knowledge as the ultimate ground and purpose of the rational forms in and through which the worlds of nature and human history exist, and since the primitive ethical community cannot immediately know itself (through the consciousness of its members) as the ground and purpose of the ethical forms of its existences, but attributes those to an external authority, the immediate unity of the individual with his community must be destroyed in the course of history through the emergence of individualist thinking.

Individualism and the ethical community

Hegel's aim, then, is to show how individualism in respect of its claims regarding abstract personality and subjective freedom is true and that its rights must be recognized, and yet how it can be fully grasped only as forms through which an ethical whole realizes itself. The argument of the Philosophy of Right purports to be the proof of this thesis.[7] The proof accepts the initial individualist standpoint in free personality and takes the form of showing how the freedom that the individual claims for himself as a separate unit can in fact be adequately achieved only through his self-determination as a member of an ethical whole. This conclusion does not, however, involve the cancellation of the individual's claims to enjoy rights as a person and a subject. It is supposed to reveal how such rights are necessary conditions for the individual to realize his nature as free being through his self-consciousness as the vehicle through which the ethical whole achieves an adequate self-determination.

The initial standpoint of natural rights individualism is then that the individual is a free being as a separate unit and as such has negative rights to life, liberty, property and contract. Of course, he has rights as such a being only if all other such beings have the same rights. So we can say that his having a right is *relative* to the rule of natural law: be a person and respect others as persons. But if this is a normative order, it is not the order of a community. In it individuals are independent units and have no notion of a common standpoint or the good of the whole.

Each individual, understood and understanding himself as immediately free, thinks that he is free in acting in accordance with his desires, by translating his desires into appropriations of the world which become manifestations of his free will in the world. In this sense, he does not form his desires by his rational will in accordance with a conception of the good, but supposes that he is free in whatever he puts his will into in an immediate way. The unsatisfactoriness of this conception of the freedom of the individual lies in the fact that it comes into contradiction with the rule of natural law, that in the exercise of one's will one must respect the equal rights of others, and hence with the requirement that one form one's desires to accord with the normative order of right. However, this is also to say that one is free not immediately but only *mediately* through the self-formation of one's will by the principle of right.

Self-formation in accordance with right is nothing other than self-determination, because the principle which forms the content of one's will is the expression of one's free nature in universal form – be a person and respect others as persons. The content of the will is determined by the principle of the free will itself and not by the particular desires, impulses, etc., which arise in the individual in the course of nature.[8]

We have thus arrived at the idea of subjective freedom, the conception of the individual as really free only in so far as he is self-determining. Of course, the content of the will should conform to what is morally good, but this must not be seen as an external principle to which the will must subordinate itself, for if the subject is to be free the morally good must be the product of the individual's own will.[9] Furthermore, although the standpoint of independent personality has been transcended, the new conception of freedom cannot sensibly be understood to involve the abandonment of the rights of the individual as person. The morally good must encompass respect for persons and their rights.

It was asserted earlier that subjective freedom involves the right of the individual to find his particular satisfaction in action, as well as the rights of the self-determining moral conscience. This right to *particular satisfaction* is an essential element in the Hegelian notion of civil society and ensures that it is not simply a version of the classical liberal idea. Members of civil society have, according to Hegel, a right to particular welfare, that is to say a right to find in the exercise of their rights as a person the attainment of their welfare. The right to particular satisfaction arises from the fact that self-determining action at this stage is the action of a particular individual, who is still understood as an essentially independent unit. The self-determining particular individual necessarily aims at his own welfare by attempting to fulfil the needs and interests of his particular personality. In this way, he seeks and has a right to seek his particular satisfaction in his self-determining action.

The particular individual must nevertheless have as his aim not his own good alone but the general good. Yet this general good is to be determined by each individual himself. In this individualist form, the morally good, Hegel claims, is an empty, abstract notion. It cannot yield any specific system of rights and duties which could be the basis and content of individuals' ethical lives. There is no way for the individual from an independent subjective standpoint to determine what the morally good requires, and the consequence can be only that the content of the subjective will is established arbitrarily by some non-moral motive presenting itself as the morally good will.[10]

Subjective freedom and objective good

This is the crucial point of transition in Hegel's thought from the individualist to the holistic standpoint. The idea of subjective freedom according to Hegel is the idea of a free will which wills only what it recognizes to be good. This good must be objective, for it cannot be anything that the subjective will arbitrarily thinks to be good, and yet be nothing other than the determination of the will's own nature. In other words, there is contained in this idea an identity of objective good and subjective will. Hegel claims that this idea is in fact that of ethical life. Ethical life or *Sittlichkeit* is the notion of an objective ethical order – an established system of rights and duties constituting a way of life for a people and recognized by them to be the good or the right way to live – which realizes itself through subjective wills, or in other words by human beings who identify their good with living such a life. Once individualism makes its appearance in the form of the individual's belief that he is essentially free, the naïve ethical community is disrupted. The individual claims that a normative order, which is a legitimate ethical community to which he is under obligation, must recognize his rights as a person and a subject. This is the point at which individualism and its rights are to be incorporated into an encompassing holism. Hegel accepts that the individual is essentially free. But, as we have seen, this freedom can be understood ultimately only in terms of the self-conscious identity of his subjective will with the objective ethical order. In the naïve ethical community, the individual's will is in fact that through which the ethical order realizes itself. But this identity of his will with the ethical order is not consciously apprehended. The individual loves the ethical order as his substance, since he identifies his moral being with it, but he thinks of its source as lying outside himself in the form of a given order established by the gods. In the mediated modern ethical order, the individual knows that the ethical substance is his own nature as free will, so that he is most completely free in identifying his will with the good of the whole. In so far as his will is the impersonal will of the ethical order, it is the whole coming to self-conscious expression in him.

Hegel's reconciliation of individualism and holism depends on the claim that the culmination of the potentiality for ethical freedom in the modern state's identification of the member's subjective will with the ethical order is possible only through the development of the individual's self-understanding as a free being as a person and a subject. Thus the perfected ethical order must contain within itself the individualist forms corresponding to the rights of personality and subjectivity. Only by learning to distance himself from the community and to cultivate his separate particular individuality can he arrive at the understanding of his freedom as identical with the self-determination of the ethical order.

Civil society

Civil society, then, is that dimension of the ethical order in which the rights of personality and subjectivity are organized into legal and institutional forms. These rights are, of course, only elements in the ethical order. They are not absolute rights of individuals independent of an ethical substance. Yet they are the necessary forms through which ethical freedom is perfected.

Hegel's conception of civil society, then, is that of a partial organization of an ethical community which allows and encourages the members to develop their separate individuality by giving them rights to pursue their particular interests without regard to the general good. At the same time, the justification for these rights is ultimately a holistic rather than an individualistic one, and it requires that the rights be constrained in such a way that their exercise leads individuals towards an understanding of the place and functioning of their rights in the life of the ethical whole. This will enable the individual to learn to associate the pursuit of his particular interest in accordance with his rights with its contribution to the satisfaction of the interests of others and the prosperity of the whole. This development of the individual's ethical understanding within civil society requires the existence of institutions which serve this purpose and thereby mediate between the extreme individualist standpoint of civil society, namely exclusive private interest, and the holistic standpoint of the state directed at the common good. Without such mediating institutions, civil society and state will be organized on radically antithetical principles which demand the complete separation of the two spheres and which render the scheme, conceived as a whole, incoherent.

What are these mediating institutions? In the first place, relations between private persons seeking their own good in a market society should not be seen as necessarily exclusively egoistic, as though the pursuit by each of his own interest was incompatible with his having an interest in the interest of those with whom he interacts in the market. In fact, through the system of market interdependence, each can satisfy his own ends only by contributing to the satisfaction of the ends of others.[11] This is, of course, to be taken only as a tendency of the system and not as an expression of its perfect harmony. But it means that it is not necessary to attribute to market actors a purely non-tuist motivation,[12] and there is no absolute opposition between private self-seeking and concern for the interest of others. Thus the market dimension of civil society should not be seen as wholly antagonistic to motivations which include the good of others and hence is not inherently in contradiction with the holistic principle of the state.

Nevertheless, if market actors are purely individual atoms in competitive interaction, it will be unlikely for tuist inclinations to be much more than superficial wishes for the prosperity of others. If the capacity for tuist motivation is to be developed, it must be supported by institutions which directly promote more ethical attitudes in the individual. Hegel thinks that this purpose is fulfilled by the classes into which civil society is formed in the course of its growth. There are three classes: the agricultural class, the business class and the class of civil servants. Membership of a class is determined by the type of work in which the individual engages, not by his wealth or relation to the means of production. Hegelian classes are more like medieval estates and make no distinction between owners and workers, employers and employees.[13]

Classes are functional groups whose activity is necessary for the good of the whole, and the individual who becomes a member of such a class through his own efforts and choice of career thereby achieves status and dignity in civil society and participates in the particular spirit and way of life of his class. The way in which this ethical education of the individual takes place varies according to the class. The agricultural class, on the one hand, not being directly drawn into the instability of market competition, is part of an older way of life founded on the family in which the spirit of individualism is barely developed. Families are themselves partial ethical orders, so that the individual member of the agricultural class is ethically formed through his participation in the family farm. The class of civil servants, on the other hand, is immediately concerned with the administration of law and policies directed at the common good, and so the individual member finds his particular satisfaction in explicit service to the community. It is the business class whose spirit is particularly governed by market individualism and hence it is this class which is especially in need of institutions for the ethical education of its members. This is carried out by corporations which are organizations of the different branches of industry and commerce on the basis of their common interests. Hegelian corporations are supposed to control entry into, and the conditions for carrying on, a trade and to act as welfare agencies for their members, all under the surveillance of the state. Through membership of a corporation, which Hegel calls an organ of the whole society, the individual learns to identify his interest with that of his group and to understand the functioning of that interest in the whole economy.[14]

The state

Nevertheless, the individual cannot through membership of civil society alone achieve that harmonization of his particular interest with the general good in which full ethical freedom consists. The harmony of civil society depends on the regulation of its affairs through a system of law, through the control of corporations, and by the pursuit of general policies directly concerned with the general welfare. In other words, civil society would not of itself, even including the state-enforced law, achieve a general good. The instability of civil society, due to large and rapid market fluctuations, together with the market's tendency to produce unacceptable extremes of wealth and poverty, requires of political actors more than the passive functions attributed to the minimal state. And it is only through participation in the state's activity that the individual can complete the development of his potentiality as a free being.

The state in the narrow sense and in its modern form is the full realization of the ethical idea. Through the state's activity in giving specific determinacy to the ethical order in the form of the institutions of family, civil society and the state itself, the ethical whole determines itself through the wills of its members and knows that it is itself the ground of the objective ethical order. At the same time, its individual members, through their participation in the state's activity and their willing the universal ends of the state as their own ends and aims know that the ethical whole is nothing other than their own substance, so that in willing its good they are determining themselves and fulfilling their nature as free beings (in its practical dimension).[15]

The political institutions through which the ethical idea fully realizes itself is that of a constitutional monarchical government. The monarch is the ultimate embodiment of the self-conscious sovereign will of the ethical whole. The representative institutions consist of an upper house in which the aristocratic members of the agricultural class sit, and a lower house containing those elected by the corporations. The administrative class is, of course, itself an essential part of government. Hegel says that the Estates, by which he means the institutions representing the classes of civil society, are a guarantee of general welfare and public freedom. But this guarantee does not consist in their particular power of insight into these matters, since they are necessarily surpassed in this by the higher civil servants. It consists in the first place in the additional insight they can provide into the way in which the administration of the government's policies bears upon civil society and in keeping government officials up to the mark through public criticism. But secondly, and more importantly, the Estates through the publicity of their debates on public business make it possible for the ordinary member of civil society to come to recognize the common good as his good.[16]

These constitutional ideas in their detail will no doubt be felt to be quite inadequate, but of interest still is Hegel's conception of the appropriate mode of representation of civil society in the state, which is directly relevant to his general notion of the necessary interpretation of these two spheres. As indicated above, Hegel's representative regime is that of a *Ständestaat*. Individuals are to appear in the state through their representatives, not as individual atoms but as member of groups and classes. His objection to an individualist-based system of representation is that this would be to put the many as atomistic units, hence as a formless mass, into the state, the result of which would be 'elementary, irrational, barbarous and frightful'.[17] Already in civil society the individual is present only as a member of a group, while the state is an organization whose parts are not individuals but groups. It is then essential that, to hold civil society and state together while preserving their differentiation, the private judgement and will of individuals which emerges in civil society should be integrally related to the state. This will be achieved in so far as the individual's private interest is formed by his membership of groups which are at the same time the entities through which he is integrated into the state.

I have been describing the state in terms of its internal constitution, but its nature as an independent ethical substance must be understood ultimately in terms of its relation to other states. For the state is essentially one autonomous or sovereign individual among other such individuals, and individuality here means the abstract individuality of the single unit. Hence relations between states necessarily take the form described above in terms of relations between independent persons possessing natural rights. Independent personality involves an *inadequate formation* of the individual's desires and impulses by the normative order of right. The international order on such a principle will therefore be unsatisfactorily rationalized and moralized, and the individual state will be subject to chance events resulting from the arbitrary element in its relations with other states.

Nevertheless, this moment, in which the very existence of the state is potentially under threat by the action of other states, is one in which the state's essential nature as an independent substance of which its individual and group members are accidents is most clearly revealed. For it is the point at which 'its absolute power over against everything individual and particular, against life, property and their rights, even against societies and associations makes the nullity of these finite things an accomplished fact'.[18]

The Hegelian state, then, in the narrow sense and on its domestic side, is essentially active in forming both itself and civil society, since it is the organ of the ethical whole through which the whole gives specific determinacy to its own nature. Is this view of the state of the slightest relevance today?[19] That must depend on whether one is prepared to acknowledge inadequacies in the dominant liberal individualist modes of theorizing and to see something of merit in Hegel's criticism of individualism. The unsatisfactoriness of the liberal view of the state is indeed recognized in contemporary criticisms of pluralism as having no place in its theory for the autonomy of the state in relation to society.

The criticism of pluralism

Pluralism can be seen as a modification of the classical liberal theory of the state. In the latter theory there is a sharp distinction between society and state, but society consists wholly of interactions between private individuals and there are supposed to be no significant or authoritative associations mediating between individual and state. The state exists to supply public goods – primarily law, order and defence – which private initiative cannot produce in sufficient quantity or at all. The state on this view should be essentially neutral between individuals' interests and provide equal protection for their rights. Although the state thus has an important function, it should have at least in regard to domestic affairs no real autonomy from society. It should act as the servant of society by making it possible for the individual members of society to realize their common interests. The liberal constitutional problem is then to design political institutions in such a way that the power political actors need to bring about the common interest will be controlled by the members of society, so that it cannot be used against them in the selfish interests of the rulers.

Classical liberal theory with its abrupt, unmediated distinction between individual and state has difficulty in making coherent the different attitudes and motivations appropriate to private institutions on the one hand and citizens on the other. One way in which this is attempted is through contrivances which align the self-interest of political actors with the pursuit of outcomes which are in the common interest. Nothing other than self-interest would then be required of such agents. Representative democracy is typically seen as such a device for uniting the interest of rulers and ruled and hence of producing the common interest out of self-interest. Even Rousseau's direct democracy, which has many elements in common with what I have called crudely enough classical liberal theory, is presented in this manner.[20]

If such schemes could be realized, they would solve the problem of politics on its domestic side by ensuring that the power of the state can be used only in accordance with its original justification. Pluralism can be seen as the descendant of this theory with the addition of intermediate associations between individual and state. These are interest groups and political parties. On the pluralist view, individuals are related to the state only through such associations. This is, of course, the more realistic view. Yet the basic liberal idea is preserved in so far as on the one hand such associations are seen only as coalitions of individual interest resting on the individual's right of association, and on the other no group or combination of groups comes to dominate the state. In this way, an approximate equality of groups, at least over time, ensures that the state will retain its ultimate neutrality towards the different interests of members of society. The inability of a few associations to acquire a dominant position in controlling the state was supposed to be due to such factors as cross-cutting cleavages, overlapping membership, the voluntary and non-hierarchical nature of associations, and general social mobility.

For pluralists the state is just the arena in which interests aggregated by political parties fight to secure dominance, but, as indicated, because of the design of the system an equilibrium is reached in which no such dominance is achieved. At any rate the policies of the state are merely the product of the pressures generated by interest group politics, and it would appear that the state is simply an instrument of such social pressures with no power of independent initiative. The so-called contemporary rediscovery of the state, then, is the recognition that state actors are in a position to form policies of their own towards interest groups by determining for instance the structure of its relations to those groups and the structure of the relations among the groups themselves. Corporatist practices which, understood in a wide sense to mean the preferential recognition given by government and its departments to some interest groups, are in fact everywhere apparent, and are taken as evidence of such state initiatives.[21]

Let us assume that the state as a matter of fact is active *vis-à-vis* civil society. It could still be the case that liberal individualist theory in one of its versions is ideally correct. It could still describe the conditions under which a state would be legitimate and its subjects would be obliged to obey its commands. Unfortunately, constitutional arrangements hitherto devised in theory or in practice have not succeeded in satisfying those conditions. The consequence would be that such active states lack legitimacy. This is obviously not a satisfactory state of affairs. However, there are various attitudes one can adopt in the face of it, such as seeking further constitutional devices to constrain the state, or resigning oneself to the crookedness of the world and the wickedness of men. One could espouse the view that the source of the state's activity *vis-à-vis* civil society in fact lies outside the domestic realm altogether in the competitive nature of its relations to other states, which forces it to acquire more and more power merely in order to survive, and to penetrate and form civil society in order to expand the basis of its power. The solution to the active state from a liberal point of view would then lie in a reform of the international order in accordance with liberal principles.

But one further possible attitude is that liberal individualist principles involve an incorrect theorizing of the relations between society and state quite independently of the nature of international relations. The relevant theory here is not the so-called empirical theory of political science, but the normative theory of political philosophy, where this is to be understood as an enquiry into the nature or concept of the state in the context of the idea of individual interest, or welfare or the good. In terms of the latter, the problem of the relations between society and state is the problem of political obligation. Given that the idea of the state is that of a person or institution with the ultimate rule-making and rule-enforcing authority over all those inhabiting a certain territory, the question is 'How can such authority exist carrying with it as it does the obligation of its subjects to obey?'

The criticism of contract theory

The traditional or early modern individualist theory of political obligation took the form of contract theory, now recently revived in a more abstract version under the influence of Rawls.[22] According to this theory, the authority of the state and the obligation of its subjects derives from a contract which rational self-interested individuals in a position of approximate equality would enter into in order to create an institution which would promulgate and enforce the rules embodying their common interest. Without the coercive power of the state, individuals in society are unable to enjoy through their spontaneous interaction the benefits of living in accordance with such rules. Such a theory expresses the typical individualist view that the individual and his interests are formed independently of his participation in the order brought about by the state. This produces the crucial liberal problem of requiring at the same time a state with creative power *vis-à-vis* society and a state that is merely the instrument through which the interests of society are given effect in the world.

Hegel rejected contract theory on the grounds that it treated the state as dependent on the arbitrary wills of independent persons, and so made it something external to the individual and contingent.[23] The state in the wide sense is, of course, for Hegel the individual's very substance. He sees the state as the product of individuals' arbitrary wills in contract theory because he treats the contract as a literal and not a hypothetical one. If the right of the state is derived solely from the rights of independent persons to enter into contracts, then because relations between such persons are for Hegel necessarily inadequately rationalized and moralized, the durability of contractual arrangements rests on the continued but contingent agreement of the parties' interests. Hegel may be criticized for not recognizing that the interest of the parties to the social contract are in fact supposed to be their rational interests in a position of approximate equality. This means that the contract is not to be taken literally, but hypothetically, as the contract that rational individuals would make in their own interest under the prescribed ideal conditions. This is indeed the form in which the theory is explicitly presented by Rawls and many other contemporary writers.

In this form, the terms of the contract are what any rational self-interested person would commit himself to whatever his particular, contingent interest because the conditions of service are the same for everyone. The conditions force the individual to universalize his interest, and thus they involve the transcendence of the standpoint of independent personality in Hegelian terms, and the adoption of the standpoint of morality, according to which the individual, in order to be rational, has to will the universal interest. But this is the point at which, instead of founding the contract on the concrete particular interests of independent persons, the theory appeals to an abstract conception of universal interest in a form vulnerable to Hegel's criticism of abstract morality. Indeed, in its hypothetical version, the contractual element is really redundant, the whole weight of the argument resting on the essentially moral and not self-interested requirement to subject one's particular interest to the demands of universality.

The criticism of Hegel

To follow along this road is to go in the direction in which Hegel's argument points. But, it may be said, can't we see all too clearly the end of this road in the idea of ethical substances of which individuals are accidents, a view to which liberal individualism, with all its incoherences, is vastly preferable? Is the idea of ethical substance so objectionable?

In so far as it depends in Hegel's thought on the idea of national and ultimately cosmic mind, I do not think that it is either plausible or attractive. The Hegelian view requires us to believe that the ethical idea (the idea of an ethical community) is perfectly embodied in the course of human history and that the vehicles of the realization of successive forms of that idea are national minds.[24] An historic nation such as the Greeks or the Romans took the idea up to a certain point and fulfilled its potentialities in respect of that form, but the inherent inadequacies of the particular form relative to the idea itself ensure the decline of those nations, and the transfer of historical destiny to a new nation. In this course of development, the ultimate driving force is that of the Ethical Idea or cosmic mind in its practical form, since it is only through its embodiment in the consciousness of finite human beings or members of a community that it can come to full knowledge of itself as the being and end of history. Individuals in this view have real value only through being instruments of the self-realization of the idea.

The question is whether we can retain the idea of an ethical community as a system of rights and duties, expressing the good of a whole in which individuals achieve their particular good by doing their duty according to their place in the whole, while abandoning the Hegelian interpretation of the underlying agency involved and understanding the whole simply in terms of an ethical relation between individuals. I believe that this is possible provided that we can accept the following ideas:

1 The good of the whole is nothing but the flourishing of the individual members. The fundamental practical good of an individual is to be a member of such a whole. But he is not essentially a member of any particular whole, and if the whole he actually belongs to is unsatisfactory for him personally or in more general ways, it is his interest and right to seek to transfer to another whole or to tranform his own.

2 The individual has to flourish through contributing to the good of the whole. His flourishing is to be understood in terms of (a) giving his

particular existence an objective value by participating in an ethical whole – his life acquires ethical value – and (b) achieving through his place in the whole the satisfaction of his separate particular interests in a healthy, comfortable and secure life for himself and his family (or hers).

3 Communism is a simple-minded and inadequate understanding of the idea of ethical community. Human beings have the capacity for autonomy – that is to say the formation of their lives in accordance with a conception of the good. It is because of this that their fundamental interest is to make themselves a member of an ethical community, or in other words, to structure their cooperative relations with others by ethical considerations. But to develop in each person this capacity for autonomous self-formation, it is necessary to grant individuals rights to form themselves with direct regard to the common good. Yet through the exercise of such rights, individuals must be led to act in ways which contribute to that good. The elements of a market society are necessary but not sufficient for this purpose, and the ethical order has to be completed through the community's self-determination through its political institutions.

Notes

1 G.W.F. Hegel *The Philosophy of Right (Ph.R)* edited and translated by J.M. Knox (Oxford University, 1952) § 144.
2 *Ph.R.*, § 145.
3 *Ph.R.*, § 152.
4 *Ph.R.*, Addition to § 144.
5 *Ph.R.*, Remark to § 185.
6 *Ph.R.*, Remark to § 124.
7 *Ph.R.*, § 36.
8 *Ph.R.*, § 103.
9 *Ph.R.*, §§ 106–7.
10 *Ph.R.* §§ 133–9. Hegel is attacking in this section the Kantian conception of morality which he sees as an abstract and empty formalism. Since the Kantian categorical imperative provides no criteria for deciding whether something is a duty or not, according to Hegel, its use or justification in fact allows any wrong or immoral conduct to be supported.
11 *Ph.R.*, § 199.
12 Non-tuism is a term developed by economists to express the fundamental assumption that they make about the motivation of market interactors. It is designed to avoid the criticism that such agents are egoists. Thus it is held that the private ends of each agent may be of an altruistic or impersonal nature and not egoistic at all, so long as his end is not to promote the interests of those with whom he is interacting in the market. Hence, non-tuism.
13 *Ph.R.*, § 201–5.
14 *Ph.R.*, §§ 250–6.
15 *Ph.R.*, § 260.

16 *Ph.R.*, § 301.

17 *Ph.R.*, Remark to § 303.

18 *Ph.R.*, § 323. Hegel means that in war states do in fact suspend civil rights, requisition their members' property, and require them to risk their lives in defence of the state, and that these practices are justified.

19 By relevance here I mean significance in terms of philosophical or more narrowly ethical theory. Is this means of theorizing the relation of the individual to the state at all plausible for us? It can, of course, be argued that Hegelian ideas have been very influential in the fields of sociological thought and nationalist practice independently of the question of the continued vitality of Hegelian ethical theory. But nowadays I suspect that most sociologists are not holists at the level of national minds and most nationalists have little to do with Hegel.

20 See, for instance, the characterization of classical democratic theory in J. Schumpeter *Capitalism, Socialism and Democracy* (George Allen & Unwin, revised edition, 1947) Ch.22, and C.B. Macpherson *The Life and Times of Liberal Democracy* (Oxford University, 1977), and innumerable others.

21 See, for instance, the essays in P. Schmitter and G. Lehmbruch eds *Trends towards Corporatist Intermediation* (Sage, 1979) by P. Schmitter, B. Nedelmann and K. Meier, L. Panitsch and G. Lehmbruch. Also the essays by S. Berger and A. Pizzorno in S. Berger ed. *Organizing Interests in Western Europe* (Cambridge University, 1981).

22 J. Rawls *A Theory of Justice* (Oxford University, 1972). See also B. Ackerman *Social Justice in the Liberal State* (New Haven, Yale, 1980) and T. Scanlon 'Contractualism and Utilitarianism' in A. Sen and B. Williams eds *Utilitarianism and Beyond* (Cambridge University, 1982).

23 *Ph.R.*, Remark to § 75.

24 *Ph.R.*, § 344.

10

What Ought to be Done about the Condition of States?

Mervyn Frost

The reader to whom this book is addressed is now less puzzled by the condition of the state in the modern world. A lot has been explained to her. She understands, for example, the conditions under which states in the Third World were established and she understands why so many of these states seem to be the personal fiefdoms of their rulers rather than national states properly so called. She has some insight into the growth of executive power in developed states and appreciates the challenges which this development poses for traditional democratic aspirations. She has seen that more and more demands are being placed upon the state and that states are increasingly unable to satisfy these demands. Thus states seem to face a crisis of legitimacy. Yet despite these insights, we suspect that our reader is still puzzled. She finds it all very well having certain features of the state in the modern world explained to her. It is interesting to have historical and social-scientific explanations provided for the present condition of states. These enable her to understand how and why the state is as it is, but they do not provide an answer to the crucial question, 'What ought we to do about the states in the modern world being in the condition that they are in?'

The question is a general one and encapsulates a host of more specific questions, many of which arise in connection with feelings of puzzlement which the ordinary newspaper reader often experiences.

She feels moral outrage that the controllers of the government apparatus in many Third World states often use it to their own advantage and at the cost of the citizens of those states. In the light of this, she feels that the international rules relating to external sovereignty and non-intervention (which she recognizes as being fundamental to the international community of states) when applied to these states have the effect of protecting an advantage which is used for immoral purposes. Yet, at the same time, she recognizes that these states are for the most part poor and ought to be aided by the developed states. Ought she to favour aid to these states or ought she to favour tough measures against them in order to bring about the democratization of their internal structures?

She sympathizes with the aspirations of various nations striving for statehood – for self-determination – but she feels that their actions in pursuit of these aims are, in many cases, barbaric. What ought she (be she a leader of a state, or citizen, or an academic) to do about such cases?

She knows that states (including her own) have a duty to protect their citizens against external aggression, but she feels acute moral unease about many of the nuclear devices installed by states supposedly to protect national security.

Racism is abhorrent to this reader, but she cannot whole-heartedly support the actions of those who are seeking to end it by force of arms. 'Are you with us or against us?' the anti-racist groups challenge her. She cannot give a clear answer.

In those states in which liberal institutions are at risk, ought she to support armed intervention in support of the crumbling institutions, or, ought she to advocate a policy of allowing people to sort out their own affairs unhindered by foreign intervention?

Our reader recognizes that these problems are pressing ones for which answers must be found. They cannot simply be ignored or returned to on a later occasion. For politicians, bureaucrats, academics, citizens – all of us – are in one way or another called upon to act on these issues. Governments have to make policy decisions. Citizens have to decide which policy decisions to support and which to be critical of. Our reader's problem is that she does not know how to go about finding a solution to these vexing normative problems. No amount of examining the conditions of states (no amount of state pathology) will enable her to answer the general or specific questions mentioned above. No detailed catalogue and examination of the variety of states will move her towards an answer to these questions. The answer will have to come from a moral theory. There is no reason to suppose that it will be an easy or a simple moral theory. Nor can we hope to construct a complete moral theory of international relations in the compass of a short article. The best we can hope to do is give a brief outline of the kind of reasoning that is called for.

The problem of bad states

The puzzlements which we mentioned all involve specific moral claims and counter-claims. Our reader is familiar with them. She encounters them daily (explicitly or implicitly) in the newspapers which she reads. Her problem is to know how to get to grips with the issues thus raised. How ought she to go about solving such problems? The problem is made all the more bewildering by the fact that the issues are clearly interrelated in complex ways. For example, Third World states make claims about being unfairly treated by the distributive arrangements currently operative in the system of states. At the same time, the developed states make allegations about the abuse of human rights in the Third World states. Our reader feels strongly that these issues are connected; that the abuse of rights in some way weakens the force of claims about unfair treatment regarding global distribution. Similarly, she feels that although all states have a right to appeal to the principle of non-interference in their domestic affairs, nevertheless, states with a poor record in the human rights field who appeal to the principle of non-interference have a weaker case than states with a good internal human rights record. Given that these issues are related in complex ways, how ought our reader to set about solving the problems raised in this field?

Let us step back a bit in order to get a wider view. Our reader is, roughly speaking, in the following position. She is reading a book on the condition of states. In it she has found that, generally speaking, the condition of states is not good. On the one hand, she has found that the developed states are suffering from overload and from the problem of ungovernability. More and more is required of the developed states by their citizens, and they appear to be in a position to supply less and less. On the other hand, the states of the Third World face a myriad of different problems. They lack legitimacy among their citizens, they are often economically weak, they are administratively inefficient and corrupt, they are not in a good position to provide their citizens with the traditional goods which states are supposed to provide, viz. protection, and they are in an even less favourable position to provide citizens with welfare services. In short, the condition of states looks bad.

Let us focus for a minute on Third World states. They, more than First World states, seem to be failing to provide even the rudiments of what states are traditionally expected to provide. They fail to provide even the first thing which is traditionally required of states, viz. that they protect the rights of their citizens.[1] Thus, with regard to these states, the question arises particularly acutely: 'Why should the developed states, citizens of developed states, citizens of underdeveloped states, you (anybody) support them?' Our problem is, given that the condition of states looks bad on all these diverse dimensions, what ought to be done about it?

It may seem as if the core problem at this point is the practical problem: 'How can we make states and the system of states work better?' If we ask this question, we have in the back of our minds some kind of mechanical image of a state as being a piece of apparatus which is not functioning properly. On this view, our problem is the mechanical engineering one of getting it to work properly.

Fixing the state

Before tackling the problem of how best to fix the problems facing states in the modern world, it is necessary to answer the prior question, 'Why ought we to be concerned with the performance of states at all?' An alternative way of putting the question is: 'If states are performing so badly why should we support them? Ought we not rather to concern ourselves with the establishment of a better arrangement such as a world society without any states? Or ought we not to seek to bring about a world government? In short, if states are failing to deliver the goods ought we not to abandon them? We now have over 160 states in the world. The vast majority of them seem to be failing. Should we not try some other mode of social arrangement?'

An answer to the very general questions posed in the previous paragraph will obviously give us an indication of what states and the system of states are for, and will place us in a much better position to answer specific questions about what ought to be done about the particular weaknesses and problems which are plaguing states in the modern world.

'What are states for? What is the point of having a world polity arranged into diverse sovereign states?' Many different answers have been given. Let us consider some of them. According to one major tradition, the point of organizing world politics in the state centric way is that it is a workable way of maintaining *order* in the world. The best known defence of this point of view today is Professor Hedley Bull. He argues that order is a somewhat more limited goal than justice or the protection of human rights, but it is a necessary precondition for those more complex goals. In the world as it is presently constituted, it is not, in his view, possible to achieve these more substantial goals. The system of states preserves order and that is the best that can be hoped for at this stage.[2]

A second answer which is often given to the question 'What are states and the system of states for?' is the answer that they are there to protect human rights. According to this line of thinking, individuals in a state of nature are not powerful enough to protect their rights; thus, they have a good reason to contract one with another to form a state which is a body with sufficient power to ensure that the rights of the contracting parties are protected. On this view, the community of states is (and ought to be, if it is not already) a set of voluntary defence associations; and the multiplicity of states which exist in the world is an indication of the multiplicity of different kinds of organizations people wish to make. According to this view, the reason one state ought not to interfere in the internal affairs of other states is that by so doing it gives the rights holders in that area a chance to form their own political contract. Well-known theorists who reason along such lines are Michael Walzer and Robert Nozick.[3]

A third answer which is sometimes given to the question 'What are states (and the system of states) for?' is the answer that states and the system of states are defensive only in so far as they maximize utility. On this view, a multiplicity of sovereign states operating according to the current norms of international relations (such as the balance of power norm) has the effect of maximizing utility, i.e. limiting disutility. This line of reasoning can be found in Kenneth Waltz's *Theory and International Politics*.[4]

A fourth answer portrays states and the system of states as a whole as dysfunctional. According to this radical view, states are there to advance the interests of a global capitalist class. States are functional to this class in that they ensure that it can maintain the conditions in which the exploitation of the oppressed class is possible. This is a very crude portrayal of a position that has been argued with great sophistication elsewhere.[5] Proponents of this view argue that, in the Third World, the state is used by the emerging capitalist élite to maintain the conditions under which it, together with the capitalist élite in the developed world, can exploit the massive supply of labour in the state in question.[6]

The details of these four approaches need not concern us here.[7] But it is important to notice what is common to all four of the approaches which we have mentioned. They all have this in common, that they see the state as a device for achieving certain ends. States are envisaged as machines which are designed to achieve certain ends. For Bull, the system of states is a device that preserves order; for Walzer, it preserves the function of protecting rights; for Waltz, it serves a utility producing function, and for the radicals it serves an essentially oppressive function. Of course, whether it does all, none or some of these things is a question that is hotly disputed among these different theorists. The radicals argue against liberal rights-based theories. The radical argument is that the system of states does not, in fact, protect the rights which the liberals claim it does. The radicals seek to show that, as a matter of fact, the system of states, far from protecting liberty, does the converse! It entrenches the bondage of the working class. The liberals argue against the theorists who stress the primacy of order that, as a matter of a fact, the system of states protects much more than simple order. However, these arguments are not crucial for our purposes. For us, the important thing to notice is that they all talk of the state as an *apparatus* which does (or ought to do) something for the people living within it.

If we think of the state and the system of states as a piece of machinery (whether it be an order-protecting one, or a rights-protecting one, or a utility-producing one, or an oppressive one), then we have in mind a particular relationship between the individual and the apparatus in question. We have in mind an individual who can, as it were, consider the machine from the outside. He can look at it while it is at rest, he can examine it in operation, he can discern whether it clangs, bangs, squeaks, rumbles, and so on. He can decide whether to maintain the machine, or whether to get rid of it, or whether to modify it ('hot it up'), or whether to redesign it completely.

Indeed, we find just this kind of approach reflected in the terms used in much political science literature, with its many references to 'function', 'constitutional engineering', 'political fine tuning', 'state apparatus', 'negotiating machinery', 'international structures', and so on. The crucial elements of this image are:

1 Individuals are beings who can, in some important sense, conceive of themselves as independent of states. On this view, individuals can conceive of themselves as standing outside of that which we call the state and can evaluate whether it is (or will be) of use to them or not.
2 The state and the system of states are devices (conceptually independent of the individuals who operate them) which serve some of the purposes which people happen to have.

On the face of the matter, it seems highly implausible to entertain an image of the state as a device which is somehow apart from the citizens of that state. We all know that hardly anybody is really independent of states. For most people live within one state or another. But it is possible to reconcile this fact with the image of the relationship between the individual and the state (and the system of states) which we are now considering. It may be done, for example, by envisaging that states are, in some sense, analogous to ships. There could conceivably be a world in which all people lived on ships. In such a world, the people would obviously be dependent on the ships on which they lived, but nevertheless the ships could still be seen as devices which the people use for certain purposes (one of which is to avoid drowning). The ship people could consider modifying all or some of their ships; they could consider improving the performance of their ships in certain ways, e.g. by putting in better navigational equipment, by using more fuel-efficient engines, and so on.

However, the relationship between people and states is quite different from the relationship between the ship people and their ships in this imaginary example. This point is of fundamental importance and will affect rather dramatically the ways in which we think about the questions, 'What are individual states (and the system of states as a whole) for?', and the subsequent question, 'What ought to be done about the condition of states in the modern world?'

The image of the relationship between the state and the individual which we have been considering is one which portrays the state as an apparatus which may or may not be useful to the individual in specific ways. Questions about what ought to be done must, on this view, be seen as questions about how to make the machine work better; how to make it preserve order better, protect rights better, produce utility better, and so on. We wish to argue for an alternative way of conceiving the relationship between the individual and the state (and the system of states).

Constituting the individual

On this alternative view, the state is not a device which may (or may not) be useful to the individual, but ought rather to be seen as a social arrangement within which the individual is constituted as such. Individuality as we know and value it is constituted within the state. It is not that the states serve the individual, but rather that without some state-like arrangement, individuals as we know and value them would not exist. It is only in the state that they are constituted in their fully fledged form.

What image may we use to portray the nature of this relationship? If the image of man and machine will not do, what image will illustrate the point? We suggest that the image which guides the practice of psychoanalysis is the one which we need here. The relationship there is portrayed as one between a conscious component and a subconscious one. In psychoanalysis, what is sought is an understanding of the conscious relationships which the patient has, together with an understanding of those unconscious ones (oedipal, for example) of which the patient was unaware. The underlying level is not seen as something apart from persons undergoing analysis, but as a component of their personality. Typically in psychoanalysis the patient together with the analyst seeks the root cause of some or other emotional disturbance which is plaguing the patient. As often as not, the analyst gets the patient to explore her relationships with her family during her formative years. The whole procedure presupposes that the patient was somehow constituted by her relationship with the family. She is not being asked to examine the condition of her family (father, mother and children) in order to find out whether that institution is in a good condition and whether she has any further use for it. On the contrary, it is recognized throughout that who she is, is determined by the family and that these relationships determine (in the past, now, and in the future) who she is. The whole process is one of making explicit to the person in question the internal linkages which exist between her and certain other key people within specified institutions such as the family, the school, the church, and so on. By getting the patient to talk about her earliest years, the analyst makes the patient aware of those relationships within which she first came to conceive of herself as a 'self' of this or that kind. She is made aware that she was constituted in specified relationships. She may come to understand, for example, that her father's recognition of her was coloured by his disappointment that she had not been born a boy, and so on. In this exploration of her relationships to the people and institutions within which she was formed, there is no suggestion that she sees herself as somehow independent of these institutions and as being in a position to evaluate them as useful or not useful. Rather she is called upon to *understand* her relationship to the people and institutions within which she was constituted as the person she is. It is only in the light of this kind of self-understanding that she can seriously tackle the question, 'What ought I to do about the condition in which I presently find myself?'

Our argument is that our reader needs to think about her relationship to the state (and the system of states as a whole) in essentially similar terms before she can decide what to do within the sphere of international relations. She needs to explore the ways in which she is constituted by the state and the system of states. Doing this is dramatically different from examining the condition of states from the external (mechanical inspection) point of view.

This way of thinking about our relationship to the state and the system of states runs counter to much modern thinking. In most marxist and non-marxist main line thought, the instrumentalist view of the state and the system of states is primary. From the Western perspective, the problem of failing states in the Third World is seen as either a humanitarian or a strategic problem. On the humanitarian view, states are seen as devices for providing people with security and welfare. In so far as they fail to do this, our humanitarian task is to find other ways of providing these goods, e.g. by means of direct aid to the people concerned; aid which bypasses the state. From the strategic perspective, shoring up shaky states is seen as a way of maintaining control over an unstable world. Thus from a Western perspective, a concern for the condition of Third World states is seen as being a means of forestalling the Eastern powers in their endeavour to spread worldwide class war with a view to creating a world order in which there will be no states.

Our reader now stands before the question, 'How am I constituted by the state and by the system of states?' This question, we have pointed out, needs to be answered before she can tackle the subsequent question: 'What is to be done about the condition of states?' In the modern state, the citizen sees herself (and is recognized by others) as a person (together with other people) from whom the authority of the state derives. She is recognized as one who (together with others) has a right to participate in the election of the body which makes laws binding on the body politic as a whole. She is recognized, too, as one who has a right to participate in the on-going debate about the state of the nation. She is recognized as one who may not be arrested by the state unless she has transgressed a previously published law. If she is arrested, she is entitled to be charged and subjected to a fair trial. And so on. In the fully fledged state, she is recognized in these ways and is thus constituted as a free person. Were this recognition to be denied her, she would be deconstructed as a person.

How might we substantiate these claims? We may do this by asking our reader to think about the way in which who she is, is partially determined by the institutions within which she participates. We may, for example, ask her to speculate about whether she could have been what we call a full, free and flourishing individual had she never been recognized as a member of a family, or as a right holder within a market with the power to conclude contracts, or a member of a club, or a citizen of a state. A little thought reveals that it is only in the context of such institutions that we come to be recognized as individuals.[8]

A key point to notice in all this though is that a person cannot be given the recognition appropriate to her being a free woman by people who themselves are not free[9]. A slave can never grant to a slave owner the recognition requisite to her being a free woman. Imagine our reader on an island with beings who insist on seeing themselves as her slaves. She will never be able to establish herself as a citizen of a free and democratic state until such time as they cease to see themselves as slaves. Her freedom depends on her being recognized as a free being by other free beings.

Our reader may now agree that she is constituted by the recognition which is accorded her within states, but she may still ask whether she is in any way constituted by the system of sovereign states. The argument to show that she is, is very similar to the one recounted in the previous paragraph. Just as individuals are constituted as being free by being citizens in the state, so too sovereign states are constituted as being sovereign by being recognized as such by other sovereign states.[10] Thus where the sovereignty of a state is suspect, this immediately reflects on the validity of the citizenship of the people within that 'state'. Thus, for you to be free, it is important that you be a citizen of a state which is recognized as sovereign by other sovereign states.

It may be asked whether it is not possible that individuality be constituted within political forms other than states? Can it only exist within a system of sovereign states? In order to answer these questions, let us briefly consider colonies and empires. As I have argued:

> People in colonies are not free, because the political entity in which they live is not recognized as autonomous. Few people would agree to their state becoming a colony even if accepting colonial status brought with it substantial economic gain. The reason for this is that in a colony the people are in a suspect position and are not free individuals in a way that citizens of an autonomous state are.[11]

Similarly, people party to an empire can not be constituted as free individuals. An empire by definition consists of a core dominating a periphery. It consists of a master/slave relationship writ large. Furthermore, an empire is by definition expansionist. An implication of this is that those political units outside the ambit of the empire do not enjoy stable recognition of their autonomy from the empire. Instead, they are under more or less permanent threat from it.

What makes the system of sovereign states so crucial to the constitution of individuality is that, within the system, states are recognized as permanent and autonomous. The core principle of non-intervention ensures that within limits each state is recognized as free to conduct its affairs as it thinks fit. The citizens of an autonomous state enjoy a form of recognition from members of other states quite different to that accorded to colonial subjects or imperial masters. The difference is crucial to the constitution of freedom.

The implications of this way of thinking about our reader's relation to the state and the system of states are important:

1 No longer can she see Third World problems as technical problems out there.
2 No longer are the problems of the Third World ones which she can leave to sort themselves out. For they are now seen to be intimately linked to her. If the other states in the world are not free states, then the sovereign state in which she is constituted as a citizen cannot be given the recognition necessary for it to be truly sovereign.
3 Her problem is to get the people out there to recognize her in the requisite ways and this can only be done by educating the people concerned. Moving towards mutual recognition involves a non-paternalistic mode of education. This kind of education involves not telling the people concerned in some paternalistic way, what they ought to know, but getting them to see the way in which both parties reciprocally constitute one another. Thus the problem is not what ought to be done to the people in these states, but how might they be convinced of the ways in which they reciprocally constitute one another. It is not a matter of what ought we to do to, or for them, but what ought we to say to them. Once they see how they are related to one another, the answers to the question what ought to be done will be more or less obvious.

Let us stand back and see what we have achieved. We have argued that people who live in states and within the system of states do not stand in relation to that state as an individual to a machine. Thus, in a sense, the question 'What ought to be done about the condition of states?', to the extent that it is understood as analogous to 'How can we fix this ship?', is not the proper question to ask. If we understand the relationship between the state and the system of states in the holist way which we have suggested (according to which we are only constituted as individuals within the context of a larger set of institutions which includes the state and the system of states), then the appropriate question to ask becomes 'What can we do about this relationship which is constitutive of us both?' This question is very different from the 'How can we fix it?' type of question in several important ways.

First, the 'How can we fix it?' type of question implies that the fixer knows what counts as having been fixed. There is no doubt about the proper criteria specifying what is to count as 'having been fixed'. The 'How may we best understand the relationship we are in?' type of question is quite otherwise. Here what is to count as a good relationship is determined by all the parties involved. One party cannot alone specify what is to count as a good relationship.

Secondly, the 'How can we fix it?' question suggests that what has to be done, is done by somebody to something. That which is being mended is not called upon to cooperate in the enterprise. Where what we are concerned about is the *relationships* between reciprocally constituting parts of a whole, the process of healing the relationship is different. Here the parties to the problematic relationship can only solve the problem by all *participating* in the process of finding a solution. Here what is called for is a deeper understanding of their reciprocally constituting relationship followed by a joint endeavour (based on this understanding) to see that the relationship flourishes fully. Just as the psychoanalyst seeks to reveal the deep interrelations between a person's early family life and her subsequent psychosis, and just as this understanding paves the way for the person to solve her own problems, so, too, must the political analyst show the connections between, for example, the hostile actions and attitudes of citizens in underdeveloped state X and the hostile actions and attitudes of citizens of developed state Y. The psychoanalyst and the political analyst will both be concerned to bring the parties to understand the historical relationships within which the present problems arose and how their failure to recognize one another properly damages them both. In the light of this understanding, the parties will be in a good position to resolve their mutual problems.

Thirdly, the 'How can we fix it?' question suggests the item to be fixed is not an essential component of the 'fixer'. She may not be in the mood to repair it, or, it may not be vital to her. The constitutive relationship approach makes it clear that a proper understanding of the whole is vital to those parties constituted within it. The parties involved cannot ignore the breakdown and remain whole and free. On this view, then, those in the First World cannot view the condition of Third World states as something of no major concern to them which they might get around to 'fixing' some day. Instead, they come to understand that the well-being of these states is vital to their own well-being. It is important not to misunderstand the point which is being made here. It is not that the well-being of Third World states is essential to the well-being of First World states for practical reasons (e.g. to ensure a constant supply of raw materials or for strategic reasons). Their well-being is essential to the well-being of First World states in the same way that the freedom of those who are slaves is essential to the free flourishing of the ex-masters. Someone cannot be recognized as a free person by someone who herself is not free. A state cannot be accorded the recognition due to a free state by those 'states' that are not free.

This point may be made clearer as follows: in order to show Ms X that participation in a particular institution is constitutive of her as a person, we may ask her to imagine that she had *never* participated in the institution in question (e.g. never been a citizen of a state) and to ask herself whether she could then be the individual she now is in the absence of such participation. Alternatively, we might ask her to imagine a people who have never participated in such an institution. For example, we might ask her to consider a group of contented slaves who have never been citizens of a sovereign democratic state and to ask herself whether such people would be only partially formed as full and free individuals for not having participated in a state-like arrangement.

Fourthly, in the light of what we have said so far, it is clear that political education is of fundamental importance for those who understand inter-state relations in the way we are advocating. For we now see that solving the problems inherent in the present-day condition of states involves the political education of all the parties concerned. They must be brought to see that they can all only be free and whole in so far as they reciprocally constitute one another in certain specified ways. However, this education is singularly difficult for it does not involve the teaching of a technique which may be clearly perceived by those being educated as being to their advantage. This kind of education is not at all like teaching a person to drive a vehicle. In a driving lesson, the pupil knows what the aim of the exercise is, and she knows that being able to drive will be to her advantage. The kind of political education which we are considering is quite different. It involves something akin to bringing a slave owner to perceive that she will be more free if she releases her slaves and comes to recognize them as equals; or bringing a contented, but unliberated, woman to see that she would be a more complete person were she to claim equality for herself; or bringing white South Africans to see that they themselves would be freer people were they to allow Blacks to participate as full citizens in the democratic process, and so on. All of these cases are similar, in that from the point of view of the person(s) being educated (let us call them the 'pupils'), normal cost–benefit type reasoning is excluded. They cannot be convinced by showing them that doing the following recommended thing will bring a payoff. There is no clear benefit (perceivable from their present position) which is being offered to them. The contented, but suppressed, housewife cannot see the point of joining the struggle for liberation, for as she understands her present situation she lacks nothing. Similarly, white South Africans cannot see any advantage to themselves in liberating the black population of South Africa. Quite the contrary, they see many disadvantages. Similarly, the rich states of the world cannot, from their present perspective, see great advantages to themselves in helping the Third World states towards greater sovereign autonomy, etc.

The progress of political education

How then can education proceed in these cases? The short answer is that those who have understood the way in which people constitute one another as free beings through participation in states and the inter-state system must educate those who have not reached such an understanding. Just as social workers attempt to educate inadequate parents to the responsibilities of parenthood, and just as feminist writers seek to reveal to men and women the repressive aspects of their present relationships and to outline a mode of reciprocal recognition which would establish the freedom of both, political theorists are called upon to expose oppressive relationships between states and to demonstrate to states that it is only by recognizing one another in specified ways that they can constitute one another as free states within which free individuals can flourish.

We are now in a position to answer the question 'What ought to be done about the condition of states?' States and citizens ought to be educated about the ways in which freedom is constituted in the relations between sovereign states. Such an understanding dictates that the plight of frail states is not merely a matter calling for the charity of rich and powerful states, but is of more fundamental concern. A self-respecting free state is one that is recognized as such by other such states. Subservient states, frail states and enslaved states cannot confer on strong states the recognition constitutive of freedom. The force of this point is clearly demonstrated in South Africa. The recognition accorded to South Africa by the so-called 'independent states' of Transkei, Ciskei, Venda and Bophuthatstwana is of no value at all in establishing South Africa as a sovereign free state within the community of states. The recognition is worthless because these are not free states properly so-called; they are slave states. As Hegel argued so well, the recognition of slaves cannot establish the freedom of the master.

Our conclusion, then, is that the establishment of a community of flourishing free states is essential to the constitution of our individual liberty. This conclusion reveals that two common approaches to the frail condition of some states are inappropriate. The first erroneous approach is that such states ought to receive the *charity* of the First World states. Such a view is wrong, in so far as it suggests that the relationship between the strong and the weak states is one-sided, with the weak states having nothing to contribute to the relationship, but their gratitude. The second suggests that Third World states are not important to the well-being of First World states and may justifiably be left to fail in their own way. We have argued that it is important to sovereign free states to be recognized as such by other sovereign free states. The faulty recognition accorded strong states by subservient states undermines their moral standing.

Those who have understood that we can only be fully free in a world in which we constitute one another in a complicated set of institutions which includes within it a system of sovereign states, ought to treat their fellow citizens and the citizens of other states (no matter what the condition of those other states) *as if they were citizens of a free state.* In this way, we can proceed with that political education which is a necessary precondition for a free world.

Notes

1 See M. Ayoob 'Security in the Third World' *Journal of International Affairs* **60**, 1 (1983) pp. 41–51, for a discussion of some of the security problems facing Third World states.

2 See Hedley Bull *The Anarchical Society* (Macmillan, 1977).

3 Michael Walzer *Just and Unjust Wars* (New York, Basic Books, 1977).

4 Kenneth Waltz *Theory and International Politics* (Addison-Wesley, 1979); Robert Nozick *Anarchy, State and Utopia* (Oxford, Blackwell, 1974).

5 See the discussion on the state in T.B. Bottomore and M. Rubel eds *Karl Marx: Selected Writings in Sociology and Social Philosophy* (C.A. Watts, 1963) pp. 215 ff.

6 For a discussion of this position, see Ralph Pettman *State and Class: A Sociology of International Affairs* (Croom Helm, 1979) esp Chs 2 and 3.

7 I have discussed the merits of these approaches in some detail in my *Towards a Normative Theory of International Relations* (Cambridge University, 1986) Ch 4, § 2.

8 See G.W.F. Hegel *The Philosophy of Right* trans. T.M. Knox (Oxford University, 1973).

9 See my discussion of this, op.cit., note 7, p. 177 ff.

10 Op.cit., note 8, § 381.

11 Op.cit., note 7, p. 179.

11

The Duties of Liberal States

Christopher Brewin

The obligations incurred by liberal states over the past 40 years have been unprecedented in their scope and saliency. For example, within Western Europe, the obligations of member states of the European Community have substantially altered their relationships to each other and consequently to the outside world. With respect to the non-industrialized states of the outside world, all liberal states acknowledge a duty of aid on a scale which is inadequate but goes well beyond all historical precedents in relations between civilizations. It also seems that the neglected subject of duties owed to enemies in times of peace and war will become important if relations between liberal states and the USSR improve as they seem set to do.

The question this chapter poses is how this substantial development can have taken place, given the notorious unreliability of any state's supposed duties towards foreigners. The answer it suggests is that many obligations are unavoidable precisely because they stem from the essential and distinctive nature of the liberal state. Thus, liberal states will support different groups and objectives than would, say, religious dictatorships. One consequence of this argument is that obligations based on will alone, whether in formal treaty commitments or in the process of long-term cooperation, are less important.

I begin with the much greater development of the Welfare State's obligations to its own citizens within the state. All liberal states have taken this route in the post-war period, which shows that controversy about what liberalism requires is compatible with an increase of obligations. The main purpose of the comparison, however, is to demonstrate the relative weakness of obligations to other states in terms of the formal criteria of universality, efficacy, generality and finality, and in the spectrum of domestic opinion. The hurried reader may choose to skip this section. The following section sets out the other part of the paradox, namely the willingness to incur obligations with respect to states, corporations, individuals, future generations and other forms of life.

I then set out two serious attempts to resolve the paradox – the universalist approach which denies the moral significance of borders, and the realist contention that the interests of particular groups or states, plus perhaps their deliberate commitments, are all that count.

My own resolution accepts the realist basis of international society, but differs in restricting the grounds for breaking obligations to those rare occasions when the *liberty*, and not merely the interests, of the state are in immediate danger. On that basis, I would like to suggest, the superstructure of agreements to enhance the prosperity and better secure the independence of separate states is both possible and desirable. Some of the practical consequences of this approach are explicitly laid out. I would, moreover, contend that the preference of writers on international relations for the language of interests over that of duties has been misleading.

Domestic and international obligations

Within liberal states, the range of views on their international obligations parallels the much more virulent debate about the extent of domestic welfare obligations. At one end of the spectrum are those who hold that what they have is rightfully theirs and that gross inequality is a price to be paid by others to preserve stability and incentives.[1] They regard their identity as an expression of their internal makeup and not as socially determined by their relations with like-minded states, with enemies, or with the less industrialized states of the Third World. While they may choose to undertake charitable or peace-keeping activities, or join alliances, this is entirely a matter for them. In their view, the variety of states and national egoism rule out any requirement to constrain their pursuit of their interests as they see them by any supposed external standards of behaviour. If the Swiss may be taken as, for the most part, expressing such views, at the other end of the spectrum one may cite the Swedes. Like domestic progressives, they are more impressed by arbitrariness in the distribution of wealth and in the protection of basic rights. Inequalities of power prevent the weaker from doing much about their own condition, and impose obligations on the stronger. Multilateral agencies and common standards help the weak and also constrain the abritrariness of the superpowers, which is itself an interest of middle powers. The Swedes regard their own identity as international, affected by the way they act with like-minded states and by the way they treat others. In short, they tend towards the Gladstonian tradition of liberalism where one's own interests are constrained by others' rights, rather than the Bismarckian tradition that the prudential assertion of interests is the only yardstick for determining international behaviour.

In general, views on international obligation tend to be more conservative than on domestic obligation. No national society would accept that its right to its own territory is subject to any international compulsory purchase order. A second corollary of the principle of self-determination is that, despite increasing awareness of the fragile interdependence of the earth, the units of international society do not have the same allegiance to the whole of which they are parts as do the citizens of most states.

An example may illustrate both the likely importance of material interests in furthering the concept of duties beyond borders, and the public's conservatism with regard to such supposed obligations. By the Treaty of Washington in 1871, Gladstone obliged Britain to abide by arbitration in settling American claims which included a claim for compensation for the losses caused by the British-built Confederate ship, the *Alabama*. Gladstone may have done this because he thought it was right; equally, he may have been using the route of arbitration to mend his fences with the USA to balance Bismarck's creation of a German Empire. We do know that the majority of his countrymen did not share Gladstone's views, and that their resentment at paying compensation for the damage caused by the *Alabama* played a part in Gladstone's electoral defeat of 1874.[2]

Since Gladstone's time, the obligations of citizens to each other have been transformed by the historical development of the state in enforcing or taking over the obligations to keep the peace, honour contracts, and aid the unfortunate. It may well be that the systematic provision of policemen, of welfare and defence agencies has lessened individual responsibility. My point is that these public arrangements have made it possible for obligations, even in the contested area of welfare rights, to be more stable over a wider area than they were before. Within the state, obligations generally pass the tests of efficacy, publicity, generality, universality and finality, by which the reliability of obligations can be measured. By contrast, obligations at the international level generally fail these tests.

First, citizens of a welfare state have available to them efficacious means of enforcing their claims. They no longer have to depend on the willingness of squires to acknowledge a duty of charity. However, in international relations, there is no international force or proportional taxation to enforce contracts or provide the means for upholding human dignity. It is possible for states to act together on finite projects like smallpox eradication and ease the strains of commitment by apportioning the costs among the richer states, but as with nineteenth-century squires, it is the states who decide whether to fulfil their duty or not.

Secondly, within the state, duties are publicly set out in standards and laws passed by a legislature. By contrast, the appeal to standards of civilized behaviour among states is vague and questionable. If the world wars of this century have not made a mockery of the concept, they have at least justified self-doubt about the permanence and efficacy of the notion of a civilized world. Since the Second World War, the restricted concept of 'Western Civilization' has been in vogue. On the one hand, this has been used by the industrialized capitalist states to assert that, by their own criteria, many other states are backward, underdeveloped or developing, but not yet fully members of civilized society. On the other hand, it has implied the exclusion of the communist states as illiberal states with whom relations are necessarily inimical. The fragile rules of co-existence between the blocs have not been the expression of a common civilization, but of an ability to define limited areas of agreement on the basis of separate pragmatic concerns. Such rules need last no longer than the pragmatic considerations underlying them.

Thirdly, within the state, we cannot selectively fulfil our obligations only to those for whom we feel affinity. Rights are legislated in general terms for which particular names cannot be easily substituted. By contrast, the number of states is so few that proper names are easily substituted. The duty to aid, or honour agreements is selectively applied in favour of those for whom we feel racial or ideological affinity, or who are useful to us in some way. When the superpowers have been actively involved, as in Guatemala in 1954 or Hungary in 1956, the Security Council cannot uphold the public maxim that self-determination should be respected.

Fourthly, the principle of universality requires rights and obligations to apply to all agents in so far as they are alike in relevant respects. However, since order within the blocs depends on disparity of power, there has been justified disparagement of this principle that what is right for us to do must be right for all. A comic illustration of this has been the expulsion of diplomats uncovered as spies by states who are simultaneously themselves breaking the prohibition against including spies among personnel accorded diplomatic immunity.

Finally, the principle of finality expresses a doctrine of legal certainty, that disputes about obligations can be referred to a hierarchy of courts and legislatures whose decision will be accepted as final. In international society, the legally binding judgements of the new European courts in Luxembourg and Strasbourg, of the Court at The Hague, or the decisions of the United Nations Security Council, are all progressive assertions that states have rights whose corresponding obligations can be brought before common juridical and political fora. But these judgements and decisions still depend on the willingness of the states concerned to enforce them as their own will, which brings us back to the first criterion of enforceability. It would seem that international obligations should be understood as expressing but not binding the wills of the states concerned. Thus a state may decide that it is in its interests to join an alliance, or a common market, or a regime specifying rules for aviation or free trade. It may take pity on refugees or migrants, the hungry or the victims of disasters or disease. It may feel a greater affinity for some foreigners than others. It is up to it to decide whether and how to undertake commitments.

The weakness of this view of obligation can be shown in logical form. If the basis of obligation is the will of particular states, then obligations cannot strictly be understood as binding will. The same authority that incurred the obligation can also decide to abrogate its obligation. Such unilateral changeability makes others' obligations inherently unreliable. Moreover, this unreliability is reinforced by the logic of Hobbesian security. If alliance obligations are accepted to make an agent more secure, it would be illogical to put one's own existence at risk by actually going to war for the sake of a larger whole or for others whose existence by definition is not one's primary concern. Hence the notorious weakness of the concept of obligation in Hobbes, and the long republican tradition of avoiding entangling alliances. The US Senate paradoxically adhered to this tradition, while appearing to agree to its reversal, in the NATO treaty. In case of war, each state is to act as it deems fit. Since, without a treaty, each state would act as it deems fit, no legal obligation is added by the treaty. The US commitment to its allies is merely a moral one in the sense that the USA has encouraged its fellow signatories to expect American help beyond the strict letter of the treaty. The same solitariness is at the root of the 'secret clause' by which the free-trading Americans and the Europeans protect their agriculture and basic industries so that they could revert to autarkic self-reliance. The Japanese have reason to feel that their commitment to the rules of Western free trade has made them especially vulnerable.

The increasing scope of international obligations

Given the theoretical and practical weakness of the concept of international obligation, it is remarkable how the recent practice of liberal states has been characterized by a willingness to incur international obligations. This can be illustrated by again considering Switzerland. In the first place, the care and deliberation with which the Swiss on traditional republican lines have avoided becoming members of organizations, trading blocs and alliances implies that international obligations are more than empty words. They feared that any formal ties which identified them with a group of states would compromise the military security they sought through the policy of neutrality. Secondly, in practice, Switzerland has nevertheless been so drawn into participation in the International Monetary Fund (IMF), the General Agreement on Tariffs and Trade (GATT) and the Club of Ten, that it is now seeking formal membership of the IMF, considering in a referendum membership of the United Nations, and may so develop its relationship with the European Community as to be effectively part of the common market.

Thirdly, this avoidance of obligations is unusual among liberal states. Like Switzerland, Sweden and Ireland are neutrals but consider themselves thereby all the more obliged to improve the international milieu by contributing to peace-keeping forces, multilateral aid agencies and the United Nations. The USA has abandoned its traditional republican dislike of foreign entanglements. Japan, the state which understandably holds that its wealth is the product of its own competitive efforts, is under pressure to adapt its internal market lest its export surplus put at risk the fragile trading agreements on which its present prosperity depends. Within Western Europe, the obligations of members to their partners include acceptance of common and enforceable legislation and common, if indirect, taxation intended to bear more heavily on the richer states of the Community. As all liberal states have been drawn into obligations to international trading communities to enhance the welfare of their citizens, so most of them have been drawn into military obligations. In both the spheres of welfare and warfare, the bulk of acknowledged obligations is contingent on the end envisaged: if you want to take part in civil aviation or a common market, join with others in paying the subscription and in formulating and abiding by the rules.

However, the enlarged scope of obligations of liberal states to each other is more than the sum of the plethora of post-war treaties and organizations to which they have committed themselves. Other obligations stem from their self-conception as liberal states. Thus, states may accept obligations on the grounds that they should not harm others by their own avoidable acts, they should do good where possible, and that they should remain faithful to their agreements and their associates, especially with kith and kin. To act otherwise, with ruthless reliance on force and fraud, would be to declare that they were not the states they conceive themselves to be. By way of unilateral reparations for past harm, the Germans have made payments to Israel. The World Health Organization (WHO), as the best-financed of the UN agencies, is an example of states attempting to do good where needs have been identified on a global scale, and those needs are being met by assessing in a rough and ready way the relative abilities of likeminded states in meeting that need. Similarly, the duty to assist in the industrialization of the Third World has been recognized, although in this instance not fulfilled. In consequence of agreements with the GATT, some protectionist measures have been accompanied by compensation to the states whose traders have been thereby harmed. It has, however, also to be said that the attempt by Prebisch to extend the scope of these obligations to include a duty by the industrialized states to avoid, and make amends for, harm to others from the present structure of the global trading system, has not been successful.

The scope of the obligations binding on states has also been enlarged with respect to corporations and individuals. The increase in trade increases obligations of payments. In addition, there are the new or enhanced problems associated with both rapid and global social and technological upheaval. Political refugees and migrants have changed the composition of many liberal states, and the rules of membership have been at odds with the humanitarianism of civilized states. The ancient but not universal obligations of men to be hospitable to travellers has given way to state regulations for admitting or excluding various categories of foreigners according to their numbers and purpose and, once admitted, a general obligation on states to protect aliens from injury. The UN and European conventions on human rights have brought individuals within the scope of international law. And unlike rights of property and status which vary in particular jurisdictions, human rights are by their nature universal.

Finally, there are obligations on states with respect to future generations of men and other living beings. Nuclear, biological and chemical weapons, and commercial activities which pollute or plunder the earth, together have put on the agenda of states individually and collectively the novel obligations with respect to what John Rawls has called the order of nature.[3]

How can this wide range of duties incurred beyond borders be reconciled with the logical and practical weakness of the notion of international obligation?

Universalist and realist approaches

One avenue has been to deny the moral significance of borders. If a maxim to avoid depriving, to protect from deprivation, or to aid those deprived of human dignity is valid for one human it must, by the criterion of universality implicit in reasoning, be valid for all humans. Henry Shue has made powerful use of the criterion of universalizability in making the case that duties to foreigners are based on stronger grounds than interests or feelings of benevolence. To take an example, he has argued that if it is right to ban the use of a technology known to induce asbestosis in those handling it, then it is as right to ban the export of that machinery.[4] The consent of foreign states and foreign workers could not be any more a valid reason for allowing its export than would the consent of domestic workers be a sufficient reason for allowing the use of that technology at home. Duties to compatriots have no priority over duties to non-compatriots. Similarly, Charles Beitz has argued that universalizability is more than a test of policy in that the present interdependent global economic system is actually universal:

> If evidence of global economic and political interdependence shows the existence of a global scheme of social co-operation, we should not view national boundaries as having fundamental moral significance.[5]

He explicitly draws the conclusion that obligations to foreigners are the same as those to fellow citizens as a corollary of working together in a single system of distribution:

> The conclusion that principles of distributive justice apply globally follows from the premise that international economic interdependence constitutes a scheme of social co-operation like those to which requirements of distributive justice have often been thought to apply.[6]

Applying the test of universalizability to a maxim, institution or policy may test its moral worth. Indeed, this test may be especially appropriate for liberal states whose justification for existing rests on the unprovable assertion that all humans have a dignity as rational beings. However, it is not the sole relevant criterion. My liberty and welfare are more likely to be secured by the mutual obligations of citizens in that such obligations better meet the criteria of efficacy, finality, generality and publicity than do obligations incurred in the global interdependent marketplace. Within the state, machinery for taxing riches and collectively enforcing rights exists with a predictability which for the foreseeable future will be lacking in their international analogues. Americans are more strictly obliged to aid the poor in Appalachia than to aid the poor in Bangladesh for the reason that Kant set out, in the terminology of his day:

> The general will of the people has united itself into a society in order to maintain itself continually, and for this purpose it has subjected itself to the internal authority of the state in order to support those members of the society who are not able to support themselves. Therefore, it follows from the nature of the state that the government is authorised to require the wealthy to provide the means of sustenance to those who are unable to provide the most necessary means of nature for themselves. Because their existence depends on the act of subjecting themselves to the commonwealth for the protection and care required in order to stay alive, they have bound themselves to contribute to the support of their fellow citizens, and this is the ground of the state's right to require them to do so.... The money should not be raised merely through voluntary contributions, but by compulsory exactions as political burdens...[7]

From a liberal perspective, therefore, priority may be given in some circumstances to compatriots. The right of a community collectively to rule itself is likely to remain a major tenet of liberalism. And as a matter of fact, historically forged communities united by nationalism and statehood, are as much realities as interdependence.

The importance of the state is also obvious from the most superficial consideration of how obligations to foreigners are mediated. There are, it is true, private aid agencies which distribute charity raised from individuals to whatever agencies they choose in the host country. But the comparison between the sums involved in government aid and private aid shows how great even in this field is the role of government. In 1980, the figure for UK official aid was £961 million as against £40 million in private aid.[8] In military and trade matters, in diplomacy and in setting the rules for immigration, the state deals directly with foreign states or individuals or indirectly through international organizations whose policy is negotiated between the states participating. As with domestic obligation, the growth of state mediation has been staggering. The paradox cannot be removed by denying the moral reality of separate states.

Nor can it be removed by simply stressing the particularity of states, or of one's own racial, religious or ideological group. The realist argument that all that concerns us is our own relative strength, and our own interests, must mean that we will fulfil our so-called obligations only when it is in our interests to do so. By the same token, we cannot rely on others' obligations to ourselves. This is to reduce the weight of the obligations depicted in the second section above to mere words papering over interests. I cannot resist pointing out that while this radical solution to the paradox may be internally consistent, it can lead to contradictory policy outcomes.

For example, European Gaullists, in stressing the primacy of national interest and power politics for all states, doubt the value of alliances and trading communities. They argue that to rely on others for security and welfare is self-deception. In terms of security, for states in Western Europe to rely on the USA for protection in war and direction in peace is to abdicate the role of the state. In ceasing to be responsible for the defence of their own citizens, they will spend insufficient attention and insufficient money. In times of crisis, their citizens will look elsewhere for protection and in consequence such states will lose their reason for existing or commanding loyalty. In terms of welfare, by ceasing to be self-reliant in agriculture and in industry, their firms will look to the USA for technology and ultimately for management.

From the same starting point that obligations can be reduced to the power-political calculations and interests of particular states, pro-US realists draw the opposite practical conclusion that European states must rely on unilateral American decisions. The reality of the NATO alliance stems from leaving the US President untrammelled by his partners, so that the decision to threaten to lay Europe waste may be credible to the Russians. It would not be credible to have joint control of the instant decision to engage in what in Clausewitzian terms would be absolute war. The Americans cannot be strictly obliged to come to the aid of Europe, but it is hoped that they will risk war because it is in their interests to protect Western Europe. For all its uncertainty, reliance on the USA is the best form of available and credible deterrent. With respect to the rules of trade, it is US leadership which underlies the readiness of the free world to accept the multilateral trading system and the obligations of the GATT. The sanction available to the Americans is more than the argument that all would lose from the lower level

206 The Condition of States

of trade to be anticipated under bilateral arrangements. It is also that in view of the inequality of power between the USA and its individual locutors, the terms of bilateral agreements would be likely to favour the Americans. It seems legitimate to conclude that Europeans who stress the interests of particular states as the sole ground of obligation cannot seriously rely either on the individual efforts of those states, nor on American leadership.

Basis and superstructure

Having argued that neither universalism nor realism can resolve the paradox of states' increasing reliance on unreliable commitments, I shall tentatively suggest that a third, more fruitful, approach is possible in accounting for obligations which may be relied on except in the most extreme circumstances. This approach distinguishes the underlying basis of state co-existence from the participatory structures which modern states have built upon that basis. On this view, states have developed an international society which transcends without replacing the repulsive basis on which it has been built.

At a basic level, international society is characterized by resemblance in that all states have sovereignty in the same world; each state repels foreign states from its jurisdiction. A self-determining state has to do what is necessary for its own existence, for otherwise by definition it would cease to exist. It is a categorical imperative. Moreover, it is the judge of its own actions even when breaking a formal obligation. By exchanging ambassadors, it acknowledges the right of other states to pursue their differing purposes as each sees fit.[9]

This concept of society has changed little since the seventeenth century. Of the changes that have taken place, the most important for a discussion of mutual obligation has been the universalization of the idea of state sovereignty. Sovereignty now carries the implication that, if it is right for us not to be ruled by foreigners, it is right for foreigners of whatever stage of civilization not to be ruled by us. This far-reaching denial of empire is a recent and efficacious limitation on those statesmen who hold that they are maximizing their interests and power as they see fit.

By definition, resemblance cannot be shared. However, on a basis of mutual repulsion, cooperative structures have been progressively built up in production, credit, information, alliances and other fields which are characterized by participation. To the extent that this has occurred, whether regionally or globally, international society is more than a collection of entities brought together in any sort of way. For participation presupposes a common sense of utility and justice. As Hedley Bull puts it, '... co-operation can take place only on the basis of agreements, and agreements can fulfil their function in social life only on the basis of a presumption that once entered into they will be observed.'[10]

This participation is in form hypothetical: if you want to participate, keep the rules. But, in practice, states may have little choice about participating in the Council for Mutual Economic Assistance (CMEA) or the GATT. Rapid and externally induced change has been important in determining the nature of many modern states. In Andrew Linklater's terminology, external obligation is replacing internal obligation.[11] States, corporations and individuals engage in economic, cultural and military tasks that can be analysed in terms of an international division of labour. There may be general rules about the rights of communities to self-determination or the human rights of individuals. There may be particular rules about regimes for wheat, or for states in Western Europe to act together in economic or military matters. States may even feel obliged to allow derogations from agreed rules for the sake of the common good. An example might be that in 1984 the European Community allowed extra milk quotas for the Irish in view of their historically lower output per cow and the losses suffered by Irish industry after entry into the common market.

If international society is conceived as dual, it is possible to comprehend the problem of how states in general can be observed to incur obligations when theoretically the concept of international obligation is grounded in a society based on mutual repulsion. The state's obligations to its own citizens entitle it to renege on its alliance and trading obligations if, but only if, in its own judgement it is necessary for its continued existence. On the other hand, the willingness to incur obligations towards other states and non-citizens follows from participation in alliance structures, international organizations and trading communities intended to realize their contingent purposes more fully than non-participation would do. There remains an ineradicable tension, in that obligations stemming from participation are limited by the state's basic egotism. However, for liberal states, the practical limitations consequent on the dualism of international society can be much reduced by considering more closely the self-regarding aims of states in so far as they are liberal. If liberal states are justified to the extent that they enhance the human potential for self-rule, then many of their obligations to foreigners are categorical, unavoidable and not merely hypothetical.

The duties of liberal states

Most obligations are contingent on agreement, on reciprocity and on the purpose for which they are incurred. However, some of the most important obligations are grounded in a state's conception of its essential and distinctive nature. A liberal state which allowed an interest group whose power derived from either numbers or wealth to ride roughshod over the human or civil rights of its citizens would be in contradiction with itself. This is more than a self-imposed obligation of which one can relieve oneself at will. Just as a man cannot be a singer unless he sings, so a state cannot be liberal unless it acts on the assumption that men in general and its citizens in particular have the potential for ruling themselves in freedom. A liberal state is justified to the extent that it successfully enables freedom to be realized.

If the capacity in human nature for collective and rational self-rule is the end which liberal states exist to promote, they cannot consistently deny that other men also have this capacity. If they therefore have a duty to promote just institutions for their own communities, they have also a duty to promote just institutions for other communities and between nations. If liberty and welfare can be best enhanced by separate states, even at the basic level of international relations the only legitimate reason for overriding the rights of foreigners is where such action is strictly necessary to preclude a clear and present danger to the liberties of the citizens of a liberal state threatened, for example, by an occupying power. By this purposive criterion, the 40 or so liberal states identified by Michael Doyle[12] on institutional criteria should enhance the liberty and welfare of their citizens by participating with others in alliances and trade, within the limits imposed by respecting the rights of foreigners affected by their actions. Brown's arguments on constraining interests where the foreseeable consequence of present policies is inimical to the rights of others would have far-reaching effects on Anglo-Saxon underpinning of apartheid, the destruction of the Amazonian Indians and the exploitation of the forests of Gabon.[13]

I will consider, first, the duties of liberal states with respect to like-minded states. These are the most far-reaching and extensive. By sharing rule in matters of warfare and welfare, liberal states have shown that progress in international society is possible. Then I will consider duties to enemies, where the greatest threat to the liberties of established republics is perceived as external aggression resulting in completely destructive war. Thirdly, I will consider the duties of liberal states to those states which are 'developing' into full participants in industrial civilization. It is here that the interests of liberal states are most in conflict with their duties.

Duties to other liberal states

Liberal states do not threaten each other with war. As Michael Doyle has argued, there is plenty of empirical evidence that 'even though liberal states have become involved in numerous wars with non-liberal states, constitutionally secure liberal states have yet to engage in war with one another'.[14]

The more difficult question is whether, in view of the inability of all but one present liberal state to defend themselves, militarily against the potential threat from the Soviet Union by their own efforts, they should unite in any way. In his day, Kant argued that republics should unite in a confederation for the sole purpose of defence at the same level of force as the threat from the large monarchies of France and Russia. He also argued that ever-increasing wars would drive them to unite if they did not choose to do so. Rousseau argued that a confederation would have to find some way of choosing a dictator with powers limited to the emergency who could direct the forces of a confederation. In our day, the European members of the NATO alliance have chosen to defend their citizens by relying on the decisive powers of the US President. Thus, they participate in NATO decisions on deployment of manpower and some missiles in peacetime, but could not participate effectively in a decision for war. However, as the US President is himself elected by Americans and not by Europeans and Japanese, it is his responsibility for US security which is direct and basic. Of course, by participating in the machinery of NATO, he has incurred a secondary and implicit obligation to defend America's allies. But from the perspective of those allies, his obligation to put the USA at risk on their behalf is not reliable. On the other hand, those states which do not rely on the USA, putting their faith instead in their neutrality, or on arming their populations, are not fulfilling their duty to prepare for war on the level of the potential if distant threat. Theoretically, the European states could better safeguard their peoples against the USSR if they recognized a duty to prepare the way for a common European defence in the hands of an elected president who could provide in his person the unity that is lacking among the states as separate entities when faced with making a decision that, to be credible, would have to be taken without consultation. It cannot be shown that the lack of social solidarity in Europe makes such a confederation impossible because the framework of the USA has already succeeded in inducing sufficient social solidarity among similar and at least equally diverse population groups. This may not be a likely outcome. The point is that as it cannot be shown to be impossible, it remains an idea which could lead states to making a more adequate preparation to defend themselves.

In terms of securing the welfare of their citizens, the liberal states are for the most part presently unable to safeguard employment by their own efforts. Where tasks are too big for single states, as in building large civil and advanced military aircraft, the states do not best meet the welfare requirements of their citizens by saying that the task is impossible. They have a consequent duty to pursue the option of joining with other mixed economies in acting so that the contribution of each state is in proportion to the task in hand and the ability of each state to contribute. They are now living in a totally different society from that of the eighteenth century when Kant dismissed economic confederation. Moreover, the simple model of the buyer and seller employed by Kant is inadequate in a world where subsistence societies are broken up by contact with large-scale commercial practices. Also, as Michael Donelan shows in Chapter 12, the states who draw up the rules are not just ensuring that the buyer and seller are free agents. They take directly into consideration the needs of taxpayers, producers and consumers who are affected by those rules. On the one hand, the Agriculture and Finance Councils of the European Community have to balance the differing interests within the participating states. On the other hand, by closing off their markets and subsidizing exports on an inner-regarding basic view of their obligations, they may be breaking their obligations to other states in at least two ways. The obligation on a large trading bloc to trade fairly is particularly strong, as is its obligation not to hinder Third World states in realizing the conditions for free and dignified lives, an obligation which will be considered below in relation to the consequences for the cane sugar producers of the European sugar regime.

Duties to enemy states

In their relations with enemy states, liberal states remain at the basic level of international society. The relationship is repulsive and adversarial. However, it does not follow that relations at this level are determined at the lowest common denominator allowed by the principle of reciprocity. If the justification of the state is that it makes possible the liberty of the people in a community, it follows that the peoples of enemy states rank as ends in themselves, and not merely as means or obstacles to our purposes. One virtue of aristrocracies was that they had no difficulty with the idea that other people were different, and did not expect them to become aristocrats like themselves. In our own day Americans, Russians and Chinese, and their leaders, all seem to assume that the world would be peaceful and pleasant if only foreigners could be like themselves. The forcible fashioning of defeated states in the liberal image by the victors of 1945 is not justified by liberal ideas. The justification that any continuation of fascist states would have meant the immediate disappearance of our own states is too implausible to rank as an argument from necessity.

In time of peace, liberal states have a duty to consider whether their actions with respect to enemy states will improve the milieu. This duty follows from the fact that poor international relations constitute the last and greatest problem in securing the liberty of citizens in republics. As the inevitability of war cannot be proved, the duty to act as if perpetual peace were possible is incumbent on liberal states, irrespective of whether our enemies refuse to treat us as ends in ourselves. This duty is non-reciprocal. The only relevance of an enemy doctrine of inevitable war with us is if this leads to the judgement that they are actually about to destroy us. The milieu is unlikely to be improved by broadcasting hostile propaganda to enemy states. Similarly, when liberal regimes choose to strengthen themselves by domestic propaganda against the evil enemy, this also is contrary to the duty to seek peace. Further, the argument that trade in pipelines, but not food, strengthens the enemy is tendentious, in that the potential danger of blackmail is remote. On the other hand, banning the sale of advanced weapons may be justifiable in that such weapons could directly put the liberty of the manufacturer's state at risk.

Spying is a more vexed issue. On the one hand, spies like soldiers may be judged necessary to the survival of our own liberty when faced with a closed and immediately hostile society. If spies are necessary, then it would be humane and reciprocally advantageous to treat unmasked spies as no more useful to their countries than disarmed soldiers. The present practice of exchanging rather than shooting spies could be upgraded to the status of a convention akin to the Geneva Convention on prisoners-of-war. Participation in such a structure might improve the milieu a little. On the other hand, spying is a game which in peacetime does not improve relations. There is a grey area. After the Second World War, the British director of military intelligence was delighted when he found that Russian soldiers with venereal disease were seeking out British doctors.[15] In order to obtain information on Russian troop deployment, he ordered the doctors to find out where the soldiers had been previously posted, on the excuse that venereal disease was contagious. However, this use of medical personnel, diplomats, journalists and tourists is bound to result in all foreigners being treated as potential spies. Since such practice cannot meet the criterion of publicity, it would seem to be only justifiable on the ground that, otherwise, liberty would be lost. As information from spies is unreliable in predicting a nuclear first-strike and at best secondary in surveillance of a conventional build-up, it seems most unlikely at present that the argument for its necessity can be sustained.

In wartime, the traditional restraint imposed on liberal states was that the purpose of war was peace and that neither the ends nor the means should make peace less possible. In terms of ends, the liberal states in 1943, followed by the Soviet Union, adopted the view that no peace was possible with a German fascist empire. The doctrine of unconditional surrender could be defended at a basic level by the claim that liberal states would risk another war if they respected German self-determination. For decades, the Western states maintained a hypocritical commitment to German unity and self-determination while intervening to remodel Western Germany in their own image and making plain their contentment with the division of Germany. The German question was a clear example of the tension between the commitment of liberal states to maintain their own liberties and their commitment to liberty and self-determination as a universal principle.

As for means, the development of nuclear war to the point of, in Clausewitzian terms, absolute war has resulted in a dilemma for liberal theory akin to that posed for Christian ethics. For nuclear war could not be justified except at the basic level of international life, where self-help in defence of liberty is the last resort. Even if it is arguable that the threat of

212 The Condition of States

sufficient nuclear delivery systems is a necessary bluff to deter any attack, a bluff does not meet the criterion of publicity. Also, to destroy the enemy is inconsistent with treating him, both as a state and as a community, as a self-determining entity. Finally, to preserve liberty by destroying the free is irrational. The conclusion seems to be that it is impossible for a state to be at once a liberal and a nuclear power. Under modern conditions, it would seem that the strict liberatarian must either hold that liberal civilization is strong enough to absorb its potential conquerors, or seek to develop conventional defence to the point where a hostile nuclear power could be deterred from attempting an invasion.

Duties to third world states

In assessing the duties of liberal states with respect to illiberal states which pose no threat to their liberties, the dualist analysis of international society is most revealing. At the basic adversarial level, decolonization has resulted in a political acceptance of the doctrine that all peoples have the right to repel the Western states from their jurisdiction. The idea that there is a naturally dominant Western race, or nation, or class, is no longer intellectually defensible. However, at a cultural level, the assumption of superiority remains. Public acceptance of the rapid deployment force available for use in the Gulf may be cited as evidence of this. It seems to be axiomatic that our interests in a continued supply of oil from the Gulf entitle us to use force to maintain continuity of supply. Yet if Arabs suggested that our continued purchase of their oil was essential to their economies, and therefore they intended to maintain a force in the North Sea to ensure that we continued to buy from them, we would be most surprised.

Western civilization and the Western state is taught in universities as the model which all others must imbibe. We have no interest in the Roman Empire after its collapse in the West in A.D. 476, or in the Greeks between A.D. 451 and A.D. 1820. We have no strong interest in Chinese civilization before 1839, in India before the eighteenth century, in Incas, in Aborigines or African tribes. Our sense of duty to aid others in adapting to industrialization could be compared to the sense of duty shown by Cortez in taking God to the Indians of Central America while taking the gold from them. In 1983, the percentage of aid to the less developed countries from the OECD countries in terms of their GNP dropped from 0.08 to 0.07[16]. While the industrialization of the Third World was enhanced during the depression of the 1980s by the phenomenon of 'runaway factories', the deliberate policy of liberal states has been to hinder this industrialization by basic-level protection of their own industries. Citing the competitive nature of international relationships, the USA and Germany rejected, perhaps temporarily, the UNCTAD demands to participate in creating structures for determining rules on commodity trade and for redistributing the allocation of money in the form of special drawing rights. The European Commission withdrew from the international sugar agreement because its own sugar regime, by favouring sugar-beet producers, entailed not merely denying access to cane producers but wrecking their alternative markets with dumped European sugar.

On the other hand, there is a new recognition that liberal states are responsible for the consequences of their own acts as these affect the nature of the regimes in the Third World and the human dignity of their expanding and urbanized populations. This is more than the formal recognition of the universality of human rights. The notion that the least developed countries have a right to special treatment for their exports in a Generalized Special Preference Scheme has been accepted, even if at present each trading bloc or country interprets this obligation as it sees fit. The Conference on the Law of the Sea provoked American disagreement, because the Reagan Administration's liking for *laissez-faire* exploitation was that of a small minority. The system of multilateral agencies to monitor and finance the needs of refugees, migrants and those without food and water may be viewed as prolegomena to a system of international taxation. The importance of agency budgets is that while for each separate state the problems of the world may seem a bottomless pit, by agreeing to act together in proportion to their abilities on finite problems, the rich can reduce what for them constitutes the biggest disincentive, the strains of commitment. Practical anthropology is necessary if states, who are not by nature angelic, are to act in accordance with, let alone from, a concept of duty. If Japan does not wish to dilute its racial purity by taking in boatpeople, it might be induced to contribute money to those countries who have taken them in. If other countries would guarantee not to discriminate against Australian exports, Australia might be induced to accept more immigration from Asia. The rhetoric of the international community against apartheid in South Africa might be backed by positive inducements to investors and the white population, as well as by the cheaper route of negative sanctions.

Conclusion

In his famous chapter on the poverty of international political theory, Martin Wight wrote:

> If Sir Thomas More or Henry IV, let us say, were to return to England and France in 1960, it is not beyond plausibility that they would admit that their countries had moved domestically towards goals and along paths which they could approve. But if they contemplated the

international scene, it is more likely that they would be struck by resemblances to what they remembered.[17]

In this chapter, I have tried to show that the domestic development of 40 or so states into securely established liberal states has important consequences for the conduct of their international relations.

Their duty to make liberty possible for their own citizens at a basic level of international relations is quite different from the view that their job is to maximize the strength of the state and the interests of its citizens. Under modern conditions, the preservation of liberty by military alliances, and of welfare by trading communities, involves the acceptance of obligations characterized by building structures of participation. This includes obligations consequent on the duty to enhance human dignity and promote just institutions, generally. In particular, there is a duty to develop the pacific union between liberal states and the obligation on liberal states in Western Europe to build a confederation with its own decision-making capacity. With respect to enemies, there is a duty to treat enemies as ends in themselves, subject to the limitation of the basic duty to protect the citizens of liberal states from clear and immediate threats to their liberty. With respect to the Third World, I have discussed some of the implications of equality at a basic level and of participatory structures in which great needs can be met by collective decisions.

The common thread uniting liberal duties in all three sets of relationships is that liberal states are justified to the extent that they make possible the realization of the human potential for collective self-rule. At a basic level, the first duty of liberal states is to safeguard this potential within their own territories. The corollary of this duty is that they may renege on their international obligations when, but only when, there is a clear and present danger to the liberty and not just the interests of their own citizens. As under modern conditions, liberal states can enhance liberty and welfare in general, and the liberty and welfare of their own citizens in particular, by building alliances and trading structures with other states, their obligations are otherwise strictly binding by virtue of their own liberalism.

Notes

1 Alisdair MacIntyre *After Virtue* (Duckworth, 1981) p. 7.

2 Paul Knapland *Gladstone's Foreign Policy* (New York, Harper and Row, 1935) pp. 41–2.

3 John Rawls 'Kantian Constructivism in Moral Theory' *The Journal of Philosophy* **77**, 9 (1980) p. 524.

4 Henry Shue and Peter Brown eds *Boundaries: National Autonomy and its Limits* (Totowa, N.J., Rowman and Littlefield, 1981) pp. 107–47.

5 Charles Beitz *Political Theory and International Relations* (Princeton University, 1979) p. 151.

6 Ibid., p. 154; see also C. Beitz 'Cosmopolitan ideals and national sentiment' *The Journal of Philosophy* **80** (1983) pp. 591–600.

7 Immanuel Kant *The Metaphysical Elements of Justice* trans. John Ladd (New York, Bobbs-Merrill, 1965) p. 93.

8 London Press Service, Verbatim Service, 133/80.

9 Murray Forsyth *Unions of States* (Leicester University, 1981) p. 10.

10 Hedley Bull *The Anarchical Society* (Macmillan, 1977) p. 19.

11 Andrew Linklater *Men and Citizens in the Theory of International Relations* (Macmillan, 1982) pp. 38–56.

12 Michael Doyle 'Kant, Liberal Legacies and Foreign Affairs' *Philosophy and Public Affairs* **12**, 3 (1983) pp. 205–34 and **12**, 4 (1983) p.210.

13 Peter Brown and Douglas Maclean 'In the National Interest' in *Human Rights and Foreign Policy* (Boston, Mass., Lexington Books, 1977) pp. 161–73.

14 Op. cit., note 12, p. 213.

15 John Cloake *Templer, Tiger of Malaya* (Harrap, 1985) p. 172.

16 UNCTAD *The Least Developed Countries: Introduction to the 2DCs and to the Substantial New Programme of Action for Them* (New York, United Nations, 1985).

17 Martin Wight 'Why Is There No International Theory?' *International Relations* **2**, 1 (April, 1960) pp. 35–48, p. 62.

12

States, Food and the World Common Interest

Michael Donelan

All subtle questions about the condition of states fade in the harsh light of this one: 'Are the people fed or do they starve?' So this chapter is about food. It is also wider. The setting in which states face the problem of food is international: they are in a world food-market; moreover, they say that they are 'an international community'. They are, at the same time, sovereign nation-states, concerned for their national interest. The wider question about the condition of states is how they can reconcile their obligation to the international community with pursuit of the national interest. I will begin with this broad question, using the concept of 'the common interest', and later return to the case of food.

In the study of domestic politics, the idea of the common or public interest fell for a long time into disfavour. Political science was predominantly positivist; it pictured a political process that consisted of the conflicting pressures of interest groups; to grace the outcome of this struggle with the high name 'the public interest' seemed humbug. In recent years, however, there has been a revival of respect for the idea on the understanding that it is a normative concept, that it refers not so much to how people behave in politics as to what they think reasonable.[1] The statesman, it turns out, cannot operate without the idea, whether sincerely, as in some countries, or hypocritically, as in others. He cannot only say, 'What is the policy that best reflects the relative power behind the competing interests?' He must also say, 'What is the public interest?'

Perhaps the idea is nowadays equally clearly indispensable among states in their foreign policies or perhaps there it is vacuous and utopian. Before setting out to explore this, one point deserves stress: idea of an international common interest could not be the only thing indispensable in foreign policy. Concern for the common interest is at most a disposition. By itself, it decides nothing. It cannot tell us the comparative value of particular interests or the efficacy of alternative measures or, above all, how to discern and face opposing power. It needs skilled, experienced prudence, courage and control. It is only a guideline without which all is self-interest and cunning, and nothing in international relations changes.

To begin our exploration with fundamentals, the idea of the common interest is part of the natural law philosophy of life. (Strictly, I should say 'the common good', but this term, though more flexible, may sound either sanctimonious or collectivist to present-day ears.) The natural law philosophy is best understood not as one among many competing philosophies but as how human beings think before their thinking is supplemented or distorted by other philosophies; supplemented, for example, by utilitarianism, distorted, for example, by racism. According to natural law, a human being is programmed in certain ways, one of which is that he is a social being. Sociality demands, first, that each of us in pursuing his interests should, in his acts and arrangements, avoid and avert injuries and ills to others; and, secondly, that conditions that affect all (laws, policies, systems, ideas) should be in the interests of all, the common interest.

The community within which this applies is, in the first place, as wide as a community of mankind. For when we examine our moral experience, one of the first facts we discover is that we do not need to give ourselves or anyone else a reason for being social with any other human being but a reason not to be. We should, in other words, avoid and avert ills to all other men unless we have reason not to; and conditions that affect us and them should be in the interest of both unless there is reason why not.

The most basic condition for the common interest of the community of mankind concerns statehood. In natural law, as I understand it, the world cannot be administered as a single worldwide state but must for practical reasons be divided into a variety of states. The purpose of each state is to create conditions among its citizens that are in their common interest. But because it is a division of a community of mankind, not radically separate, it also has a purpose in relation to the other states of the world; namely, to seek with them conditions that are in the common interest of all their citizens. Customary international law, universal treaties, the diplomatic system, a balance of power, the migration laws of states, international interest rates, the ideas of self-determination and human rights are examples of conditions affecting all the citizens of all states. States create these conditions or influence or seek to alter them or to impose them (this last, for example, by ideological propaganda or armed intervention) and their purpose, in the sense of their reason for existence, is to do so with an eye to the world common interest.

Similarly, when a state is a member of a group of states, its purpose is to create conditions that are for the group common interest of all the citizens of the states of the group. Let the example of the European Community serve, with its customs union and accompanying rules, its common policies, its directives for the harmonization of national laws, and its elements of international economic management, all of which create conditions under which the citizens of the member states live, and should be in their common interest.

The North Atlantic Alliance is an example of a group that exists to seek the group common interest (in brief, peace among its members) and also, more prominently, the joint common interest of the citizens of its member countries with the citizens of the Soviet Union and its allies (in brief, peace between them). Simple examples of joint common interest, that is, where the partners are not alliances of states but single states, abound. In every bilateral relationship of states, from a Sino-Soviet military alliance or a Spanish-Moroccan commercial treaty to an Anglo-Argentine territorial dispute, the purpose of the states, their *raison d'être*, is to seek the joint common interest of their citizens. That is, it is reasonable that they should judge arrangements on these grounds.

We have, then, three levels on which foreign policy proceeds and states exist to seek the common interest: world, group and joint levels. I do not mean to suggest that the three can be exactly distinguished in practice. An interaction between two states in, say, a territorial dispute, while a matter of their joint common interest, will almost certainly affect the world common interest in that, for example, an international waterway, a rule of international law or the balance of power is involved. Similarly, states searching for the group common interest have to consider the effects on the world common interest, as, for example, the effects of the European Community's Common Agricultural Policy (CAP) on the conditions under which all agricultural producers and consumers trade and live.

I shall use the example of the CAP and the world common interest to take this discussion into greater detail, but before leaving fundamentals, I should mention some obvious objections to what I have been saying. Nationalists will object to the conception of the state that I have preferred. The state, they will say, is not to be seen as a mere collection of individuals but rather as a person, 'Argentina', 'Britain', 'China'. Its interests are not to be reduced to the interests of its citizens; it has a national interest and a national honour that they do well to serve. Least of all should the state be considered a mere administrative division of mankind, a functionary of alleged common interests of its members with those of other states. The state is the final community.

We should concede something to this way of thinking. Algerians, Brazilians, Chinese and Danes have interests and honour not merely as private persons but also as nation-states. Attempts to thrash out with them the common interest should respect this fact. Still, it is they that have interests and honour, not an abstraction, the state. The state is not a person but a community for creating conditions such that persons can prosper.

A less heady objection is that states, contrary to my picture of them, are not essentially condition-creating entities; they act towards one another in many other ways. I reply that this is only apparently so, and that on a closer view, such acts (e.g. of diplomacy, propaganda, spying, economic pressures, force, etc.) are the use of the instruments of statecraft to the end of condition-creating. They are so directly or by reforming the instruments, as when some are banned or new procedures such as intergovernmental organizations are set up. Alternatively, such acts are indeed not condition-creating, and express a different, second role of states, the state as entrepreneur, engaged in state production and state-trading, or as a charitable organization, as in overseas famine relief. But these roles, however important, are subordinates to the distinctive role of the state in creating the conditions under which its citizens and those of other states live.

A last objection brings us full circle. Supposing we grant that the state is to be understood as essentially condition-creating and, furthermore, in the domestic life of the nation, not arbitrarily and chaotically but in the common interest, are we really obliged to conclude that its essential purpose is also condition-creating for the common interest in its relations with other states? That it does in fact create conditions there also, we may readily concede, but the idea that its purpose is to do so with a view to an international common interest may strike us as vacuous and utopian.

I reply that having argued the case for this idea, so to say, forwards from a conception of man and the state, I should now argue it, so to say, backwards from the daily business of international relations. I will take a particular case of state policy making, and the reader shall judge whether the idea of an international common interest works and whether the purpose of the state is to seek it, subject to prudence, or whether the idea is a fantasy.

The case I shall take concerns France and the world wheat trade. In discussing it, I shall allow my opinions to show through but that is merely in an effort to avoid insipidity. I should like to stress that my purpose is not to persuade the reader that a certain policy on the wheat trade would be in the common interest; I do not presume to do that. My purpose is to set out the matter in a way that makes tolerable reading and enables the reader to judge whether the idea of an international common interest is applicable to it at all.[2]

The world's largest food crop is wheat. Five producers have large surpluses – the USA, Canada, the European Community (EC), Australia and Argentina – which they sell to deficit countries in competition with one another or give away as food aid to the poorest countries. The EC, principally France, began to have surpluses in the 1970s, and, to enable it to sell these, it uses export subsidies. This policy is a condition under which its producers and all other wheat producers in the world, their competitors, and all consumers trade and live. The question is whether this condition is in the common interest; more precisely, should French statesmen continue to support EC wheat export subsidies, or should they stop doing so and seek a rule under the General Agreement on Tariffs and Trade (GATT) against subsidies by any country?

An ancient procedure for answering such questions is discussion by those affected. The EC discusses wheat subsidies subsidies internationally but in a restricted way. It subscribes to GATT Article 16.3 whereby states should seek to avoid subsidies on primary products and, if they do use them, should not thereby take more than an equitable share of world trade. It proposed (ineffectually) during the Kennedy Round of GATT negotiations in the 1960s, the 'binding' of support levels (that is, an agreement that such levels would not be increased). During the Tokyo Round in the 1970s, it helped negotiate the Subsidies Code (1979) that sought to clarify, *inter alia*, Article 16 and the meaning of 'equitable'. Agricultural subsidies are on the agenda of the Uruguay Round, and limited agreements may be reached. However, these multilateral discussions and many others with producer countries are arguably superficial. For production and export subsidies are not an isolated act of policy but are a part of the EC's whole policy for agriculture, the CAP; and the CAP it will not allow to be decided internationally. The CAP, it believes, is essentially a domestic matter.

The procedure of deciding a policy on domestic grounds, treating the views of the rest of the world and the effects on it as subordinate, is in the common interest in many of the affairs of states. This is true, for example, of the constitution, the legal system, the welfare system. That such matters ought to be decided locally and not by the world as a whole is the most obvious reason why the world is divided into separate states. Provided each national system is, in its own way, in the common interest of the citizens of the nation, the variety is good. But as liberal theorists have taught us, policies for the economy of the state and for the security of the state and its conflicts with other states create conditions under which not just its own citizens but the entire citizenry of some, perhaps all, other states live, and so a unilateral approach is unlikely to make for the common interest. The part is here deciding conditions for the whole. Of course, this opinion refers to broad policies and systems. The thought of thrashing out the details of the CAP not merely in the EC but in a world forum would drive a Community bureaucrat to retirement, and indeed seems impractical and unnecessary; but the principles of it might best be.

Even if this is the best method of deciding the common interest, obviously French statesmen should not adopt it without some prospect of cooperation by others. They would need, first, cooperation within the EC. The current standard view among its members is that the principles of the CAP are the best balance achieveable between their various national interests and that therefore there is no point in submitting these to discussion in a wider forum such as the GATT. The thought here is sometimes that member governments and citizens would not tolerate the influence on their affairs of a world perspective. Sometimes, it is that the business of working out the common interest of the members of the EC is already hard enough, and that to try to take into account the interests of the entire world is an impossible ambition that would destroy the lesser good. The question for French statesmen is in either case whether or not to maintain a prudent pressure on their own citizens and on fellow members towards a world perspective.

France would also need the cooperation of states outside the EC. The existence of the EC and French policy within it are in part a reaction to the power of the USA. The principles of the CAP, while reflecting continental European traditions, are partly to be explained by a French belief that the EC should not depend on US food. More than this, though the USA is generally well disposed to multilateralism to a degree unprecedented in previous dominant powers, unilateralism in its agricultural policies does something to explain the unilateralism of the EC. The wheat policies of the CAP, for example, were formed at a time when the USA was engaging in subsidized production, storage and exports, practices that it now objects to under the CAP, without much willingness to be influenced by European views. The question for French statesmen is how far the USA is basically willing to adopt a multilateral approach and to seek the common interest, including concern for the problem of internal balance within the EC and how far accordingly effort on their part in this direction would be worthwhile.

This much on procedures; next on the substance of the matter: do Community wheat export subsidies, by whatever procedures decided, create conditions that are in the interest of all? The current international phrase for the interest of all is 'food security', by which is meant an uninterrupted supply of food at stable prices that citizens can afford to pay. For rich states, 'uninterrupted' and 'stable' are what matters most; for poor states, 'afford' is the vital issue, or in other words, malnutrition and starvation. All states face instability if they fail.

French statesmen might press for a world answer to the food security problem as follows: all states would agree to unrestricted, unsubsidized trade in wheat; those with a comparative advantage in the cheap production of wheat would supply those whose advantage lies in other products. This would make for the cheapest prices for bread and, by ending subsidies to agriculture, to the lowest burden on taxpayers. The poverty-stricken in the Less Developed Countries (LDCs) that could not afford even these prices would continue to be helped by food aid from rich surplus countries or by money from the rich to finance food purchases from food surplus LDCs, and for the longer term by aid to agricultural development. As to price stability and uninterrupted supply, a bad year in some countries would be balanced by a bumper crop in others. For worldwide bad years, such as 1972–4, which frightened the world into coining the phrase 'food security', governments would need to build up and release international stocks. In sum, the world would follow, in the twenty-first century, the example of nineteenth-century France. Immemorial recurrence of regional dearth and riot was ended there by the making of one great unified market.

States at present do none of this. They prefer to rely on a national policy, each regulating home production and exports and imports for itself. Some (broadly speaking, the poor countries) are provisionist, meaning that they are mainly interested in low food prices for their consumers, achieved with the aid of imports and consumer subsidies. Others (broadly speaking, the rich countries) are protectionist, meaning that they are as interested in preserving a strong domestic agricultural industry as in low prices for their consumers. The EC is faced with the fact that its wheat production costs are higher than those of such countries as the USA. It protects its farmers' incomes against imports by border levies. It protects them against their own over-production by buying up surpluses and storing them, and subsidizing exports. Thanks to these and other support policies and great advances in farming methods, the EC achieved by the 1970s an agricultural industry flourishing as never before, something it prized socially. It attained food security as to many types of wheat (and many other foodstuffs) by the route of self-sufficiency, autarky. It began to have large wheat surpluses for export.

The EC and the other great producers engage, it is true, in frequent negotiations aimed at international cooperation, but in doing so they are caught in a contradiction: their purpose in seeking international cooperation is to facilitate their national policies, but their national policies prevent international cooperation. Early in the life of the EC, in 1961, the French Minister of Agriculture, Edgard Pisani, and his colleague Wilfrid Baumgartner, put forward in the GATT a Community plan that had many features that looked to the common interest. The proposals failed, however, because all could see that in the end they favoured the domestic producer over the exporter, which was the position of the EC at that time. In achieving national price stability, state policies, especially the CAP, have increased international price instability. The Wheat Trade Convention of 1967, made to promote stability internationally, broke down in 18 months under the weight of subsidized national over-production and US export subsidies. The successor agreement in 1971 could provide for no more than 'consultation'. There was and still is much interest in a new wheat trade convention, centring on internationally managed wheat reserves to keep wheat prices stable but this is unattainable or, if attainable, unworkable given that governments simultaneously claim autonomy, not least the EC. Moreover, in debating the level at which prices should be stabilized, governments defend national positions, and these are incompatible. At the one extreme, the USA sees an advantage in low world prices; at the other, the EC's consumers are less restive and its taxpayers make savings on export subsidies the more that world prices climb towards EC prices.

At this point, someone might say, you paint too gloomy a picture. Contradictions and conflicts and much confusion are to be expected even among states seeking the common interest. The idea of an internationally agreed regime for wheat on the lines sketched earlier may sound very fine in theory, but arguably states should never relinquish the final power of decision on the feeding of their people. This is sometimes thought to be a matter in the last resort of strategic security but that is not the basic point, especially for the EC. Strategically, the EC would probably do better to have Australia and the western hemisphere as its granaries than to rely on a large domestic agriculture dependent on large chemical and energy imports. The basic point is that in peace as much as in war, the first common interest of the people is enough food and the state has the final responsibility for ensuring this. Furthermore, such are the complexities and unpredictabilities and constant changes of the world food outlook that one might well be sceptical of detailed schemes for international control. One might well expect deep legitimate divisions of opinion on what should best be done. Arguably, then, the best system is one in which states attempt no more than to discuss their national policies with each other, to frame them with an eye to the common interest, and to co-ordinate them as far as possible. At any rate, it would be wrong to assume that to speak of seeking the international common interest is to speak of an international regime.

Let us move on. Granted a world where, rightly or wrongly, there is no international regime for wheat, should French statesmen continue to support wheat export subsidies by the EC? Is it the best available policy in the common interest? That is, do these subsidies create the best possible conditions for all the people concerned, the citizens of EC countries, of other wheat exporting countries, of customer countries?

A French statesman's first response to these questions might be that they are the wrong ones. Question the CAP if you wish, he might say, and I will answer you; but granted the CAP granted, that is a policy of self-sufficiency, export subsidies follow inevitably. For, in the first place, to maintain our farmers, we have to support prices at a level that maintains an adequate income for the least efficient of them. This tempts (*alors, que voulez-vous?*) the more efficient to over-produce. Hence, there is a surplus. In a second and more penetrating perspective, we must support agriculture on a scale at which, even when a harvest turns out bad, we can still feed ourselves. Hence, since in most years the harvest turns out good, there is a surplus. Now, what shall we say of this surplus? Is it bad? *Pas du tout!* It is a further provision against a bad year. Do not forget the fright the world had in 1972–4. As has been justly observed, in agricultural affairs, the only guarantee of enough is too much! The surplus has to be stored. Where? Obviously in granaries. Here beetles can attack it. There is a further, more intelligent method. It can be stored in an export trade which can be cut off in a bad year. It must be so stored! The surpluses are so large that for the EC, one must say *exporter ou étouffer*. And exports, such are our high production costs, require subsidies.

In all aspects of national affairs, broad policies (here the CAP) entail narrower policies (here wheat export subsidies). This does not, or should not, stop us scrutinizing the separate costs and benefits of a narrower policy apart from its contribution to the broad. If it does not stop us where the criterion of scrutiny is the national interest, no more should it where the criterion is the common interest.

In any case, it is questionable how far export subsidies really are entailed by the CAP. Perhaps a scale of support for Community agriculture could be devised which, while maintaining its generally flourishing condition and in particular its ability to cope with a bad year, including surpluses stored in granaries, cut out the further surpluses 'stored' in the export trade. Disturbed by rising costs, the EC is making some effort to put a ceiling on production. On the present scale of support, surpluses available for export are likely to double over the present decade. One may doubt whether even the present export volume, leave alone double, is needed to fulfil the aims of the CAP.

Perhaps, though, a great wheat export trade is in the interests of the EC for other reasons. The only apparent reason is that it contributes to the balance of payments, which is to say, that it permits imports. Perhaps other products than wheat would do better in this role. Since the EC does not have comparative advantage in wheat, it is making an inefficient allocation of resources in growing it. Its taxpayers have to pay its producers about as much in subsidy on every ton of wheat they export as the overseas customer pays in price. France is a net gainer from the export subsidies but there are other costs. In the days of Britain's North Sea oil boom in the 1970s, President Giscard d'Estaing used to refer to French agriculture, of which the most spectacular feature was the soaring wheat exports, as 'our oil'. The cost, alas, was the creation of a veritable equivalent of the North Sea on the land of Europe, the perpetuation yet again of the man-made treeless melancholy of Picardy, and the destruction elsewhere in France and the Community of much varied husbandry and habitat under interminable, featureless waves of wheat. This was not agriculture in its proclaimed role of *gardien de la nature*. Nor was it agriculture as guardian of the ancient rural personality of the nation. It was an *agriculture commercante* of bankers, chemical and engineering companies, and oil importers.

If we now turn from the interests of the EC to the interests of the other great wheat exporters, the USA, Canada, Australia and Argentina, we should first note that they think the EC's subsidized wheat exports perverse and disruptive. These four have the best conditions for raising wheat at the lowest cost; they have long acted as granaries of the world; a very high proportion of their wheat has always been raised for export. For the EC to refuse any longer to rely on imports for its home consumption was strange enough but doubtless its right; for it to enter into artificial competition with them in other markets was aggression.

Comparative advantage, it is true, cannot be the only principle for the common interest in world trade. Just as sometimes countries need to ignore the comparative advantage of others, so sometimes they need to waive their own comparative advantage and restrain their potential exports of some product or other. The reason in the one case as in the other is to avoid national dependence on a few industries and to promote a wide variety, for all manner of economic, social and strategic reasons. However, this consideration seems hardly applicable to the 'Four'.

Theoretically, the EC's subsidies are intended only to enable its exporters to match the prevailing world price, but it seems that sometimes the subsidies undercut world prices and that at all times they exert some downward pressure on world prices. However, since the main price-setter is not the EC but the USA, the far more important effect of the EC's subsidies is that they have enabled it, starting from nothing, to carve out a large slice of the world market. The resentment of other exporters in the 1970s and 1980s was much reduced by the fact that all were benefiting from a great increase in the world market, but it was enough to provoke the USA into calls for the limitation of the EC's wheat export growth and new measures of assistance to its own wheat exporters. These measures were in turn resented by the EC and Canada, Australia and Argentina, all of which had suffered from US subsidies in the 1960s.

Much of the EC's success has arisen from growing wheat consumption in the Middle East, especially Egypt. The EC argues that the Middle East is a traditional European market; the USA argues that so far as wheat is concerned, deficit countries are traditionally supplied by surplus countries, and the EC competes in the Middle East only by subsidies. The USA has retaliated with large subsidized sales of its own to Egypt.

We come, then, to the interests of customer countries. The salient point is that many of the LDCs could not feed themselves without large imports of wheat at low prices. The fear is often voiced that these countries are caught in a vicious circle: because they cannot feed themselves, they import, and because they import, their agriculture never grows strong enough for them to feed themselves. This fear is especially acute about wheat and other food given to them by rich producers under food aid programmes. A reasonable conclusion to be drawn from the controversy on this matter might be that, with suitable agricultural policies, imports usually need not depress local agriculture; that, in any case, food aid will be indispensable for many years to come for the very poorest; and that when countries succeed in growing richer, the pent-up demand for food inevitably outstrips the capacity of even a growing local agriculture and leads to great purchases from abroad.

Egypt, for example, once the granary of the Ottoman Empire and exporter of wheat to France, now imports three-quarters of its wheat needs, about a third from the EC, mostly from France. With a population of over 50 million, increasing by more than a million each year, it can do no other. For many generations, its agricultural policies have usually favoured cash export crops over subsistence crops; in the last century, cotton; in recent years, horticultural produce for export to neighbouring countries. In some LDCs, such policies favour the richer people and their rich overseas customers at the expense of feeding the people, but it seems that in Egypt at the present time, they may be in the common interest. Great improvements have been made in Egyptian wheat production and, apparently, for the moment anyway, no more could be done without inordinate inputs. To increase high-price exports and continue low-price wheat imports seems the best policy.

It does not follow, of course, that the EC should be one of the suppliers; other countries might do better. The EC's unique claim to the role is that its subsidies exert some downward pressure on prices. This can be seen as a form of aid to importing LDCs such as Egypt. Apart from this, the role could as well be filled by the USA and Australia. Alternatively, the EC might seek to aid agricultural development in LDCs by encouraging exporters among them. Thus, the Pisani–Baumgartner Plan proposed to use the proceeds of EC levies on agricultural imports to finance food exports from food-exporting LDCs to food-deficit LDCs. The savings made by ending EC export subsidies might be usable for the same purpose. At present, EC aid policies, including food aid, are decided, like the CAP and export subsidies, mainly according to what suits the EC; but we are discussing here what might be done from the perspective of the common interest.

An enquiry into whether a given condition (here EC wheat export subsidies) is in the common interest cannot be confined to its effects on each of the parties separately (here the EC, other exporters, customers); the effects on relations between them may also be important. Thus, the EC's campaign of wheat exports has to be considered in terms of the usual drive of states to win friends and influence in the world. The wheat sales to Egypt are in line with the Mediterranean policy of the EC, as yet a somewhat inchoate affair, which roughly amounts to seeking a preferential relationship with the countries encircling that sea, as with those of Africa. The tussle with the USA over wheat sales to Egypt probably concerns more than wheat. However, the evidence publicly available is slight, and the matter can only be alluded to as possibly of importance to a French statesman seeking to assess whether the developing pattern of relationships in the Levant is in the common interest. The broad point is perhaps worth making that on average over the years, the wheat market seems to be equally balanced between buyers and sellers. Egypt is no more likely to become dependent on purchases from France than France on sales to Egypt.

The future, especially when we widen the question to the world's future, is still more speculative. Apologists for the EC's wheat production point to forecasts of coming world needs. Western Europe has pushed its way from dependence to self-sufficiency in wheat: as a producer it is surpassed only by the Soviet Union, the USA and China; as an exporter, only by the USA and Canada. No doubt this has been possible only by encouraging the brilliant technical advance of EC agriculture with production and export subsidies. But these subsidies are trifling compared with what is at stake for Europe and the world. Exact forecasts are subject to many doubts, but all agree that the world's need of wheat will grow greatly over the coming decades. How is this need to be supplied? Consider what else has happened as EC production has grown: Latin America, a grain exporter before the Second World War, became an importer after it through population growth and mismanagement of its agriculture; two further whole continents have lately gone the same way, Africa and the Soviet Union; they too cannot feed themselves. The capacity of the USA to fill the world's needs is well known to be boundless, that of Canada, Australia and Argentina is doubtless considerable. Does the common interest require that the USA and these others should attain so dominant a relationship to the world's food? Ought not Europe, even at some economic and financial cost, to accept a role as a world supplier?

An alternative line of thought, here as earlier, is that a European Community, as brilliant politically as technically, would prefer to help reverse the agricultural decline of Latin America, Africa and the Soviet Union. Fear of a world food empire of four is perhaps little eased by the prospect of an empire of five. The possibility of creating a wider distribution of power seems more inviting.

A last question concerns the effect on international relations of an EC role in world food supply achieved by the use of export subsidies. The EC's subsidies cause friction between itself and the most important country in world politics. The reason is not simply that US commercial interests are injured, but that the prevailing idea in the USA and in most of the world is that, in the common interest, free trade should be the norm; import barriers and export subsidies have to be justified. Perhaps this idea is destined to collapse under a mass of arbitrarily imposed national barriers and subsidies. If so, one kind of friction will disappear, that between a rational idea and arbitrary action, to be replaced by the frictions that an arbitrary world will generate. The EC will have its share of responsibility for this. Perhaps, on the other hand, the norm of free trade is destined to be replaced by a new international idea, that, say, of *libre échange concertée* under which export subsidies such as the EC's will play an accepted part in world commerce. A Community that seeks the common interest has the responsibility of working out such an idea and showing that it is intelligent.

I will not attempt to sum up this discussion or to draw conclusions. As I explained at the beginning, my aim has not been to persuade the reader one way or the other about the wisdom of the EC's wheat export subsidies. No doubt much more would need to be said on both sides before one could form a definite opinion about that. My aim has been to discuss a detailed matter of state foreign policy in terms of the idea of 'the common interest', and to let the reader judge whether that idea could be used by statesmen and citizens in foreign policy or is absurd.

Notes

1 See Virginia Held *The Public Interest and Individual Interests* (New York, Basic Books, 1970); William J. Meyer *Public Good and Public Authority* (Port Washington, Kennikat Press, 1975); John Finnis *Natural Law and Natural Rights* (Oxford, Clarendon Press, 1980); and Michael Novak *Free Persons and the Common Good* (Lanham, Md., Madison Books, 1989).
2 I am especially grateful to the following authors: D. Balaam and M. Carey eds *Food Politics* (Croom Helm, 1981); J. Cathie *The Political Economy of Food Aid* (Aldershot, Gower, 1982); A. Chisholm and R. Tyers *Food Security, Theory, Policy and Perspectives from Asia and the Pacific Rim* (Lexington, Mass., Heath, 1982); J. Chombart de Lauwe *L'aventure agricole de la France de 1945 à nos jours* (Paris, Presses Universitaires de France, 1979); S. Davies, *Markets, States and Transnational Corporations – Power in the World Grain Trading System* (Ph.D. Thesis, University of London, 1983); Francois Duchêne, Edward Szczepanik and Wilfrid Legg *New Limits on European Agriculture* (Croom Helm, 1985); F. Grogan *International Trade in Temperate Zone Products* (Edinburgh, Oliver and Boyd, 1972); S. Harris, A. Swinbank and G. Wilkinson *The Food and Farm Policies of the European Community* (Chichester, John Wiley, 1983); B. Huddlestone *Closing the Cereals Gap with Trade and Food Aid* (Washington D.C., International Food Policy Research Institute, Research Paper 43, 1984); T. Josling *Agriculture in the Tokyo Round* (Trade Policy Research Centre, 1977); and M. Tracy *Agriculture in Western Europe 1880–1980* (Croom Helm, 1981).

Index

The Condition of States

Bangladesh, 78
Barber, Peter, n100
Baumgartner, Wilfrid, 222
Begin, Menachim, 88
Behrman, J. H., n164
Behrman, M. R., n100
Beitz, Charles, 203–4
Belgium, 103
Beloff, Max, n100
Benelux states, 109
    and Customs Union, 110–11
    and European Integration, 110–11,
        114
    and negotiations for Euratom, 110
Benn, Tony, 73
Bergson, Abram, 147
Bergson, Fred, n165
Berlin, 107
Berrill, Kenneth, 87
Bevin, Ernest, 76, n84
Biafra, 67
Bierstecker, J. J., n163, n165
Bismarck, 61, 62, 64, 65–6, 76–7, 82,
    199
bismarckian tradition, 199
Blunden, Edmund, 135
Bophutatswana, 29–30
borders, moral significance of, 203
Botswana, Bechuanaland, 21, 22, 23,
    25, 27, 28, 29, 31, 32, 34, 36, 38
bourgeoisie, comprador, 58
Boyce, Peter, 86, n100
Brams, Steven, 90
Brazil, 161
Bretton Woods System, 116
Bright, John, 68
Britain, 87, 137
    and aid, 205
    as authoritarian democracy, 72–4
    and European Union, 103–5, 109,
        114, n123
    role of Parliament in foreign policy,
        80–81
    and World War II, 80, 126
Brown, Peter, 208, n215
Brussels Treaty Organization, 102
Bull, Hadley, n17, n58, 186, 187, 206
Bullock, n83

bureaucratic analysis, 2, 144

Callieres, François de, 87, n100
Cambodia, 89, 140
Camp David Agreement, 116
Canada, 24, 26
    Foreign Take-Overs Bill, n164
    Gray Report, n164
    and wheat regime, 219, 224–5
capital flight, 130
capitalism,
    adopted by new states, 31
    colonial administrators' suspicion of,
        31, 32
    relation with liberalism, 48
    and state, 4–5, 6–7, 8–9, 145, n163,
        n164, 187
capitalist states, 200
Carter Presidency, 70, 75, 97
Central African Federation, 23
Chad, 35, 51–2
    civil war in, 51–2
    colonial state in, 51
China, People's Republic of, 20
    and international economic order, 57
    and Kuo Sung T'ao, 87
    and Sino-Soviet split, 99
    and Tiananmen Square
        demonstrations, 86, 94
    as wheat producer, 227
Christian Democracy, 102, 103
Churchill, Winston, 70, n84
    and civil military relations, 135
    and European Union, 104
civil war, 78
Claude Inis, n84
Clausewitz, Karl von, 70, 127,
    129–30, 132–3, 136, 140–41
Cobden, Richard, 68
Colonial Welfare Acts, 30
'common European home', 160
'common fate', 160–61
Commonwealth, 95
    changes in, 28
    as mechanism of decolonization, 24,
        29
communications revolution, and
    foreign policy, 81, 92

national champion, 156
national interest, 4, 37–8
  definitions of, 10
  in European Community, 119–22
  France and, 74
  in modern state, 49–50
  as opposed to duty, 198
National Socialist foreign policy, 64
nationalism, 2, 3, 14, 15, 49, 62–3,
    65, 83, 102
  as basis of statehood, 33
  opposed to natural law, 218–19
nationalist movements, 26, 32–3
nation state, concept of, 33, 37–8, 102
  in Europe, 105, 120, 121–2
natural harmony of interests, 45
natural law, 146, 151, 217
natural rights individualism,
  in Hegel, 170, 172, 175–6
  and radicals, 187
Nazi-Soviet Pact, 91
neo-corporatist theory, 4
Nepal, 22
Netherlands, 103
New Realism, 4, 11
New Zealand, 99
Newfoundland, 26
Newhouse, John, n123
Nicolson, Harold, 76
Nietzche, F., 138
Nigeria, 21, 22, 32, 34, 38, 89
Nikiforov, V. N., n18
Nixon, R., 68-9, 75
Nkrumah, K., 31, 33, 34, n42
non-aligned movement, 28
Non-conformism, 73
non-intervention, 191
Noriega, General, 86
North Atlantic Treaty Organization
    (NATO), 92, 95, 102, 104
  and Europe, 120, 209
  Lisbon Meeting, 106
  natural law view of, 218
  realist view of, 205
  and US President, 209
Northedge, F. S., n17
Nozick, Robert, 186
nuclear weapons, 57, 73, 136, 137

de-nuclearization, 58
Numieri, 52
Nuremberg War Trials, 127
Nyrere, J., 23, 34

Offe, Claus, 161
oil price increase, 30
  and Europe, 116–17
  and use of force, 212
one-party states, 25
organization for European Economic
    Cooperation (OEEC), 91
Organization of Africa Unity (OAU),
    28, 34, 89
Organization of Petroleum Exporting
    Countries (OPEC), 116–17
Ottoman Empire, 8, 52–3

Paine, T., 68
Palestine Liberation Organization, 93
Palestinian struggle, 52
Palliser, Michael, n100
Palmerston, Lord, 61
Pan European Union, 103
Pan Slavism, 65
Pearl Harbour, 69
periphery, 9
Perpetual Peace, 58
Peru,
  and multinational companies, n165
Pettman, Ralph, n196
Pinello, A. J., n165
Pisani, Edgard,
  Pisani-Baumgartner Plan, 222, 226
Piscatori, James, n59
pluralism, 1–4, 10, 143–4, 146, 176–7
plurality of legal orders, 14, 143
Poggi, Gianfranco, 151
Poland, 138
Polisario, 89
Portugal,
  and decolonization, 20, 21, 25, 34
positivism, 216
Poulantzas, Nicos, 6
power politics, 6
Prebisch, R., 202
Protectorates, within the British
    Empire, 21–2